GIRLS
NEED
NOT
APPLY

GIRLS NEED NOT APPLY

Field Notes from the Forces

KELLY S. THOMPSON

McClelland & Stewart

McClelland & Stewart and colophon are registered trademarks of Penguin
Random House Canada Limited.

Library and Archives Canada Cataloguing in Publication data
is available upon request

ISBN 978-0-7710-7095-2
eISBN 978-0-7710-7096-9

Book design by Jennifer Lum
Cover photograph by Raquel Hounsell
Typeset in Bembo MT Pro by M&S, Toronto
Printed and bound in Canada

McClelland & Stewart,
a division of Penguin Random House Canada Limited,
a Penguin Random House Company
www.penguinrandomhouse.ca

1   2   3   4   5   23   22   21   20   19

Penguin
Random House
McCLELLAND & STEWART

To my sister, Meghan.
18 July 1981–17 August 2018
My biggest fan. My tiny defender.
You always said I could, and the result is all for you.

And to the women who see themselves in these pages.
Change is coming.

CONTENTS

Author's Note

As is the case with most memoirs, certain events have been compressed, eliminated, or rearranged. My memory—which generally leads to me being referred to as the Thompson Family Elephant—does have its faults. The experiences in these pages are also funnelled through my own perception. Names, for the most part, have also been changed for privacy.

The ever-changing nature of military life also applies to the terminology used. As an example, while I joined the Canadian Forces and the Canadian Air Force in 2003, these organizations are now referred to as the Canadian Armed Forces and the Royal Canadian Air Force. In most instances, the terms used in these pages are the ones that applied at the time I served.

PART ONE

From Civvie Street via Black Cadillacs

Officer Cadet Thompson
May 2004-July 2004

1

The route to basic training, from Barrie, Ontario, to Saint-Jean-sur-Richelieu, Quebec, wound coincidentally through Ormstown, where my Grandpa Thompson was buried. Dad and I stopped by after lunch at the Husky diner on the side of Highway 401, where I had a chicken club, sloppy with mayo. Dad had insisted I needed support on the drive, although it felt more like he was escorting an unruly deserter, since he'd brought his own car to get himself home once the new officer cadet—me—was delivered to the Forces.

Grandpa had died two years earlier, when I was sixteen, and I hadn't been to his grave since. Not much had changed about Ormstown: the streets were still haunted by clunky farm machinery; still dotted with brick houses that appeared abandoned or derelict. But Grandpa was here, in the soft ground, and I wanted to take root in the muck that sucked at my shoes, plant myself like a frothy hydrangea so that my impending military career would wither before it even sprouted.

After 9/11, I'd convinced myself that the attack on the Twin Towers demanded that I carry on the Thompson military legacy, which extended back four generations on both sides of the family. Nearly two years later, the memory of a burning

New York was still sharp enough to stir the patriotism I'd felt when I watched the news from my grade twelve English class. Yet I was terrified, somehow already aware that military life and I weren't exactly well-matched; unsure of a future with a rifle instead of a pen in my hand, because I'd always thought I wanted to be a writer, never a soldier. Dangling like a carrot was the free university degree that I was two years into, paid for by the Forces, and the chance to do something that felt more important than putting my words onto the page—something in service of others instead of myself. Grandpa—who served in the Korean War and had encouraged my stories and now lay at my feet—would have understood my uncertain reasoning. Yet for Dad, a thirty-five-year veteran, the only legitimate reason for enrolling was protecting Canada.

I was going to be a logistics officer in the Canadian Air Force, a fact Dad encouraged but also ribbed me for, as the air force was known as the cushier environment within the Forces. In the four generations of military Thompsons, all had been army men, enlisting in the combat arms or support trades as non-commissioned members. I was breaking pattern by being a woman, enrolling as an officer, in the air force, in a support trade with a human-resources focus—a path that was more focussed on paperwork than rifles. I didn't want one of the "sexy" combat jobs that involved countless tours to war zones, lugging a rucksack on my back. I didn't want to have to shoot anyone, and knew my odds of having to do so would be significantly higher if I joined the army. Ultimately, I just wanted to help people in a way I saw as being suited to my personality, and in that desire I was straying from protocol, already the family's black sheep.

Dad and I stood shoulder to shoulder in front of Grandpa's grave, my Volkswagen Beetle parked on the dirt road near the church cemetery behind Dad's car. Even in May, the ground was soggy with moisture, my Doc Martens sinking into the earth and liquid seeping through the seams despite Dad's overaggressive polishing of the toe box. His eyes were trained on the headstone as though he needed to memorize the inscription. Our family, without ever saying it, resented Grandpa's burial so far from home. All of us felt aimless in our mourning without a grave nearby. But army brats have no particular origin, no one place that demands allegiance. Instead there is a series of locations, places once called home, punctuated by blurry memories no longer important. Home is wherever the family is at that moment, and so finding a final resting place might as well be done with eyes closed and a finger jabbed on a spinning globe. I shivered with the knowledge that my life would continue to follow that same wobbling path of disintegrated roots, moving every two or three years, a life of goodbyes and nice-to-meet-yous.

Whether Grandpa Thompson was in the ground beneath my feet or hovering in the air like a cartoon angel, I knew he would have been proud of me. He had been a soldier turned babysitter extraordinaire, who cared for me when Mom returned to work and my older sister Meghan was at school. Our days were filled with my stories, which he encouraged and enhanced with questions about character and plot. When storytelling was over, sometimes I'd ask him to put lipstick on me, but then I'd cry because he never stayed inside the lines like I was told to do in my colouring books. Other times he would pop his dentures out of his mouth and drop them in my hand, still warm and full of saliva, insisting only I knew how to brush them properly. On nice days, I would zip around the driveway on my bike while he chain-smoked from a plastic lawn chair on the porch. I lived for his approval, which he gave steadily and assuredly. With him I didn't feel the usual pang of anxiety rising from deep in my

5

stomach. By contrast, Grandpa-less nights were spent nibbling on my cuticles (which I feared made me a cannibal, a word I'd looked up in my parents' large dictionary), and then worrying about the fact that I was worrying. Nerves were in my genes— another generational trait—but those before me had proven that anxiety could be overcome.

Staring at Grandpa's gravestone, I settled on the floating-angel vision and pictured him hovering above me, showering me with that approval. I licked my dry lips and pushed back wisps of wild hair. I'd cut my bangs to an inch long, so the hair burst forth like it was saluting, a style I rationalized would be easy to tuck into my new beret, not thinking of the effect sans hat.

"It's weird to think of him in there," I said, although I sensed I shouldn't be talking. I looked from earth to sky, waiting for some sort of sign, and yet I didn't believe in signs.

My father kneeled in front of the grave and placed a weary hand on the top of the rough granite edge of the headstone. "Dad," he whispered. His jeans were damp around the ankles and his moustache quivered above his stalwart lip. The only reason Dad had time to drive to Quebec with me was because he'd been placed on medical leave from work at Base Borden after he was paralyzed by depression and stress. Certainly, his bouts of tears had become more common as he neared the end of his own military career, a medical release after more than three decades of service. Although neither he nor Grandpa T could ever say the words *post-traumatic stress disorder*, both men carried the weight of its symptoms as though they'd gained a hundred pounds, the mental condition's burden impossible for family and colleagues to ignore. My anxiety was bred into me, Dad's was a product of military experience, and enroute to basic training, I wondered if the war I'd inevitably be facing would crack me in half like it had the men of my family.

Dad stood and brushed invisible dirt from his pants, sniffed hard, and put his arm around my shoulders. "He would have been so proud of you, Moo."

At the mention of the nickname Grandpa had given me, I leaned into Dad and breathed in his cologne, which was mixed with a whiff of cigarette smoke. My throat tightened as I stuffed my hands into my pockets, desperate to delay the continuation of the drive.

"He was proud of you too, Dad."

My father snuffled and grunted, turning towards the wind, eyes closed and listening. I swallowed over and over, clenched my fists and relaxed them. Clenched and relaxed. I'd read this small act staved off tears or anxiety or something like that, yet the action did nothing but carve half-moons into my palms. Dad walked towards his car without another word.

"Wish me luck, Grandpa." I rested a palm on the headstone, shocked at how cold it was, then followed Dad in a wobbly line back to my own waiting car, careful to avoid stepping on gravesites. Finally, the sun emerged, a beam reflecting off the car until I had to shield my eyes. Perhaps it was a sign.

The commissionaire at the entry-gate booth looked bored as he waved my car to a stop with the flap of an age-spotted hand. I rolled down my window and peered out into the semi-darkness.

"Kelly Thompson, uh, reporting for duty."

He scoffed as he checked his clipboard. "You're not in the doors yet, girly, and this isn't a screening of *Platoon*. Save that for the guys in there." He gestured towards the Général-Jean-Victor-Allard Building—the hub of training for Canadian Forces soldiers—which loomed behind him like a giant cement accordion. The structure zigzagged back and forth, boasting rows of glass windows that sparkled as the base's streetlights flickered into action. The information packet on the Canadian Forces Leadership and Recruit School (or CFLRS) in Saint-Jean noted that if the building was stretched straight, it would measure a kilometre and a half. It was referred to as the Mega; looking at its span in front of me, the nickname felt appropriate.

"I'll need some form of government ID," the commissionaire said. I handed over my driver's licence and waited while he returned to his hut and phoned in the name, watching Dad in my rear-view mirror. I drummed my fingers on the car door armrest, nails cut short. "All right, you're good to go. Sign your life away right here." He passed me the clipboard, a pen attached by a string, and I scrawled my signature in loopy teenage cursive. "Good luck in there." A press of a button lifted the gate and I drove into the parking lot while simultaneously rifling through my purse for a mint. My handbag also contained two packages of Kleenex, a makeup bag, hair pins, bandages, and lavender-scented hand cream—a veritable vanity emergency kit.

The joining instructions directed me to two green metal doors, chipped and weather-beaten. I unloaded the trunk of my car and stood with the luggage my parents had bought from the Bay, which had shiny spinning wheels that made my belongings float across the rough pavement.

"Ready?" Dad wasn't smiling, wasn't even looking at me. The question was lost in the breeze, his back to me, halfway to the green doors.

Inside, the Mega hummed with activity. Throngs of soldiers walked through the halls, stood in lines, or milled by the vending machines. To the right, a break area had rows of chairs where uniformed bodies slumped with exhaustion, combat boots stretched out into the aisles, the smell of dirt and bodies permeating the air. There were also others like me, dressed in business casual as required, looking just as unnerved as I felt.

At the entrance, a soldier sat in a booth like a bank teller. I approached with my hands hanging awkwardly at my sides, looking nothing like the capable officer I intended to become.

"Hi there, I'm Kelly Thompson. I'm supposed to start basic officer training tomorrow morning, the initial assessment period."

"Stand behind the yellow line," the man barked.

"I'm sorry?"

"The yellow line," he insisted, pointing sharply with his arm extended. "Remain behind the stripe on the floor." Underneath my shoes was a thick strip of yellow, similar to lane markings. My eyes followed the route as it meandered down the hall, disappearing beyond the first zig of the zags like the yellow brick road. I stepped back one pace and cleared my throat, eyes going to Dad, who typically wasn't one to let people speak to me so harshly. But he watched motionless from the break area, where he'd taken up residence between two recruits, looking both out of place and right at home in the melee.

Once my toes touched the back of the line, the man nodded approvingly. "Name?"

"Kelly Sara Thompson."

"Officer Cadet Thompson," he said, correcting me as he assessed his paperwork. "You can approach." I stepped forward. "You'll be in 13 Platoon. Report to room D12 at 1900 hours." The man slid a package towards me and checked my name off his list. "Sign here. Inside this envelope you'll find the key to your pod, a meal card, and the rules and regulations of the Mega."

"I'm sorry, what's a pod?"

The man ignored my question. "Everything you need to know will be in your packet. You can find your room with this map." He pulled out a photocopy showing the layout of the complex, my current location highlighted in blue. "You are not permitted to use the elevators at any time during your training. Understood? You are also not permitted onto any floor other than your room floor and the basement level, from which you will access the mess hall and your training classrooms through the stairwells." He probably repeated this mantra in his sleep, having dictated the rules to countless cadets and recruits who stormed the green doors.

"But I'm on the twelfth floor."

"And?"

"So how do I get my bags up there?"

"You carry them, Officer Cadet. Welcome to military training. Head over to that room and unzip your luggage, leave it open, and take several steps back."

I did as instructed, while mentally preparing myself to haul sixty pounds up eleven flights of stairs. "I'm sorry, what's the purpose of this?" I asked as he plunged his hand into my bag. There was no regard for my careful folding, organization of toiletries, or diligent wrapping of shoes in dust covers.

"Seizure of contraband and other unacceptable materials," he responded, not looking up. "Any alcohol, medication other than that prescribed to you by a doctor, or weapons?"

"No."

"Well then, you have nothing to worry about. Are you currently on any prescription medications you'd like me to be made aware of before I finish searching?"

My voice came out as a squeak and a rash of heat rose up my neck. "Birth control." Cough. "I'm on birth control." Should I tell him about my reasoning for the pills—Trevor, my high school boyfriend back home in Ontario?

The man nodded and then continued. I held my breath as he rummaged through my things, praying that the lipstick-sized vibrator would go unnoticed in its hiding place, tucked in a sock. It did, but when he stood and waved at me to indicate the inspection was complete, he had to pry off a pair of my underwear that had caught on the strap of his Ironman watch. His face reddened as he tucked the cotton bikinis back in my bag and told me to hurry up to barracks, then shuffled out of the room. I hauled my bag back into the hallway, feeling sheepish.

"Well, Moo, you all set?" Dad checked his watch, then looked around him like his own memories might sneak up from behind the yellow stripe. I eyed his lined face, curious. Was he worried what military service would mean for his daughter's mental health, knowing what such a future might hold? Wondering how much of his history would be repeated? I couldn't be sure—his thoughts were masked by his typical get-in-get-done attitude.

It had been ten minutes since I'd walked through the green doors. Ten minutes, and so much had changed.

"I think so."

But I wasn't. I wasn't set at all, legs turned to Jell-O and cheeks alight. He pulled me in for the style of hug he'd adopted since I'd grown breasts, his body forming a C-shape over mine as he patted my back uncomfortably. I didn't want him to go— his clothes still scented with the tinge of home. Panic lurched into my throat, synapses of anxiety fired across my skin. I wasn't ready. I would never be ready.

"Good luck, Officer Cadet Moo. You can call collect any time, okay? And you have your mom's cell phone for emergencies, yes?" I nodded, and held up the early-millennium Telus model that was nearly the size of a banana. "Work hard. No one can hurt you unless you let them. Remember, it's all about teamwork, and it's also a mental game to give you a taste of military life."

I still wasn't sure I wanted to taste military life. I only wanted the essence of it, the glory and the comradeship I'd seen in those recruiting commercials that had dominated television since the war in Afghanistan began. But I couldn't voice these thoughts, not at this stage, not with the ink still damp on my service contract and a free degree hanging in the balance. Dad gave me a quick kiss on the head and then I watched him walk away, my last connection to freedom, spinning his car keys in his hand.

After hauling my bag to the twelfth floor, I pushed through a set of heavy fire doors and arrived at the pod, which was akin to a university residence but without the stacks of empties and the band posters held up with sticky tack. Inside the pod were five bedrooms, each containing a sparse-looking twin bed—sheets and woollen army blankets stacked in a crisp pile at the end— opposite a desk, closet, and window. At the back of the pod I found a bathroom that looked to have been built in the 1970s, lined in orange tile, with a bathtub-shower combo behind a separate door, two sinks, and an orange toilet stall.

I tossed my luggage onto my assigned bed and swiped at my sweaty face, the sound of roommates unpacking their own belongings echoing through the hall. Before long, I met the three women I would share my pod with—the fifth bedroom remaining mysteriously empty. There was Norla Doffer, who appeared too young to be in service; Mary Huang, a woman of indiscernible age; and Leahn Kelper, who introduced herself with a raised eyebrow and commented on how cute my chubby arms were. "They're like a baby's!" she said, cooing at a line of flesh on my forearm. I wasn't aware I had chubby arms, and from what I could tell, Kelper and I were incredibly similar physically: round curves on muscular frames, blonde hair, blue eyes.

We arrived at room D12 fifteen minutes early for our platoon briefing, finding it bustling with cadets, some lingering near the doorway and others settled in a series of folding chairs. Most were university-aged and I picked out four other women, obviously united in their own pod family. Twenty-two of us in total, an odd size considering platoons are usually sixty soldiers each. The walls sported annotated pictures indicating various rules and regulations: Fire orders. The proper room layout for inspection. The rank structure and correlating symbols.

Four uniformed men entered and stood at the front of the crowd, each intentionally stern. I felt cowed into silence by their stances, respect already emanating from me like body odour. These men looked ready to kick ass, if necessary, and they were going to show me how to be the same way.

"Okay, 13 Platoon. I'm Petty Officer Hopper. This is Sergeant Bruvelle, your course sergeant; Master Corporal Gagnon, section one commander; and Master Corporal Persaud, section two commander. We will be your staff for the duration of your initial assessment period of basic training, also known as IAP. Due to the time constraints of your semesters at university, you will complete nine weeks of IAP this summer, followed by five weeks of BOTC, Basic Officer Training Course, next summer. After graduating university and completing basic, you will separate into your selected occupations for training in various locales across Canada."

Training progressed in steps designed to teach us first about the military as a whole, and later our specific roles within it. IAP and BOTC taught officer leadership and generally how the military worked. From there, we would break down into our occupation-specific courses. As a logistics officer, I would train at Canadian Forces Base Borden, while others went to Portage la Prairie to become pilots or Gagetown to become engineers. We then took courses geared to our environment—whether that be army, navy, or air—and, finally, were educated within a specialty, which for me was human resources. My military education was designed to remind me that I was an officer for the Canadian Forces, then an air force officer, then a logistics officer, then a human resources officer, in that order of importance.

"You are the civilian university platoon," Hopper continued. "Also on course in Saint-Jean is a platoon of Royal Military College cadets, and another of direct-entry officers who have already completed university.

"Now, some items first and foremost. Whenever an officer walks into your area or leaves it, or when you are under inspection in your pods, you will call 'ROOM' and collectively come to attention in your seats or while standing, like this." He checked his arms to his sides, making tight fists that ran parallel to his body. Several cadets mindlessly mimicked the action. "Is that understood?"

"Yes, Sir," the crowd said in unison. It came so naturally, the robotic response we'd learned from movies.

"I AM NOT A *SIR*," he bellowed, as we jumped in our seats. "I am a non-commissioned member, which means I actually work for a living, dammit. I said when an *officer* leaves or enters the room. Officers have bars on their ranks, NCMs have chevrons or crowns. You will learn this tomorrow." Hopper straightened his shirt collar, collecting himself. Anyone who has grown up in the military has heard the endless NCM-versus-officer debate. NCMs are known for doing the tough work in the field while wielding weapons; officers for sitting at their desks and wielding orders instead. So it didn't feel odd to have our chosen professional route put down by the very people who would train us.

"I expect you will conduct yourselves accordingly, now that you are members of the Canadian Forces. Be advised that for the next four weeks you are confined to barracks. This means you are not to leave this floor except to eat, exercise outdoors, or do laundry. That's all from me for today. Sergeant Bruvelle will arrive for inspection at 0730 hours, after your morning physical training. Our first lesson tomorrow will be on rank structure, but in the meantime I encourage you all to spend the night preparing your rooms and ensuring that they meet our very high standards of cleanliness. Am I clear?"

Hopper looked around the room, his stare connecting with a few wide-eyed and frightened individuals. Then he did an abrupt about-turn on his heel and left, his air of authority lingering behind him.

"Now," Bruvelle said with a heavy French accent, pacing back and forth at the front. I could not imagine him cracking a smile, even for his own children or at funny cat videos. "I am not here to babysit you, but I care about your well-being while you are on course, and it is my hope that you will all succeed in your training."

"This guy scares the shit out of me," I whispered to Kelper, who hushed me with a finger raised to her lips, either because I'd been loud or because this was not a sentiment to make known.

"You are expected to be physically fit, mentally capable, and also in possession of strong leadership skills. Those who do not have these capabilities have already been weeded out in the recruitment process. You will assist each other in your training, as you will quickly learn that without the support of your fellow troops, you will fail.

"After this evening, all of your personal belongings will be locked up in the extra room in each of your pods for the duration of the confinement period. For inspection, you are expected to showcase your room as indicated on this poster."

My palms began to sweat at the idea of parting with my bag and the childhood stuffed penguin buried down the shaft of my leather boots. There would be no family photos. No comfy clothes. Nothing that smelled or reminded me of home.

"Also," Bruvelle continued, "fraternization is strictly forbidden and is punishable by formal charges. You are not, at any time after eight p.m., to be found in a pod of the opposite gender."

Our eyes roved across one another, assessing for weakness, attractiveness, and capability. Male stares lingered for so long that I expected the men to hold up score cards, as if we were competing for Miss Canadian Forces. I wrapped my arms around my waist and hung my head in inexplicable shame.

"Tonight, you will all be assigned cleaning supplies. I advise diligence, because I hate nothing like I hate a dirty floor. Physical training—PT—will take place at 0500 hours, breakfast afterwards, so ensure you have enough time to eat and return for inspection at 0730. The platoon will be divided into two sections by alphabetical order. Aaron to Juniper, section one with Master Corporal Gagnon; Kelper to Yan, section two with Master Corporal Persaud, on this side of the room."

Just hours into my military experience and I felt paralyzed by nervous uncertainty. What did my last name start with again? Was I to sort into my section by *Kelly* or *Thompson*? As we self-organized into our groups, I stumbled and bumped shoulders with a tall blond man who looked a few years older than me. He smiled an apology, his face noticeably stubbly, a change from the boys back home who barely required the swipe of a razor— my boyfriend Trevor included.

"Grab your supplies and we'll see you bright and early," Bruvelle said. The staff funnelled out of the room and the platoon heaved a sigh of relief, then buzzed into chatter.

"Sorry about running into you there. I'm Joe Shorrocks." The blond man extended his hand to shake mine.

"Kelly Thompson. Nice to meet you."

"Looks like we'll be spending a lot of time together. Same platoon, same section." His pale eyebrows arched below a receding hairline not befitting someone so young, while a hint of laugh lines spread from his eyes, making him seem worldly. Within a few minutes, I learned that Joe was in his third year of an environmental physics degree at the University of Calgary, was twenty-three years old, and he was going to be a pilot. It seemed to be the way we took stock of one another: Location. Degree specialization. Age. Occupation.

"What about you, Kelly? What are you in school for?"

"I'm at York University taking Professional Writing, with a focus on books."

"That might be the answer I'd least expect in a place like this," Joe said, gesturing at the barren cement-block walls, ivory laminate, and grey slatted blinds. "So, you want to write?"

"Since I was in grade one." At six years old I'd created a book about springtime, full of crayon illustrations, and dreamed about my writing career as I watched my classmates flip through the construction-paper pages.

"Thompson!" Kelper hollered at me, rattling a bucket of cleaning supplies. "Let's get to work." I felt compelled to listen to my podmate, her bark sharp and confident.

"I should run. Nice to meet you, Joe. Good luck."

"See you around."

Kelper, Huang, Doffer, and I returned to our pod with our cleaning gear. In the common room we unloaded the arsenal: an aerosol can of window cleaner, some generic liquid the colour of Pepto-Bismol, an old cloth mop without an apparatus to wring it out. There was also a roll of brown paper towel, the kind found in elementary school bathrooms that doesn't absorb a damn thing.

"God, are they going to have us on our hands and knees with a toothbrush or something?" Kelper asked.

I poked at the dated linoleum floor with the toe of my shoe. "This place already looks pretty clean to me."

"There's always room for improvement, even when there isn't." Doffer grabbed hold of the mop and pulled long strands of black hair from the cotton fibres, her nose scrunching in disdain. "Reality is, we're going to fail this inspection just like we did in my first basic training attempt." She looked around, waiting for us to ask questions about this; when we didn't, she continued. "We'll fail every inspection for the first few weeks because they don't care how hard we cleaned or how flawless our uniforms are. All part of the brainwash. What they care about is that we suffer together." Doffer dropped the mop onto the floor. "Can't see this thing cleaning the toilet, much less our floors. Dibs on the windows."

Each of us took an item and moved about the pod, scrubbing the common areas and then our rooms. I filled up the bathtub with water, added some of the lemon-scented pink liquid, and set to work mopping, taking care to scrub in the corners with the spare toothbrush Doffer gave me. We cleaned until midnight, sharing pieces of our life histories while passing each other in the hallway. *I've got a dog named Beans . . . Never had a boyfriend . . . From London, Ontario . . . Getting a degree in science . . .* A bastardized attempt at getting to know one another. The only words no one said were: *I miss home.*

2

The morning came early and abruptly. I woke underneath my scratchy wool blanket to Huang waving her arms wildly in the doorway of my room, her body a silhouette of anxiety.

"Thompson! Physical training. PT right now!"

"What?"

Huang stood at the end of my bed with her hands on her hips. My alarm, set for 4:30, hadn't gone off yet.

"Come, Thompson. Up. Dressed."

Everything Huang said came out like an order. After peeing and sweeping my hair into a limp ponytail, I stumbled down the blue stairs and lined up in the main Mega hallway in the basement with the rest of the platoon, our eyes swollen with sleep and our noses running in the chill of the subterranean air. Having not yet been assigned uniforms, we were a mash of civilian sweat-wicking fabrics, shiny new sneakers, and zip-ups to protect us from the cold. Everyone was fifteen minutes early, but Bruvelle and Persaud were already approaching, looking like the bulldog and the terrier from the *Looney Toons* cartoons, Persaud requiring two steps for each of Bruvelle's. They walked up and down our cadet cluster, assessing. Nerves grumbled in my stomach, or perhaps it was just hunger.

At home, I lifted weights, played basketball, hiked; I was fit on a generic level. But I didn't *train*, a term I'd previously only used in conjunction with Olympic athletes but which now seemed a common phrase amongst my platoon-mates. So although I was a perfectly healthy teenager and one hundred and thirty-five pounds, I couldn't run worth shit; couldn't fathom making some misguided, active choice to go for a jog when runners always appeared miserable. Why suffer that kind of thing when you could exercise by holding a personal dance-a-thon in your bedroom, bouncing to Ace of Base remixes?

The course staff sorted us alphabetically by our last names, then formed us into two lines in the echoing hall. "From now on, when we come to collect you for lectures or exercises, you will be waiting for us like this," Bruvelle said. Ahead of me was Joe Shorrocks, the blond man I'd bumped into the prior evening, and a guy named Brad Verner was behind me.

"Morning," whispered Joe. He looked chipper and well rested.

"Hey." I rubbed sleep from one eye and turned to shake hands with Verner. "Looks like us three will be pretty cozy the next couple of months." Verner smiled crookedly, hair shorn close like most of the men, kindness in his face. Both of them were so tall that I could never see what was ahead when we marched.

As we followed Bruvelle out into the semi-light of Saint-Jean, most of us were still half asleep, pillow creases on our cheeks. We were led into a series of warm-ups, including pull-ups, push-ups, and archaic stretches, before starting to jog around the Mega campus, our breath burping frosty clouds in the May morning air. *How in the hell*, I wondered, *are pull-ups part of a warm-up?* Lumbering forward, I took in the looming structures, the manicured lawns, the other platoons looping around the complex in the same bedraggled fashion. A smattering of buildings lined the perimeter, drill halls and trailers akin to high school portables, except this campus sported ten-foot-tall fencing and concertina wire, more to keep us in than to keep trespassers out.

Despite looking the fitness part, ten minutes into PT I knew the next nine weeks would be physical hell, but I didn't yet know enough to be ashamed of that fact. I sunk back from the ranks, losing sight of Shorrocks and Verner, even the tiny bouncing head of Huang. I choked and gasped for air, legs like rubber, cramp in one side then pinching in the other, quite literally the only person who couldn't keep up with what was an embarrassingly slow pace. Persaud dropped back to my side. He appeared equally miserable.

"Thompson." Wheeze. "Catch up to your platoon, Thompson." Gasp.

"I'm trying, Master Corporal."

"Try fucking harder." Gasp. "Keep up. Up, up."

I lurched forward, a desperate attempt, but my legs pounded clumsily, weighed down by Persaud's penetrating stare.

"This is fucking easy," called out one of the cadets, muscles bursting from his rolled-up T-shirt sleeves. The guy hadn't broken a sweat, wasn't out of breath, and I wanted him to die on the spot.

"You think that helps your platoon-mate, Officer Cadet? Is that teamwork?" Bruvelle demanded, his ears alert to any gripes. "For the rest of PT, you will run circles around the platoon as we move forward. You understand? And you sure as hell better keep up." Bruvelle jabbed his finger in the air for effect without even panting, chatting as though he ran on diesel, not oxygen. The cadet's mouth curled into a sneer, considering the order an easy one. But after several minutes of lapping us, his shirt was drenched in sweat and he clutched a cramp of his own. Dragging myself behind my peers, miserable and nearly in tears, I relished every moment of his suffering.

How much time passed? Thirty minutes? A hundred? Did we run five kilometres or seventy-five? After the first few minutes, every step felt like a kilometre, and my body nearly collapsed in relief when we reached the front doors of the Mega. We lined up in our wobbly ranks, everyone panting and gasping.

"Pitiful," Bruvelle said. "Some of you"—he paused to make eye contact with me—"need to train better, or you should have come more prepared. You are only as strong as your weakest link. You are dismissed for showers and breakfast. Ensure you are back in your rooms for inspection by 0730. Understand?"

"YES, SERGEANT!"

"Dismissed."

"I think he was talking to you," Kelper said casually as we entered the stairwell. I stared with desperation up the eleven flights of stairs that might as well have been eleven hundred.

"Sorry?" I thought I'd not heard her properly. Or that no one would be that rude—at least, not to my face. In high school, my girlfriends had rarely spoken their minds so openly. Instead, we gossiped and wrote hateful notes behind one another's backs, plastering on saccharine smiles when face to face. I didn't know how to approach Kelper's brutal honesty, which was merely a statement of fact. I wasn't yet an officer. I was a young woman, insecure and aware that, on my first day, I'd failed to meet the standard set for all of us. So I blinked at Kelper with wide eyes, my hand resting on the railing, saying nothing.

"It's not good to stand out like that. Not on day one. Not in such a small platoon. You have to keep up."

I watched as she bounded up the stairs like a gazelle, leaving me at the bottom with my mouth wide open in shock. At a distance, Kelper and I could have been mistaken for one another, and yet she seemed to possess a natural military prowess. Already, I felt the first inkling of female competition stirring in the back of my throat, like the warning of a coming cold, so I took the stairs two at a time until I arrived at the top and gagged from exertion. I burst into our pod just as the shower became free, and by the time I emerged clean, the bathroom windows full of steam, my podmates had already gone down to the mess hall, leaving the weakest link behind.

With just five minutes to eat, I plonked my tray on the long folding table, next to faces I vaguely recognized from the run, eating too quickly to taste the food. The watery scrambled eggs turned my stomach, but I shovelled them in anyway, feeling ravenous. Collectively and mechanically, we pushed food into our mouths. Shovel. Chew. Swallow. Repeat. Another check of my watch before I dashed up the stairs, arriving at my pod out of breath yet again. One day in, and I already hated those fucking blue stairs.

My podmates and I waited in our rooms for inspection, each of us at the foot of our bed, arms at ease and folded behind our backs as though we already knew the drill moves. We stood feeling awkward in our civilian collared shirts and khakis—all of us attempted adult versions of ourselves.

During our pod-cleaning mania the night before, I'd discovered that I was the only one who hadn't already experienced some form of basic training. Kelper had been a reservist and had done milder versions of Regular Force training during summers in Meaford, Ontario. Huang was on her second round of IAP after failing the year prior, although she didn't elaborate on the reasons and we didn't ask. And Doffer had been "re-coursed" to this year after an injury the previous summer.

"Re-coursed?" I'd asked.

"It's when you fail out and have to repeat the course," said Kelper, sounding unimpressed. She didn't seem one to tolerate failure.

"It's not necessarily because you failed," Doffer had said, her voice hurt. "I was injured." Doffer made it to the final week in the field before breaking her foot, an injury she highlighted by showcasing a pudgy appendage with toenails about a month's worth too long.

I was the basic training virgin, and the term had the same connotation as its sexual variety. My only frame of reference was movies, and even at eighteen I sensed that the film industry had lied to me.

"So, we just stand around here, waiting for the sergeant to show up?" I asked now, calling into the hallway. *What's the point of stupid inspections?* I'd asked Dad on more than one occasion. He routinely inspected the troops in his unit, returning home to lament about uniforms with dangling threads or improperly cleaned weapons, shaking his head at his soldiers' ineptitude. *The point*, he said, looking annoyed to have to answer such a question, *is discipline*.

"That's the idea." Kelper sneezed twice.

"Anyone else nervous?" Doffer said. No one answered her. "ROOM!"

Bruvelle pushed through the pod's heavy fire door, heading straight for Huang's room, which was closest to the entrance. We came to attention at the order, although we'd not been told exactly how the move was performed, so I slapped my right foot to the ground so hard that it stung up my thigh. I felt like an idiot. "Officer Cadet Huang, attention! Remainder, stand at ease!"

What followed were terse questions and closet doors sliding, desk drawers being opened, and questions I couldn't hear. Huang's answers were spoken in sharp bullet points: "Yes, Sergeant. No, Sergeant. No, I didn't, Sergeant." Huang seemed to think that the louder she spoke the more effective the words; each syllable was like a hammer to glass.

A few minutes and Huang was done. Nothing to worry about; I could do this. Next was Kelper. Then Doffer. Bruvelle and Persaud were just around the corner, so close I could smell their aftershave and laundry detergent. Bruvelle directed Doffer to stand at ease and I was next. Breathe in. Breathe out. Repeat.

I clumsily came to attention when they arrived at my door, and Bruvelle rushed within an inch of my face, his breath hot on my nose.

"Did we ask you to come to attention, Officer Cadet Thompson?" My new name had so many syllables that by the time the words had left Bruvelle's lips, I was uncertain if Officer Cadet Thompson was a separate being.

"No."

"No *what*?" he said, voice raised and tight.

"No, Sergeant!"

He nodded, eyebrows bobbing over chocolatey eyes. "Part of training is learning not only to give orders, but to take them, Officer Cadet Thompson. Understand?" I nodded. "I ASKED IF YOU UNDERSTOOD, OFFICER CADET THOMPSON. YOU ANSWER QUESTIONS WHEN SOMEONE ASKS THEM. NONE OF THIS BOBBING YOUR HEAD BULLSHIT."

"Yes, Sergeant!" How could I have been so stupid? It was the same rule that had applied to my upbringing, which should have prepared me for this life.

Sergeant Bruvelle moved about the room like a jaguar, while Persaud stood post in the doorway, filling the exit that led to my freedom. Bruvelle flung open my closet and the doors rattled on their track system, revealing the layout that the poster in the D12 common room had depicted. All items were lined up in perfect order: soap, razor, laundry soap, deodorant, and so on.

"Officer Cadet Thompson, what is this exactly?" Sergeant Bruvelle held up my two-blade Gillette between his pointer finger and thumb, as though he risked exposing himself to an unspeakable virus. His lip curled with disgust.

"Uh, it's my razor, Sergeant." My response came out like a question, my uncertainty making my inflection rise up at the end.

"I'm not blind, Officer Cadet Thompson. What I want to know is what the fuck is all over it."

"Excuse me, Sergeant?"

He rushed the razor to within an inch of my face. Between the rubbery ridges of the handle—if I looked very closely—there was a bit of scum, some water, and tiny blonde leg hairs mixed with a crust of shaving cream. "Did you actually do any work last night or did you just go to bed and cry? Did you think that you worked hard enough? That this was enough?"

How did he know I'd wanted to cry?

Perhaps what I should have done, on my first day of basic training, was say out loud what had been swirling in my head for months: *I'm not sure I want this.* Instead, I swallowed and reached out for the razor and all the shame attached to it.

"DID I ASK YOU TO TOUCH THE RAZOR, OFFICER CADET THOMPSON? DID I GIVE YOU THE IMPRESSION I WAS FINISHED?"

"No, Sergeant." The tiniest squeak. A whimper, even.

He slammed the razor back in its place on the top shelf and gave a cursory glance at my tidy closet. Persaud smirked from the doorjamb, his arms clasped behind him and chest flexed. When Bruvelle wordlessly turned on his heel and the pod door shut with a whoosh, I had to bite my lip and wring my hands to keep from falling apart.

"Well," said Kelper as we all emerged from our bedrooms.

"That wasn't bad, was it?" Easy for her to say, the woman who hadn't been screamed at.

"How do we know if we passed?" I asked, wiping sweat from my forehead. My voice sounded wheedling and desperate. I had never failed anything before.

"We'll find out later in the day," Kelper said, checking her makeup in the bathroom mirror. "Marks always come later. They like to keep us waiting."

I learned my lesson in the weeks that followed. I bought a secret toiletry kit from the all-purpose military store, Canex, and kept it stashed in the one-foot-square personal cubby hidden in the closet that was always uninspected, where I also kept my box of tampons and my birth control pills. This kit contained the items I would actually use daily—a razor, soap, shampoo and conditioner—crusted with residue and shower mould. The twins of each of these sat on my shelf for the sole purpose of inspection. Each week I would take my display soap and scrub it in the sink to wear it down, before patting it dry with paper towel and carefully cleaning any errant soap scum left in the dish. I'd then place it with exactitude on the shelf, to the left of my razor, aligning it just so. My inspection-worthy soap let me keep up the facade that I was using these museum pieces with diligence, and not just pretending. But having these decoys also gave me a sense of belonging: my podmates were often perched at the sink next to me, scrubbing their own bars of Ivory until the letters were no longer legible in the white blocks.

3

Sun streamed through the window of the military hospital where I sat with the rest of my platoon. I tugged at a loose thread on my new uniform, wrapping it around my pointer finger and giving a sharp tug. Loose threads, uneven nametags, and untucked sand traps (the material that was stuffed into our combat boots and prevented dirt from collecting in our footwear) now made my anxiety rear up. We strove for perfection, and anything less was a source of stress.

During the first week of IAP, we had acquired the uniforms that assimilated us into military culture. We were hustled through the clothing depot to receive bag upon bag of kit: three olive green combat uniforms (the final year of use of these 1970s designs before they moved on to the pixilated camouflage), five T-shirts, socks, coats, rain gear, webbing that would carry our daily necessities in the field, a rucksack, an air mattress, sleeping bags, bivvy bags, ballistic glasses, helmet—the list went on. We were also assigned dress uniforms—air force blue or army green or navy black—along with parade shoes that were to be polished to a gleaming shine. I held the blue material in my fingertips, the wool rough on my skin.

Once we'd signed all the paperwork to take ownership, we

lugged the gear onto trucks that transported everything back to the barracks, then we were ordered to spend the rest of the week sewing tiny white labels onto each item to mark them as our own. For security, we were told. *Trust us. Deployed overseas without your stuff labelled? Shit goes missing. And don't even get us started on the laundry system over there.* Every task we executed was a preparation for deployments in another world. I spent days writing the first three letters of my last name and the last three digits of my service number on tiny scraps of white fabric using a Sharpie, then crudely stitching these scraps onto my kit until my fingers bled. THO 898. I wrote it so many times that I detached from the epithet, unable to conjure up an image of the soldier who personified the alphanumeric code.

With all my labels sewn ahead of the rest of my platoon, I had retreated to my room where I closed the door and practised donning my olive green uniform, straightening and untying, lacing and tucking. Pants bloused from combat boots. Boots polished on the leather and the soles. Waist and hip ties in a bow with the extra cording looped around the buttons. Rank epaulettes square on shoulders. Then I would slowly turn and face myself in the full-length mirror, uncertain. The woman reflected was a kid playing dress-up. I would raise an eyebrow to question this stranger, and see if her actions mimicked my own. They always did. I was always surprised.

Now well into week two of IAP, we waited in the sunlight. The military hospital, or medical inspection room, was housed in a portable building set off from the Mega and was relegated to yet another military acronym: MIR. Inside, it was like most hospitals, with bright fluorescent lighting and a strong smell of antiseptic. But the MIR staff wore uniforms—the only separation between us and them was the scrub-style smock worn over their military T-shirts.

Thirteen Platoon sat in a row of chairs in the waiting area, grateful for the chance to stare mindlessly at the television, a break from the past week of fitness and educational training, all of us painfully exhausted. The penalty for looking sleepy was having to stand at the back of the classroom for the duration of the lesson, and since our feet were still adjusting to the heavy and poorly designed combat boots—which we heard the staff refer to as Black Cadillacs, a hilarious moniker considering they were more Pinto than Caddy—no one wanted to stand more than necessary. My toes and heels were covered in oozing blisters that seemed impervious to 2nd Skin gel treatments. I had taken to affixing double layers of duct tape that I would soak off in the sink every second day, peeling off layers of epidermis along with the adhesive.

We'd not been told why we were at the MIR, but then we were never told why anything was happening. Half of the mind-fuck of basic training was in the not knowing, the wondering what was coming, the haunting concern over another standard we could never quite meet. As someone who thrived on routine, the uncertainty of the days ahead had me continually chewing on my secret supply of Tums. I never told my female platoon-mates about my nerves, instead pretending chalky mint was my breath's natural scent.

"Thirteen Platoon, welcome." A sergeant appeared in front of us with a clipboard, her hair pulled taut in a bun. "Today you will undergo some routine blood work, as well as receive your immunization booklets, which you will keep for your entire careers. As you know, the Canadian Forces has operations all over the world, and for that reason we need to ensure that you are properly immunized against all possible risks during deployments, for the sake of operational readiness. Sound good?"

Operational readiness referred to a soldier's ability to be prepared for deployment at a moment's notice, and we were always expected to be prepared. Operational readiness was power. Injury was weakness. Week two, and this was already clear.

"Yes, Sergeant," was the answer, even if it wasn't. There were a few needle phobias in the room—unvoiced, of course. Verner looked ready to vomit, and another cadet had started to nervously fiddle with the buttons of his tunic. Everyone had their Kryptonite.

"We will call you in alphabetical order, so in the meantime, just try to stay awake." The sergeant gave us a knowing wink. I revelled in the idea of sitting for the next hour, staring numbly. Anything other than having to be engaged. I wanted to read a book, jot down journal notes at leisure, or take more than three minutes to eat a meal. I wanted to be alone with my thoughts and pretend I still had some of my own. I could feel myself unravelling just two weeks into our confinement to barracks with the same twenty-two people. Every. Waking. Moment. And yet alliances were being formed. Verner and Joe were my allies, harmless flirting aiding our connection.

Joe leaned in and bumped my shoulder with his. "Needle time. You nervous?"

"Nope."

"Yeah, I've never been someone who freaked about needles." Next to me, Verner leaned further back in his seat, keen to stay out of the conversation. "Kind of a neat idea though," Joe said. His blue eyes turned up to the television. "Being able to go anywhere in the world after a few shots in the arm."

"I think it's a little more complicated than that," I said, laughing. "You know, like there's the whole deployment and war part."

"Well, there is that." We smirked at the dark humour rippling through us. Back home, I would have reached out and touched

31

Joe, his arm maybe, and smiled. Here at basic training, all I could do was avert my eyes and pretend I wasn't hopelessly charmed by his kindness.

When it was finally my turn, I received three or four injections in my right arm, then the same in my left arm, then another in the fleshy meat of my ass.

"What's that one for?" I asked at the start. Poke. Poke. Pinch.

"It's a booster." Pinch.

"For what?"

The medic—a nervous male corporal who looked concerned at the idea of asking me to drop my pants—didn't answer. The immunizations weren't given in the same gentle fashion as the flu shots my mom, a nurse, gave. At Saint-Jean, the syringes plunged deep and forcefully. Dad had often talked to me about his deployment in the 1970s to the Golan, when the daily anti-malaria medication was a pill the size of a small marble, with side effects almost worse than the disease it prevented. So, after the first vaccine, I didn't question what was being put into my body, because there was no point. My body was no longer my property. While the corporal attempted to draw my blood, I was silent as he reinserted the needle several times over, digging into my skin in search of a vein.

"Good," said Bruvelle when we were all seated back in the waiting area. Verner sunk into the wheelchair that he'd been put in after he fainted when they were taking his blood. Once his greenish pallor dissipated, his face burned red when we wouldn't let up about it.

"Now that your arms hurt like hell, you'll all be ready for your fitness test tomorrow, am I right?" Bruvelle smiled, the first time we'd witnessed it, and I stared at his white teeth, perfect gums, rosy tongue. We couldn't hide our collective groan, and I'll be damned if he didn't appear to enjoy the sound.

—

The next day, we entered the echoing gym for our fitness test, and I winced at the heaviness in my limbs from the immunizations, the backs of my arms the colour of lavender. The course staff lined us up at the edge and directed us to separate by gender, as Bruvelle clomped around the wooden floors in his combat boots, his hands on his hips.

"Feels like we're in a fucking POW camp," someone whispered. There were a few perverse giggles because it felt bizarrely true, as though Bruvelle might at any moment be selecting who'd be chosen for work duties and who'd be sent to their death.

"That isn't fucking funny, man." Another whisper. "My grandparents survived the Holocaust."

"Whatever. Get over that shit."

Somewhere along the line, death-related commentary had become our new normal, so we could no longer see the crassness of the words spilling from our mouths. The same went for profanity. Off-colour jokes about war and genocide seemed necessary, to cope with what we might be asked to do one day.

"Get over it? The world isn't over it, asshole. Why do you think I put up with this training shit? It's for them. My bubbie and zayde."

A soldier's motivation for enrolling in the Forces varied from person to person, of course, but some reasons were considered more honourable than others. For a good three-quarters of the cadets I had met, we'd grown up as military brats and knew nothing else, so it seemed the natural progression of life. In the same way some people fall in love, get married, and have kids, army brats answer the call to finish high school, sign up, deploy. Like me, some of my fellow cadets were inspired to join after the 9/11 attacks, and also like me, others wanted a free education.

There were a few who just really wanted to be in the military (definitely not like me)—for them it was a lifelong passion.

I hate people like you, Kelper had said to me while we sewed those damn labels on our shirts, all of us cross-legged on the floor of our pod common room. *People who just want a free degree.* I'd argued that I'd never said that was the only reason. I wanted to serve too. It was part of my family history. But my assertion did nothing to change her opinion, and I hated myself for craving her acceptance.

By the very nature of our close proximity in the pod, and the fact that fellow females were scarce, Kelper and I spent a lot of time together, even though I found her to be abrasive and egotistical. The confinement to barracks and intense experience of training meant that we quickly shared more with one another than we would with the average person we'd only known two weeks. And yet, whether it was our physical likeness or the fact that we were both soon-to-be officers, the competitiveness between us ensured an unspoken distance. I would trust her in war, but not at a house party with my boyfriend.

Of all the tests I knew I'd face in basic training, I was most worried about the fitness test. Passing was a requirement for any qualified soldier, but most people saw it as a minor hurdle, barely a challenge, because *nine men's-style push-ups is nothing,* Kelper had insisted. I fiddled with the hem of my T-shirt as a man approached the eight women of our platoon. He wore a black Personnel Support Program shirt, the chest labelled with a PSP logo, and shorts that left little to the imagination.

"We will now commence with your physical fitness test," he said. "The standards are as follows: for women under thirty, you must complete nine push-ups, achieve a score of fifty on your hand grip test, do fifteen sit-ups in a minute, and achieve level four on the shuttle run, also known as the beep test. Clear?"

"Yes." We paused awkwardly, unsure of how to address the civilian guy who held our futures in his hand. He then prattled on about the male requirements, and other age bracket standards, none of which I heard. I just wanted to pass, which I'd already done during the test at the recruiting centre—so I could do it again here under the watchful eye of twenty-one peers, right? And yet those push-ups were always a question mark. Those nine push-ups were my potential downfall.

The PSP guy ran through the running requirements of the beep test that would assess our cardiovascular strength. Run to this line and touch it before the next beep, each tone sharp like a gunshot. The timing of the next beep was always unknown, but with each half level the speed increased. When the test began, I managed to slog through the run—which wasn't saying much considering achieving a level four could have been done by a clumsy five-year-old—although my panic over the push-ups had me stop before I overexerted. The rest of the platoon continued as the *beep, beep, beep* pulsed from the old-school boom box. Level five. Kelper hitting level six before stopping. Some reached level eight. Level ten. Joe and another cadet made it the furthest, eventually collapsing, sweaty and red-faced, as the rest of us clapped at their achievement.

"All right, Officer Cadet Thompson," said the PSP guy, checking his clipboard. "Have you been shown how to do the push-ups?"

"Yes." My dad had showed me at home. Legs straight, back without a curve, hands tucked directly under the chest, not splayed wide like I'd seen gym rats do. *You're in great shape. You should be fine*, Dad had said, eyeing me as I tried and failed to push myself from the floor to the count of one. Since then, I'd been attempting sets three times a day until my limbs gave out.

"Okay. Off you go, then."

I lay on my belly, grey PT shirt damp with perspiration, then said a little prayer to the fitness gods. I arranged myself, concentrating on keeping my palms tucked under my shoulders, even though the floral-scented hand cream I'd applied earlier that morning was now resurfacing, slipping into slimy anxiety. With a deep breath, I pushed.

"One, two, three, four, that's right, five, six, seven . . . nope, that one wasn't low enough. Seven. Lower. Seven. Lower."

I did thirteen push-ups but half of them didn't count since my arms were not perfectly parallel with the floor. "I can't go lower," I huffed. "My boobs are there." The fitness test had apparently not accounted for tits. Defeated, I flopped to the ground, puffing to catch my breath. My face was hot—from exertion swirled with embarrassment—all eyes on my failure.

"Sorry, I can't pass you," the PSP guy said flippantly. "You'll have to train to improve. You can retest in a few weeks."

"And what happens if I fail that one?" I asked. My palms were slick, and I rubbed them over and over on my shorts, like he might give me another try. Like it might make a difference if my hands were less moisturized and lily-tinged.

"Then you get put on PAT platoon for the rest of the summer and do nothing but fitness training."

PAT, which stood for "personnel awaiting training," was an acronym whispered secretively, like saying it out loud might conjure a ghost. If basic training was shitty, then PAT represented a new level of hell: nothing but workout after workout, and the rest of the time desperate with boredom while awaiting the next serial of IAP. I could not imagine anything less pleasant.

Three other cadets failed the fitness test, one male and two females, and my cheeks burned as the four of us were filtered away from those who had passed, shamed by our own ineptitude. I struggled not to cry as the PSP guy explained what we could do to build muscle mass—*Train. Train. Train*—before we were handed our failure forms, which were resigned to Bruvelle. Kelper watched me from the sidelines, hands on her hips, eyebrows arched in judgment. She had done well, better than some of the men. Despite equality measures in place, most military females I met grudgingly accepted that sometimes we were unable to physically match the men because our bodies were designed differently. *Women bring other stuff to the table*, Doffer said once. Our pod had nodded in agreement but remained silent. What no one voiced was whether or not that "stuff"—those qualities that made women in the Forces different but no less useful—would ever be as respected as one's ability to do push-ups.

This duality was always present, lingering behind my personal motivation to keep up but also to question the status quo. I wanted to be good enough, fit enough, strong enough, but also wanted to be recognized for the characteristics that could make me shine—empathy, intelligence, kindness. Sitting in the gym, watching Kelper, staring at my fitness report, I worried that recognition might never come.

"Did you actually stop running at level four, Thompson?" Bruvelle stared incredulously at my form. Everyone else had reached several levels higher than me on the run portion, even my fellow failures. At least they had that going for them.

"I wanted to make sure I had enough energy for the push-ups, Sergeant."

He looked at the form—failure marked with an *X*. "Well, a lot of good that did you."

The following weeks in basic training settled into a routine that was comforting only in the knowledge that it was preparing me for something bigger. I did push-ups whenever I got the chance, face pressed against the floor, until I passed my second attempt at the fitness test. Other than PT, mornings and afternoons were taken up with classes on rank structure, chemical and biological warfare, drill practice, and learning about the ever-changing organizational structure and the countless acronyms of the Forces. We learned to assimilate to the rules, which were incalculable and seemingly pointless most of the time. No food in the pods. No fraternization. No leaning against the walls. No hands in pockets. No apologizing, despite persistent hounding over flaws and failures. No walking on the "Queen's Grass," which was apparently all grass in the vicinity of the Mega. No talking back. No leaning on your elbows against your desk. We were constantly corrected, always under scrutiny. And also, thanks to the confinement to barracks, we were almost never alone.

At night, I vacillated between instantaneous sleep and hours of worry. I worried about Trevor finding someone else. About postings and promotions ten years down the line. About not fitting in. About who I was becoming whenever I put combat boots on my feet. I would fall into bed with the intention of pouring those worries into my journal or weaving them into stories with a new Kelly heroine, because it had become painfully clear that heroine Kelly didn't exist, not on the page and not in Saint-Jean, Quebec. She was a dream being, fictitious, stuck in a creative writing classroom.

Usually, I would fall asleep with pen in hand. I had to start setting the alarm five minutes early, so I had time to scrub streaks of blue ink from my cheek.

4

Somewhere into week four, we stood in ranks outside the Mega, blinking in the early morning sun, bogged down by our loaded rucksacks and weapons. All told, we carried more than sixty pounds each, a challenge when my own weight maxed out at not much more than twice that.

Birds chirped overhead as they soared through the husky maples. The only other sound was the rustle of nylon on cotton as we adjusted our packs and shuffled our feet. Bruvelle, Gagnon, and Persaud came lurching around the corner in their own gear, and came to a stop in front of us.

"Platoon, today we will conduct a seven-kilometre ruck march in honour of D-Day," said Bruvelle. "This will also serve as practice for your battle fitness test, which involves a thirteen-kilometre ruck march, fireman carry, and shell scrape dig, which you will complete at the end of the course. You will keep up with your fellow troops and not break ranks. Remember that this march, today, is not about fitness. It is about honour." His eyes connected with ours and I swallowed down nerves. My failure of the fitness test still loomed over-head like a cloud. "Now, line up with your fire buddy and we'll do a warm-up."

Our platoon followed Bruvelle through a series of hip rotations, ankle rolls, and neck turns. Verner and I had been assigned as fire partners, akin to the buddy system in kindergarten; we were responsible for always knowing each other's whereabouts, and protecting one another at all costs. *Your fire partner is your lifeline. You go nowhere without him or her*, said Bruvelle on the day he matched us all up. We would sleep in the same tent in the field, eat at the same time, be mimicking shadows of conformity. I liked Verner—his affable laugh, his large, gentle body. Like true fire buddies, we looked after one another.

"Well, you ready for this?" Verner dug a finger under his helmet strap, which he'd not adjusted properly, so it pressed deeply into his skin and left marks each time he wore it.

"Hey, it's just a matter of one foot in front of the other, right?"

"Right." Verner sounded unsure as our fellow troops lined up ahead of us. "Except they'll make us walk at some stupid-ass pace to meet some stupid-ass arbitrary timeline."

"Such is military life."

With a roll of our eyes, and following an order from Bruvelle, Verner and I pushed off on command, trudging forward in the June heat, lined up like green dominoes. Joe's blond head bobbled in front of us—his fire partner, Huang, at his side, her legs moving double-time to maintain the pace, which she somehow managed to keep.

Rucksack marches were a matter of tuning out the mind, not thinking about the pressure, the weight, the impending distance that stretched ahead. Left foot, right foot. Repeat. To pass the time, I counted my breaths, imagined how I would arrange my new Toronto apartment before my next year of university and did a cost analysis on furniture I needed to buy. Anything but focus on the growing blisters and weak muscles, the oxygen in too-short supply, the glowing orb of the ruthless sun.

The platoon was collectively fading, with only two kilometres left. Where the first portion of the march had generated shouts of support from the ranks and some casual chatter, exhaustion swept across us like a wave. We were surrounded by the sounds of boots shuffling over the ground and laboured breathing. And although I'd so far showcased below-average physical abilities— a strike against me in such fitness-minded company—I had morale aplenty. I saw providing motivation as a potentially redeeming quality.

"Come on, 13 Platoon!" I gasped, shoving a triumphant fist in the air, my back hunched forward to accommodate my pack. "You can—"

I blacked out. Mid-sentence.

I woke lying on my side to the blur of Verner and Joe within inches of me, kneeling on the ground, their faces shiny blobs of white silhouetted by the sun. My face was smashed between the grass and my ruck. Suddenly, I was grateful for my helmet and its smelly strap.

"Jesus, Thompson, you okay?"

Oddly, I felt completely and totally fine. Not groggy or nauseous. Not even overly tired. It was as though a switch had been flipped from off to on. Someone tugged my pack from my back and I rolled off of my rifle, the barrel having been pressed awkwardly into my ribs, leaving a long bruise from breast to clavicle.

"Stay there, Thompson," said Bruvelle. "Don't get up." He motioned to the course staff, a flurry of combat boots moving towards us. My platoon-mates hovered over me, some rolling their eyes at my weakness, others squatting to my level in concern. I wrestled myself onto my elbows.

"Really, I feel fine. I can keep going." Once semi-vertical, I felt completely capable of finishing the march. It was as though my body had just needed a moment of rest on the soft earth. "I didn't even feel dizzy. It just sort of happened." I put on a chipper tone to hammer at the thin layer of nerves nestled under my helmet. My career hung from a string of spider silk, easily undone by the swipe of a hand.

"Keep going my ass," Bruvelle said. "Only place you're marching to is the MIR. Verner, you take her pack back to the Mega. Thompson, get yourself to the hospital. Platoon, back in ranks. We'll be finishing without them."

Without them. His words gnawed at me, and I suddenly had an overwhelming headache. In an organization that prized teamwork above all, those two words did more damage than my rifle ever could. I watched from my spot on the ground as our platoon stumbled onwards, kicking up plumes of dirt. Joe turned to offer a weak wave of support over Huang's head.

"Well," Verner said, slinging my pack onto his stomach and offering me an arm to heave myself up. We stood a moment, hands locked, until I was certain I could walk unaided. "Thanks for getting me out of finishing that bullshit." We laughed as we stumbled towards the MIR, taking the direct path from the perimeter fence, just a few hundred metres. "But next time, try to be a little less dramatic about it."

At the hospital, the doctors checked my vitals and peered into my eyes with pointed lights, all turning up nothing. But they insisted on arranging some tests in the town of Saint-Jean.

In the meantime, *soldier on,* the doctor said. Soldier on. Keep going. Push until you break and can no longer rise from the ground.

In mid-June, five weeks into our course, the course staff called me to the bowels of the Mega, a place where I imagined administrative machines were powered by failed cadets on hamster wheels. Bruvelle informed me that the doctors wanted to rule out any underlying heart issues, and a series of cardiac tests had been coordinated.

"You will report to the Saint-Jean hospital at 1300 hours today. Do you have a vehicle?"

"Yes, Sergeant."

"Then we will provide you with directions." Every time Bruvelle talked, it sounded like he was reading from a technical manual, each word carefully pronounced and robotic. "You are expected to report back to this office immediately after your appointment and make up for any lessons you miss. Check in with your fire partner for his notes. Understood?"

"Yes, Sergeant."

At the appropriate time, I made my way to the parking lot where my metallic blue car glinted in the sunshine. Sitting in the driver's seat and getting out my key, I'd never felt so free. I hadn't left the Mega since I walked through the green doors back in May. Our barracks confinement restrictions had been lifted, but all of us were too tired to venture out, though we had plans to do so this coming weekend.

The hospital was easy to find, sitting on the river that wound its way through the town centre. I fumbled through awkward French until I was able to make it clear who I was and why I was there, feeling silly in uniform, surrounded by civilian families who toted toddlers and jiggled babies in strollers.

"*Ici, ici,*" said the receptionist. She gestured to the cardiac waiting room where I sat for half an hour, thumbing through two-year-old magazines. Finally, a man in his early twenties emerged from a room with a clipboard, and gestured for me to follow and then sit on the paper-covered exam table.

"*Parlez-vous français?*"

"*Un petit peu.*"

"*Je vais utiliser cette échographie pour examiner votre cœur.*" He held the ultrasound wand in his hand and motioned it over his chest. "*Votre chemise.*" He picked at his own shirt with his pointer finger and thumb, mimed a bra removal, then swept a curtain back so I could remove my tunic and T-shirt and replace them with a gown, open at the front. When I opened the curtain again, he pointed at the table, the whole exam a game of charades.

A squirt of gel emerged with a fart from a squeeze bottle while the technician pressed the wand into my breasts with medical interest, squinting as he went. I watched the screen, indiscernible swirls of black static, and wondered if my secrets were spilling from my most important organ, revealing the anxiety mixed with my military blood. Both Grandpa T and Dad had reported to hospitals for chest pain, their fears manifesting as angina. Here in the stark hospital room in Saint-Jean, my heart sounded strong and unbroken, but so had Dad's and Grandpa's at my age. It was war that had done them in. Maybe, after a trip to Afghanistan, I'd return with my blood flowing the wrong way, my cardiovascular system a knot of pain.

The technician typed things into the computer. Test complete, he handed me a towel to wipe off the gel but did not swing the curtain closed. When I manoeuvred to get dressed, he shook his head and dangled a set of cords.

"*Non, vous avez besoin de ce moniteur cardiaque. Pour deux jours.*" He held two fingers in the air like a peace sign. Apparently, I was to be fitted with a forty-eight-hour heart monitor. I laughed out loud when he produced the device, which shattered any further images of myself as a real soldier. The technician stuck gummy electrodes across my chest and below my ribs; they were connected to a Walkman-shaped apparatus via five different-coloured leads. I hooked the device to the belt of my uniform as though it were just another piece of necessary gear, fitting right next to my knife, fork, and spoon set. (*You call it KFS, Thompson*, Kelper had explained when the kit was issued, rolling her eyes at my apparently unchangeable civilian ways.)

"*Vraiment?*" I raised my palms to the technician. *Really? You want me to go back to training like this?* He offered a sympathetic shrug and handed me an appointment card to return the monitor in two days.

I arrived back at the Mega just as my platoon-mates were in the middle of a lesson on the structure of military command. They watched as I took my seat between Verner and Joe and tried to disappear despite two of the electrodes sitting high on my chest—easy to see.

"Dad, I'm like a pariah around here," I whispered into the payphone in the pod hallway that evening, the open corridor white and revealing. He'd accepted my collect call but sounded annoyed. At my potential illness or that I was calling during dinner hour, I couldn't be sure.

"Moo, you can't become a MIR Commando already."

"A what?" I was quick to anger, but immediately tempered myself. Respect for my dad was extended the same way it was in the Forces rank structure: unequivocally. And he wasn't trying to be mean, but rather parroting the terms the military had ingrained in him and he expected me to adopt. I twirled the heart monitor's wires around my finger and tugged gently on all five leads at once, feeling them pull at my skin.

"Someone who's always going to the MIR for something new. You'll get a reputation. It's like crying wolf."

"It isn't crying wolf if there's actually something wrong with you, Dad." Tears slipped down my cheeks. I couldn't help it.

I let them drip onto my chest, wondered briefly if I could electrocute myself with my own emotion.

"Sometimes you just need to keep quiet about things."

"It's hard to keep quiet when you're blacking out in the middle of ruck marches. Jesus Christ, Dad."

"Language, Moo."

I scratched at my chest, where allergic-reaction blisters had begun to form underneath the electrodes. "I'm not going to pass, Dad. I'm not sure . . ." I paused. Swallowed twice. ". . . that I'm cut out for this."

"You are . . . You are," he said again with more conviction. "You can do this. Hell, you've never quit a thing in your life."

It was true. "It's embarrassing, Dad. Sticking out like this. I feel like a failure." A fellow cadet walked by without making eye contact.

"Just stick with it, Moo. Gotta run and help your mom with dinner. Love you." Dad hung up the phone but I lingered, pretending to hear the words he hadn't said—that being unable to reach a certain level of fitness wouldn't determine my quality as a soldier, that he would be proud even if I was deemed physically weak. Being physically weak felt so different to me than frailty on a grander scale, but the more time I spent in training, the more my interpretation of strength was mutating into the military's definition—not the feminist ideal I thought I'd espoused in high school simply for enrolling in the first place. The effect was the slow disintegration of my self-worth.

I tried to call Trevor but he was out with friends, his mom said. Did I want to leave a message? He'd gotten a cell phone. Had I tried that number? I called the new number twice, both times relegated to voicemail, his greeting message jovial with civilian freedom, the life I'd left behind.

For the two days that followed, as hard as I tried to hide

them, the heart monitor wires kept poking out of my uniform like unruly, multicoloured chest hairs.

"Thompson," Persaud soon barked at me. "Get that fucking thing under control."

"I'm trying, Master Corporal."

I tried so damn hard, but in the absence of tape and since I was confined to barracks and unable to buy any, I resorted to tying loops of green paracord—thin cording meant for tying down tenting material and for other odd jobs—around my chest to keep the wires in line; anything to avoid more attention. When I took my tunic off at the end of the workday, exposing my wired-up body, I laughed along with my platoon-mates at my newfound nickname: Robo-Thompson.

The monitor offered no conclusive results. *You're fine,* the doctor said. No reasons for the episode, as though the whole thing was some elaborate cry for attention, when really I craved the anonymity that my comrades seemed to find in their uniforms. But on every future march, I fainted as if someone had snapped their fingers, turned off a light switch. Heart, normal. Blood supply to the brain, normal. vo2 max, completely healthy. In my head, perhaps? Doctors gave me a clean bill of health and sent me on my way with no solution and no reduction in duties. The blackouts felt like an aggressive push, a glaring hint that maybe soldier life wasn't for me. The proof was surely in those very blackouts—even my body was buckling in revolt.

5

The weeks had started to blend into one another, but we were near the end of June, with less than a month left of IAP. In front of us, the Mega campus obstacle course warbled like a mirage, the rising heat distorting our vision. It looked like a grown-up version of a playground.

Our platoon stood shoulder to shoulder and I shuffled my feet, eyes on the course that loomed ahead. Ten-foot walls. Monkey bars over pits of mud. A maze of low-hanging ropes to be leopard-crawled under. Bruvelle, Gagnon, and Persaud hovered nearby, chatting amongst themselves. *No one cadet can win this race, platoon. It's all about teamwork.* Persaud in particular had been hammering home this fact until I thought I might barf the next time someone uttered the words *teamwork* or *cooperation*.

"Why is Quebec so stinking hot?" Joe, born and raised in the Prairies, had struggled to adjust to the humidity, the constant sag of moisture on towels used at five in the morning and still damp by nightfall. Beads of sweat gathered at his temples.

"The joys of global warming." I sucked my teeth in anticipation, slung my thumbs under the loops of my webbing straps.

"I think they watch the Weather Channel to see which day would be the shittiest to make us run this gauntlet. It's always when they tell us we're going to be indoors all day, and I don't wear sunscreen, that they switch it up, stick us outdoors, and I'm a tomato by noon." Joe was the only one amongst us concerned about the likes of melanoma—things grown-ups worried about. Besides, our skin was mostly covered by our uniforms; all except our hands and faces. "You never seem to burn." Joe gestured at my hands, creamy brown with melanin, fingernails crusted with dirt from field exercises and weapons cleaning, just like the rest of my platoon. I'd never felt such pride at matched filth.

I scoffed, self-deprecating and suddenly shy. "I have a lot of other problems. Have you noticed I haven't actually completed a single ruck march? Couldn't even pass my fitness test on the first go."

"Hell, don't be so hard on yourself just for not being an athlete. You're doing great. You have an awesome attitude and that's a huge part of it. Think of all the other things you bring to the table." I didn't want to tell Joe, someone I was increasingly attracted to, that my attitude was shit. I beamed him a fake, confident smile as I focused on wrangling a finger between my ribcage and sports bra, trying to ease the pinch of elastic.

Joe had been permeating my imagination more often as the weeks went on. Was it the Basic Training Effect that made me want him? The shared experience, the exhaustion, the pressure and stress making him more attractive than he would have been on civvie street? Nearly every guy in basic who treated me decently seemed sexy, even when I didn't find them physically attractive, which was something I chalked up to simple proximity and sleep delirium. Flirting while we sat in the common room on weekday evenings—always polishing boots or ironing shirts— was a given, reminding us we retained part of our civilian selves. And once confinement to barracks had ended, we hung off each other during weekends spent drinking at the mess or dancing in local bars, kissing in furtive corners—fraternization rules be damned. We'd even had a weekend home to see family and friends, and on arrival, Trevor seemed juvenile to me, always partying at bars, even though I was acting the same way in a different environment.

I watched Joe, the sun in his eyes, his straight back and gentle smile. No, my attraction to him was something else.

"Just be careful, okay?" Joe said, his jaw tensing.

"Careful? This course booby-trapped or something?"

"Your fainting." Joe pushed at the dirt with the toe box of his boot. "Freaks me out. Don't want to see that happen on the rope tower or at the top of a ten-foot wall."

"I'll be careful." I was embarrassed, charmed, and simultaneously annoyed at his concern, because I was a soldier, yes, but I was also young and horny, and uncertain of where the line between independent woman and wannabe lover was to be drawn. But Joe's concern was warming because part of me wanted to be cared for. Eighteen years old and I just hoped for a guy to lay his suit jacket over a puddle instead of expecting me to splash in it with him—ironic when basic training had me fighting to be one of the guys.

"Hard to be careful when I don't even feel it coming," I said to Joe. To ease the stares of platoon-mate judgment, I'd taken to joking aloud about what I saw as indicators of my military ineptitude: not passing the PT test, fainting on ruck marches, the Robo-Thompson heart monitor. If I joked about it, I felt others would see me as less weak.

"Well, if you don't feel good, just holler, okay? I'll be there."

I nodded, knowing he would, then I cast my eyes to my combat boots and turned a shade of pink that couldn't be attributed to the sun.

"Feeling the hype," Kelper said, elbowing me in my side

and snapping my attention back to the course ahead. My pod options for friendship were limited—Doffer's religious ways put me off, and Huang didn't seem to associate with anyone in the platoon, always disappearing behind her closed door—making my connection to Kelper one of convenience. She often lamented about her hardships: her recent relationship collapse, her twisted ankle that she "soldiered on" with (*Not like you and your fainting, Thompson*), or frustration over her inability to leg-press whatever the guys were lifting that day.

You can be sexy and a military officer, she said once, gazing in the mirror as she dabbed on eyeshadow. It wasn't clear who she was trying to convince with this statement, because—like the rest of us females—Kelper seemed on a constant quest to defend her equality within the Forces, which depended on her physical capabilities, something the military confirmed for her because her fitness level was on par with the men. Kelper, while earning the respect of the male troops, had a grating presence, a fact Joe confirmed one night over rum and cokes in the mess. *The guys don't really like her,* he whispered. Meanwhile, I seethed with jealousy as my positive qualities, like kindness and compassion, went underappreciated. I'd been told that thoughtfulness opened doors, which had proved true in civilian life but hadn't translated to the military.

"I fucking hate monkey bars," I said. "Guy in grade one used to pull down my pants whenever I crossed them, and I'd be hanging in the air with my ass out."

"Try not to let that happen here," Kelper said, laughing. "It'll only give the guys what they want." Her eyes sparkled with competition, her joviality evidence she didn't consider me a threat to her personal best, much less her ability to attract the men of our platoon. In a weird way, I longed to be Kelper: my complete and total opposite, despite our similar looks.

"Platoon!" Gagnon donned a pair of army-issue sunglasses that made him look like an insect. "You will complete the course together. Help each other with the challenges, understand?"

"YES, MASTER CORPORAL!"

"On the count of three . . ." Persaud checked his stopwatch. "One, two, three, GO!"

We zipped towards the first obstacle, a series of logs stacked high or arranged low, like staples jutting from the earth. Over, under, over, under; a game of soldier whack-a-mole. My combat boots made my legs feel like lead as I ran, Kelper ahead of me with wisps of blonde hair trailing from her helmeted bun. A cadet fell coming out of his final log roll and slid on the grass, his face scoring a foot-long divot. No one stopped to help him, instead jogging past with hollered words of encouragement when it was clear he wasn't seriously injured. The chlorophyll smear across his right cheek mixed with the blood now seeping from above his right eye. A cadet's warpaint.

The leopard crawl and other challenges flew past. Next up was a series of wooden walls of increasing heights for scaling. I lumbered clumsily towards the first wall, four feet high, and threw myself over. I paused at the six-foot partition that came next, then stepped onto the back of a cadet who hovered in a stool position, reaching upwards for another platoon-mate to help pull me towards the sky, our bodies an orgy of dirt-crusted hands and thick leather boots.

"You feel that, Thompson?" An anonymous cadet cupped me from underneath, his paw pressed firmly into my bottom. His palm could have been flat, open, nothing but a supporting foundation. Instead it was curled inwards like a bear claw, clenching and unclenching, my flesh clamped between his digits. "You're a little more than a handful back here." He pushed me up, grip still tight, and with the wooden slats of the wall underneath digging into my armpits, I pulled myself upwards, feeling dirtier as the humidity and dust coagulated on my skin.

"Fuck off." I was out of breath, my chest rising and falling at frightening speed. I gagged—from exertion, surely, not the slimy sensation of tentacles creeping over my unwilling body. Not from the brief acknowledgement that this squeeze of my buttocks was a potential premonition of what I could expect throughout my career. I hovered on the precipice, feigned catching my breath. Straddling the top of the wall, my platoon-mate looking up at me with a toothy sneer, it occurred to me to say something. To yell out. Kick him in the face. Cry. Bring my concerns to the course staff. And yet I felt like I was without options; I could not hold both definitions of myself in the palms of my hands—soldier and burgeoning feminist.

My teammates and I were bound together in this venture, a fact continually reiterated by the course staff. If we didn't support one another, failure was inevitable. So I dutifully leaned down to offer my groper a hand. We landed on the other side of the obstacle with a thud. I eyed him, searching for a feeling of regret, of shame, but came up wanting while the flesh of my ass throbbed as though the mark of his handprint were painted in camouflage.

"Go, go, go!" An oblivious Gagnon jumped at the finish line, his face red with excitement. I was crying or sweating, moisture trickling down my face, dampening my T-shirt. Once at the rope tower—which extended upwards twenty feet, across twenty more, then down again—I reached for the first rung while Kelper stalled next to me, her fear of heights clearly mounting in her stomach, eyes wild. She clenched her bottom lip until I thought it might bleed.

"I'll be right next to you," I said as her hands went tentatively to the rope. "The whole way, okay? Don't look down, and keep your eyes on me." The yellow nylon dug into my hands, the structure wobbling under shifting weight as the rest of the platoon careened to the bottom of the other side. Kelper's hands moved like she was swimming through jelly. "It's all in your head. One foot in front of the other, Kelper." I stayed with her the whole way, crawling slowly up and across the obstacle, ensuring her eyes stayed on me. At the top, about to descend, she turned to me full of panic, face white.

"Hurry up! Be safe but hurry the fuck up! You can do it, Kelper!" Our platoon-mates jumped and hollered, halfway between anger and excitement. What would the response have been if I were the one with the fear of heights, paralyzed at the top? There was no time to consider it.

"Grip and flip, remember?" We grabbed the rope on the other side of the tower with both hands, and flipped over until our bodies flopped against the netting and made for an easy manoeuvre to the bottom. I'd hoped, even knowing it was fruitless, that conquering the rope tower would end like a TV mini-series: females united in completion of the challenge, linking arms and tottering towards the finish line. Side by side, no one the winner, slow fade. But Kelper beamed with pride before jetting ahead to the final obstacle, her temporary weakness forgotten. I was completely unsurprised.

The last challenge was a wobbly rope bridge. The staff stood at the end like fans irate with their losing team. "Before you cross this line, I want to hear angry voices. You are soldiers and you will yell and scream and terrify your enemy. Do you hear me?" Bruvelle shouted.

It seemed an odd request, but we weren't a group accustomed to talking back. When I got to the other side of the bridge, fresh from my "angry noise" experience, Bruvelle singled me out.

"THOMPSON! What the hell was that?! I said sound ANGRY!" I thought I had sounded furious enough, but apparently not. So I redid the obstacle, with my entire platoon watching, Kelper arching an eyebrow while she drank from her canteen, as I screamed my heart out with the rope bridge wobbling underneath me, stabbing the air with the imaginary bayonet of my rifle. I collapsed the moment I crossed to the other side, embarrassed, exhausted, and now legitimately angry. Cadets slurped on their water canisters in the shade while I sat panting in the sun where I'd landed, noticeably on the outside of the semicircle they formed.

Joe approached. "They like to pick on you a bit, eh?"

"Easy target. You know." He did know. I wiped sweat from my forehead with my sleeve.

"You're doing great. You're smart, you work hard. Don't let them get you down." He smiled wide. Joe was always smiling, his two front teeth turning towards one another as though whispering a secret. How long since I'd heard a word of encouragement, much less since anyone had recognized how badly I needed it? When he placed his hand on my back in the most platonic way, I leaned into the attention like a neglected animal. Eighteen—a kid really—feeling simultaneously strong and weak, and at that moment, relentlessly in love with Officer Cadet Joe Shorrocks, the only person who I felt saw my strengths.

"I'll try." And I would try. I would try so fucking hard.

"I'm going to marry him," I told Mom on the phone that night, surprising even myself as I wrapped myself like a cat in the metal payphone cord. I had never wanted to get married—that was my sister's main interest—so hearing the words fly from my mouth made them feel trite, storybook-like, but no less true. I hadn't wanted marriage because I wanted a career, a library of books, and a house that I would buy alone and decorate to my tastes. For some reason, I couldn't see those desires coinciding with a permanent relationship.

Besides, I was dating someone else.

And I was sleep-deprived.

And I was emotional as all hell.

And my whole, entire life was changing, out of my control.

I could almost hear Mom rolling her eyes. It was nearly time for bed. My PT gear, which I'd taken to sleeping in so I could roll out of bed before Huang's wakeup call, showcased a series of purplish welts that could each be traced back to the obstacle that had caused the injury. Three-inch line under the ribs: rope tower. Stripes of black across the arms: wooden wall. Five dime-sized circles across my ass: eager, heated hands.

"There are so many emotions flying around in a place like that," Mom said. "Don't get too caught up in them."

I wanted to cherish my attraction to Joe, cultivate it, make it mine, because love was something shiny and joyous—so different from my small taste of military life. I didn't tell my female comrades or remaining platoon-mates about how I felt. I didn't revisit the subject with Mom. I didn't call to tell my best friend. From then on, it was only within the pages of my journal that I shared my secret—that I was in love with Joe, and that I wasn't sure how to fall in love with the Forces.

6

Like prisoners of war, we sat in the back of a two-ton truck on a sweltering July day, forcedly huddled together. Attached to our hips, our webbing kit was a part of us: stubby one-litre water bottle, gas mask in a protective bag, ammo pouches, raincoat. The truck screeched to a halt and we lurched forward collectively, heads bobbing under the weight of our Kevlar helmets. As usual, we had no idea where we were or what we were doing there.

"Everybody out." Gagnon lowered the truck tailgate and jerked his finger at the waiting landscape—nothing but stretches of sandy rolling hills and skinny pines.

"We could be in Afghanistan already for all we know," someone said, and we chuckled nervously. Had they slipped us sleeping pills at the mess and dropped us into a war zone? Nothing seemed impossible.

We automatically lined up in ranks. "Platoon"—Sergeant Bruvelle pointed at the only visible structure, a squat cement hut with a flat roof—"today is your date with the gas hut." He paused for a response, but we hadn't been told to give one, so we blinked back at him. "You will now be issued your chemical, biological, radiological, and nuclear warfare suits, also known as the bunny suit, along with a pouch of decontamination sponges and a filter."

"YES, SERGEANT!"

The CBRN protective garment, or "bunny suit," was woven from dense grey fabric lined with charcoal, with a hood that made it look like a onesie snowsuit. On top of this went rubber galoshes and gloves—and, finally, our gas mask. I lugged the twenty pounds of kit to the shade, running my fingers over the rough canvas and tugging on several of the rusty zippers.

In basic training, CBRN drills were called randomly throughout the day, instigating a series of proceeding tasks:

1. Squeeze eyes shut and hold breath. (Do not heave in a big breath . . . Just. Stop. Breathing.)

2. Tear open Velcro cover of mask carrier and remove mask from bag.

3. Hook thumbs into elastic straps, slip mask under chin, pull straps over the head, and tighten.

4. With remaining breath, exhale to force out contaminated air, cover filtering canister with palm, and heave in to check the seal. The mask should suction against the face.

5. Repeat "GAS, GAS, GAS" loudly in acknowledgement to warn others.

We ran through this drill countless times, aiming to meet the ten-second deadline to be sealed in and ready for battle—literally. Those who didn't meet the ten-second requirement were deemed "dead" and ordered to the shameful sidelines for the rest of the lesson. But now there was the added complexity of a suit, gloves, and boots. Until the moment I eyed my own bunny suit, the practices had felt akin to Broadway costume changes; there was comfort in knowing there was no gas and the trial was all for show. But as I held a decontamination sponge in my hand, I realized a time might come where I would need this training, likely in some place far from home. I could die, or be asked to die. I absent-mindedly fingered the rubber galoshes, warm from the sun.

"GAS, GAS, GAS!" Bruvelle called, and we were in our masks in record time. "What the fuck are you waiting around for?!" he cried, pointing at the bunny suits that lay at our feet. "Your lungs are fine, but what about the rest of you? Your skin is melting!"

The following minutes offered a depressing display of military prowess, or rather the lack of it. We stumbled all over, fumbled with the awkward bungee-corded boots, couldn't get the rubbery gloves tugged on tightly. If we were in the real world with mere minutes to prepare for nuclear holocaust, 13 Platoon would have perished on the spot.

"That was horrible!" shouted Gagnon, his pale face now red with frustration. "Do you all want to die? Again!"

Again! turned into another three iterations of removal and reapplication. Once fully dressed, my platoon-mates milled around in various states of hilarity like bug-eyed aliens. Some cadets used each other's suits as punching bags, their rubber fists bouncing off the protective layers, grunts muffled by masks.

"Time for laps," said Gagnon, who hopped up and jogged ahead. Laps? In CBRN gear? It felt awkward and strange, but we clambered to our feet and ran several loops around the gas hut before forming a line outside the door as though queuing for a ride at Disney World.

"They're making us sweat on purpose," someone grumbled from inside their mask. "The moister your skin, the more the tear gas stings." The comments sent a flurry of panicked gossip slowly down the waiting line.

"Well," Joe said, turning to face me. "You ready for this?" He comically pulsed his azure eyes wide, then squinted, then opened them wide again; the only way to express emotion in the damn bunny suit.

"This kind of thing, it's all in the head," I said, scuffing my boot into the sand as my voice bounced around my rubber mask. I was eerily calm, despite the twenty other pairs of eyes that peered nervously from their enclosed masks. It was a strange thing, to put yourself purposely in danger, especially when horror stories of training gone wrong—burnt skin and seared eyes—had been whispered throughout the Mega. But for once, my anxiety dissipated, no room left in my brain for fear. As the door to the metal hut swung open, we moved in an orderly fashion. No pushing. Everyone gets a chance on this ride.

The hut was fabricated from cement blocks, offering a waiting area with a large window that looked onto the main chamber, like in a surgical theatre. This central compartment contained an old-school metal hotplate with a frying pan on top, and an exit door painted red. Outside was our end state. The red door was freedom.

Pushing into the gas area, we crowded into a tight circle so we could see one another as the course staff hurried in behind us and shut the metal door with a heavy clunk. The platoon warrant stood in the viewing section, fists on hips as though waiting for the bell at a boxing match. Officer cadets versus tear gas. Four-to-one odds on the gas.

Gagnon gave a thumbs up, and we did too. *Yes. Ready.* He then pulled apart several capsules and sprinkled powder across the frying pan, which sizzled and sparked to life. A curl of white smoke rose into the air, and next to me my platoon-mate Chapley, whom I recognized only from his stance, furled his fingers into his rubbery palms. Soon it was difficult to see one another through the smoky haze, all of us gender-neutral astronauts, shapes and curves hidden underneath layers of rubber and carbon. Joe, my alphabetical marker, disappeared into the gas cloud, and I felt my lungs pinch and I gasped for air as though I were drowning. I reminded myself of my training. Calm breaths, in and out.

"Platoon, you will now engage in cs gas decontamination procedure, removing the mask, using the sponge and wiping exposed skin, before putting your mask back on," said Gagnon, his voice garbled behind his own mask. "Skin will sting and eyes will water. Do not breathe in. Do you understand?"

For most of the basic training elements—the fitness test, the obstacle course, weapons training—we could see the value in the task, because they improved our soldiering skills. Other times, the staff's demands seemed to exist solely to damage our bodies and squash our spirits. But although their faces were covered with gas masks, the seriousness of the staff's concern penetrated the layers of filtering charcoal in my bunny suit. This was no joke.

"Perform decontamination procedure!" Gagnon hollered.

I paused, hands hovering at my sides like I'd been challenged to a shootout. Opening a slippery pouch, removing my mask, and completing decontamination in the space of one breath would prove a challenge I wasn't up for. But with eyes squeezed shut, I felt for the decontamination sponge package, tore it open, and tucked the package into my belt. Ready. Next, I took a huge, calming breath before I stuffed my mask into my carrier and slopped the oily mixture from the sponge across my skin. My ears echoed with the sounds of coughs and chokes, liquid hitting floor, Velcro tearing. My body throbbed for oxygen and my face pulsed with each heartbeat. Once safely back inside my mask, having huffed out the last of the toxic air and checked the seal, I shook with adrenaline. My skin itched, as if from an allergic reaction, and I coughed a phlegmy hack until my lungs settled and the tickle in my throat subsided. But I had done it. First try and all.

One unfortunate cadet had committed the cardinal sin of taking in air while decontaminating, coughing until he'd turned a strange shade of purple. Another cadet had thrown up, leaving behind a pile of what appeared to be scrambled eggs and milk. The two were escorted out to catch their breath and were forced to run the gauntlet again. The rest of us burst through the red door, collapsing as though we'd never expected to breathe fresh air again.

I was struck by how bizarre the gas hut experience was; but more importantly, that it didn't feel bizarre at all. That I had knowingly allowed myself to be tear-gassed hadn't knocked on the door of concern, because IAP was teaching me that questioning orders only resulted in more suffering, and in that way the staff were doing their jobs—preparing us for real lives as soldiers.

And I had succeeded.

Recovery was slow, even for those of us who had done the gas hut right. We coughed and wheezed, torn between using our canteen water to soothe skin or to ease parched throats. Our decontaminated faces were tinted Oompa Loompa orange, and sand stuck to the oily film like it would to suntan lotion. Also, despite the fact that I'd stuffed tissues up my nose as a makeshift plug, the world did not contain enough tissues to manage the onslaught of snot. It streamed from our noses and mouths, dripping out onto the ground and making soupy dirt at our feet. But despite bodily fluids offering endless comedic opportunities, we ate our boxed lunches in silence. We did not complain about the sandwiches with single slices of mutant cold cuts, or the apples that were so bruised that we secretly chucked them into the brush. No one used their gas mask to pretend to be Darth Vader, and snot jokes dried up with the mucous itself. Pre-gas hut, the joking had made the possibility of imminent danger feel less real. On the other side, we felt like we'd passed a test that had propelled us into the officers we would become.

Returning to the truck, we coughed and teared up the whole trip back to Saint-Jean. Our uniforms were covered in a thin film of the gas, dried into a white powder, effectively choking us the entire ride.

7

After weeks of weapons practice, we were excited to get on the firing range. Not out of some messed-up desire to shoot people, but because we were learning that our C7 rifles were an extension of ourselves, and we cared for our weapons as if they were small children in need of tending. I called my C7 "Betty" and lugged around her seven pounds of metal like she was an extra appendage.

We stored our rifles in our bedroom closets, behind a series of three keyed locks. While we were occupied in daily lessons, the course staff perused our rooms, ensuring no items were left where they shouldn't be and no contraband was tucked into secret locations. Should these inspections result in the discovery of an improperly secured weapon—left on the bed, or a lock not clicked shut—the result was a serious fine and a platoon-public berating. The message was loud and clear: in the wrong hands, mixed with the right amount of carelessness, our rifles could mean death.

Our obsession with our weapons' whereabouts manifested in countless ways. A cadet from the other female pod kept waking her roommates with her militarized sleepwalking and gunfire noises, and she'd be found by her bed in the prone position, eyes squeezed tight as if she were mid-aim, finger on her weapon's trigger. *Rat-tat-tat-tat!* Sometimes she returned to bed on her own, but on other nights she had to be guided from her post. *It's your turn to get her. No, I did it last night!* Someone would relent and wrestle the unloaded weapon from her hand until she woke with a start. Hell, Huang used to jostle me awake and I'd be mid-push-up. So we understood the behaviour. What we didn't get was how, while sleeping, our platoon-mate managed to disengage the three locks with which her rifle was secured.

Before the range, we had to ensure we were comfortable with all weapons protocols, and our knowledge was assessed by the weapons handling and safety test. Training—and later, the test—involved a series of stoppages and safety procedures: clearing the weapon when handing it over to someone else; loading a round in the chamber; emptying said round. I learned about how the breeze affected aim and sights and triggers; where to hold my hands; and how to flick from manual to semi-automatic gunfire without throwing off my shot, eye narrowed on the sight at the tip of the barrel. The main take-home was this: don't shoot anyone without really, really intending to.

We waited in a lecture hall, as one by one each cadet was led to a separate room for testing, emerging afterwards to drop their bolts into the "passed" or "failed" box that sat at the front of the hall. When my name was called, I entered the classroom with Betty clutched in my left arm, and shivered as the three assessors barely looked up from their forms. The wall was lined with targets, which I wouldn't actually be shooting at in the safety-testing phase, and a few sandbags lay stacked in a corner. Otherwise, the room was empty except for the three chairs and folding table at which the assessors sat.

"Take the prone." The weapon technician gestured with his pen and I slumped onto my stomach and stretched my legs wide for balance, the classroom floor cool under the glaring fluorescent light. Soon the technician relayed a series of orders, his voice laconic as though he was tired of the routine. For the next ten minutes, I completed the directed actions on the pretend range, then turned with anticipation to the corporal assessing me. I was proud. Betty and I had performed a well-coordinated dance.

"Officer Cadet Thompson, fail." He didn't look up as he marked my form.

"Really?"

"You didn't clear the chamber before passing it over to the master bombardier. He could have shot off his fucking foot."

The course staff weren't supposed to swear at us. But this guy, who appeared to be even younger than me, had announced his propensity for profanity during our first weapons class. *Something I fucking announce first is that you'll notice I swear a fucking lot. It's not meant to be fucking offensive or anything, it's just the way I fucking talk. Anyone here object?* We'd shrugged our shoulders. Didn't care, especially since profanity was by then so firmly planted in our vocabularies. Only religious Doffer raised her arm. *Yes, me, I find it offensive.* The corporal had turned to her, hands on hips, assessing her wordlessly. He didn't stop swearing.

"Are you sure I failed?"

He raised an eyebrow and I dismounted from my high horse in silence, trudging into the lecture hall to drop my bolt into the "fail" box.

Afterwards, I diligently practised safety procedures with Joe, who would issue sharp commands while my fingers flew over Betty in response. When we were tested on our ability to strip our weapon down to the bolt, tidily laying out all its pieces in order for inspection, I had the best time in the platoon, even when the course staff turned out the lights and made us do it by feel alone. The following week, I passed the damn safety test.

So, once our safety knowledge was up to snuff, Bruvelle announced that the range test was imminent. The bus ride to the Farnham training area, where the range was located, took approximately an hour from the town of Saint-Jean, and was a welcome change from classes and exercise. I was nervous and excited. Another test. Yet some of my characteristic anxiety had been dissipating, replaced instead with a hope that one foot in front of the other would get me to my destination—to completion. I didn't have time to worry. I could only make room for so many emotions in IAP, and I chose to focus on the ones that would help me succeed.

"So, is Betty ready for some action?" Joe turned to me from his seat by the window, and patted Betty's flash suppressor like he would a dog.

"Betty? She's always ready. Like her momma."

"Maybe I should name mine."

"Well, it's not like giving her a name made her work for me any better or anything."

"Still," Joe said, tapping the plastic handguards of his own weapon until they rattled. "Feel like I have more of a relationship with this thing than anything else here." I wilted into the seat at the idea that he might feel more connected to a piece of metal than the breathing half-soldier, half-girl next to him.

"All right," Bruvelle called from the front of the bus as it ground to a halt. We lurched forward and then sat up straight. "Everyone off and file in ranks."

We stepped off the bus into the sparse, sandy terrain of Farnham, the range looming in the distance, roundels calling out to my bullets. We were ordered to put on our ballistic glasses, which until that time had remained unused, tucked in our webbing pouches.

"I guarantee I'm sexy in these," Kelper said, twisting at the waist to blink at me from behind oversized frames. Irritatingly, the shape of the glasses suited her face.

"Well if you are, then we all are," I said, laughing, as I pushed my glasses up the bridge of my nose. I didn't want to know what I looked like. I'd nearly given up on caring other than on the weekend, when civilian clothing was permitted.

"You chicks maybe," barked a male platoon-mate. "Us guys look like douchebags."

"Well, between uniforms designed with pockets on the hips and these sexy bitches, it really is a woman's world, eh?" I spun for effect, Kelper and I bumping each other and vogueing like we were in a Madonna video. We were soldiers, sure. But we were also teenagers.

"Thirteen Platoon!" Bruvelle shouted. "We will head into the hut to hand out your ammunition, which you will load into each of your magazines with thirty 5.56-calibre rounds. Everyone's bullets will be counted afterwards, and no one is to take home any rounds or shells as trophies, you understand? These aren't collectibles. This is live ammunition that could hurt people."

We filtered into the range hut and lined up to accept our bullets like we were receiving communion. The boxes of ammunition around us, we sat on the floor cross-legged like children, popping bullets into our magazines and stuffing them back into our mag pouches, two on each hip for easy access during an actual battle, with one magazine clipped onto our weapon. The occasional round skittered out of someone's hands, the metal pinging off the cement floor until the cadet scampered cat-like to retrieve it under the watchful eyes of the course staff. I stood, swinging my metal-laden hips from side to side.

"I feel like a belly dancer. I jingle when I move."

"You're basically a soldier Shakira," Joe said. He hefted his own magazines in the air. "Didn't expect them to be so heavy."

Indeed, the ammunition and its importance hung weightily from our hips, and I stopped jiggling mid-laugh, hands resting on the pouches like a drummer silencing a cymbal. After Bruvelle called for us to line up for the safety brief, we marched in an orderly manner towards the targets, feeling like superheroes.

Minutes later, I lay in the prone position, my C7 rifle balanced on sandbags, chest pressed uncomfortably into the hard ground. I pointed the barrel towards the target and squeezed one eye shut, focusing the sight on the intended destination of my bullets. I cocked the semi-automatic and aimed, finger hovering over the trigger. As I regulated my breathing, the smell of rifle cleaning oil—CLP—filled my nostrils. I'd cleaned my weapon the night before, lubricating the metal with greasy stink until traces of carbon laced my fingerprints.

"PLATOON, FROM ONE-HUNDRED-METRE RANGE, FIVE ROUNDS!"

My finger flicked off the safety in a smooth movement.

"PLATOON, AT YOUR TARGETS IN FRONT, AT YOUR OWN TIME, FIRE!"

I took a few more deep breaths before I fired my first five shots in a jolted sequence. The rifle butt jerked erratically against my cheek. It would bruise. The result was a shit grouping, with one bullet having missed the target entirely and the rest scattered like confetti across roundels of blue, white, and red.

"What the fuck, Officer Cadet Thompson? Just be grateful you weren't being tested yet." The master corporal running the range flittered his greying moustache, then moved down the line to scold some other ineffectual shooter. "We're going to try that again," he shouted to us. "This time, try to hit the goddamn targets. Your official testing begins *now*."

"Hey, Thompson," said my platoon-mate Chapley. Someone I would have called a friend. "Maybe it's just your tits getting in the way."

I feigned my usual laughter at the objectification, as if to say, *I can take a joke. I'm just one of the guys.* I returned my focus to my weapon. But the more I thought, the more I wondered if my tits weren't indeed the entire problem all along; if, given the chance, I might choose to lop them off to revel in the possibility of being taken seriously.

"Never mind," I said aloud, not caring whose concentration I was breaking. Calm. Breathe in deep, breathe out slow. At that pause, that break between fresh air and faintness, I squeezed the trigger once. Twice. Five calculated times.

I got the second-highest mark in the platoon. On the very first try.

8

It was Sunday evening, the second last week of IAP, so close to the finish that I could almost taste the flavours of home. All that stood in the way of Mom's spaghetti was surviving the fields of Farnham and one more week of classroom lessons. Lined up in the Mega basement at the bottom of the blue stairs, we jostled heavy rucksacks on our backs, trying to create a semblance of order in the chaos. It took me ten minutes to stand properly, first having to squat on the floor while Kelper hefted the bag onto my back, then employing my thinning thighs to heave upright.

We'd spent the entire weekend packing gear into tight spaces of our rucks, utilizing every D-ring, snap, and buckle. The staff warned us against eliminating any items from our ruck that were included on the kit list; they would be weighing bags to ensure we had every last pair of socks. We each carried a sleeping bag inner, sleeping bag outer, sleeping bag carrier, webbing, rain gear, ground sheet, bivvy bag, flashlight, KFS, canteen, two-litre water bladder and carrier, one-litre canteen, gas mask and carrier, three pairs of extra socks and underwear, four T-shirts, air mattress, two spare uniforms, ablution kit, ballistic glasses, gloves, helmet, C7 rifle and cleaning materials, and other little niceties. The result was between fifty and sixty pounds of life-saving gear to be humped through Farnham. I'd packed everything into black garbage bags for waterproofing, the plastic crackling every time I moved. Armed to the hilt, ready for anything.

Our weeklong field exercise was where our Mega training was taken from theory to practice with our small party tasks. Unlike the range or the fitness test, small party tasks tested leadership and organizational skills—the characteristics that were meant to define us as military officers. In the Farnham training area, we would break into sections, with the to-be-tested soldier serving as leader before the next person took their turn. For their assessment, each cadet was given a pretend scenario with a challenge to overcome, to be executed by their "staff"—the remainder of the section. Create a rope bridge. Erect a radio contact system. Perform a grid search for a missing weapon. It wasn't just the completion of the task that mattered, but the how. Assessments examined if troops were given firm orders, clear guidance about how the operation would be carried out, and regular breaks. Get the job done but protect your troops at all times, a concept that was the culmination of all the lessons we'd learned.

"I can't believe we're expected to carry all this," Kelper said, shifting her weight. She wobbled unsteadily. "I weighed in at sixty-one pounds."

"Seventy-three," I said, pointing to my back. "I need a lot of snacks." I'd been losing so much weight that glances in the mirror no longer revealed someone I knew. Kelly Thompson had become Officer Cadet Thompson over the last seven weeks, my curves turned to sharp points.

All of the current platoon serials in the Mega were headed to the field simultaneously for their testing—approximately two hundred cadets in total. We rumbled towards Farnham in a convoy of green and white buses, smelling of clean clothes and just-washed hair, and I sensed we wouldn't enjoy this kind of freshness for a while. We had no television access at the Mega, so over the weekend I'd called my family for detailed weather conditions, frustrated with the answer. Hot as hell. Humidity 100 per cent.

We arrived at the gates of Farnham as the sun was setting, and we were unloaded in the sand. Our rucks were waiting nearby, clearly labelled with bands of coloured duct tape on the straps. And then, before there was time to think, the course staff led the march through the sand towards the thin woods.

Our platoon had spent little time in Farnham, visiting the training area occasionally to practise small party tasks or topography skills—and always, it seemed, in the damn rain, making the area appear desperate and sagging. In the haze of night falling, Farnham looked like the backwoods of the military bases I had grown up playing in—sandy and coniferous, moon-like in its barrenness. A weird part of me felt like I'd come home.

Less than a kilometre into the march and, as per usual, I was falling behind. "You'll want the new issued socks," Dad had said during a brief visit home the weekend prior. We cadets had only been issued the standard grey woollies, which gave everyone itchy rashes that spread like poison oak. The new sock system, which my dad proffered from his own kit, came with black compression socks and a thick green overlay, guaranteed to wick sweat from my Black Cadillacs. Five minutes into our march, I regretted even tugging the socks from their plastic packaging, my feet sliding too much between the layers, the friction unbearable. A firm hump was taking shape on the ball of my foot, like I was stepping on a lime-sized marble.

When we arrived at the bivouac site where we'd be setting up camp, I dropped my rucksack to the ground, no longer concerned that I had lagged back and more so thrilled that I'd finished the approximately six-kilometre march. The biv site was akin to a camping compound in a provincial park except there were no facilities, shelters, or tent pads. Instead there were rough clearings between the trees; smatterings of leaves and piles of mud where previous cadets had set up camp. Fire partners were to zip their groundsheets together to form a cover, then tie them to trees to create a sleeping shelter, which was bizarrely nicknamed a "hooch."

"Jesus," I said to Verner, my fire buddy, pushing sweaty hair from my face. "I think I'm dying. Or my foot is going to fall off."

"Once I'm home," Verner said, out of breath, "if I ever suggest going for a hike, I hope someone slaps me into sense." He spread out his groundsheet and motioned for me to dig mine out of my bag, his helmeted head casting a wary shadow as the moon rose. I reached into my ruck for the groundsheet, conveniently stored on top. With sticks serving as improvised camping poles, we laced sections of our makeshift tent into the trees, unfurled our air mattresses and sleeping bags, and fell asleep before anyone could order us otherwise.

The next morning, we were told to take off our boots and sit inside our hooches with feet facing outwards so the course staff could assess foot wellness after the march; on display like we were animals at the county fair. We knew that, during war, poor hygiene could be a quicker death than a bullet—images of trench warfare and gangrene providing the evidence. I regarded my foot's new blood blister and prodded it with my finger; it throbbed like Rudolph's nose, a beacon in the bivouac.

"I'll call her Frankie," I said to Verner. We snickered, as if giving it a name were the most normal thing in the world. The course staff marched through our maze of tents, checking feet without getting too close to our already-intense body odour.

"Jesus, Thompson," Persaud said as he approached. "What the fuck?" He pointed at Frankie.

Indeed. *What. The. Fuck.*

"Don't pop it. Prone to infection," he said.

I nodded, and fished for the socks lost inside my sleeping bag. Persaud was already turning to walk away and I was nearly free, but then he whipped back in my direction and stormed towards me.

"Are your fucking toenails painted, Thompson?" he seethed, veins throbbing near his temple. He moved closer, invading my personal space in a way that made my pulse race. "Do you know that this means we have no way of determining if your toenails are receiving proper blood supply?"

The weekend before, the fated weekend in which Dad had given me the damn socks, I'd visited Trevor, diligently painting a French manicure to detract from the oozing blisters and dry skin that covered my feet. I imagined there would be bigger issues at hand if we needed my toenails to determine my general health, but basic training left no room for logic. I'd dared to bare my pale pink desire to a world of army green.

"I didn't think of that, Master Corporal."

"Only you, Thompson." He swung his head back and forth as though he couldn't fathom my stupidity. And then, almost as an afterthought: "And why in the fuck are your lips so glossy?"

"It's just lip balm, Master Corporal." I rubbed my lips together self-consciously. "It has sunscreen in it."

He opened his mouth to say something, then closed it again, muttering as he walked away. I decided to keep it to myself that I also had a tube of hand cream in my pocket because my hands kept splitting open and bleeding. I would wake up at night with streaks of blood up my arm, as though I'd waged a mini war in my sleep.

Pleasures in the field were small and came mostly in the form of food, although *food* became a word with a definition as loose as our stools after eating it. Lung in a bag. Cat food. Bun bullet. Just some of the tasty items on the ration pack menu.

Individual Meal Packs, also known as ration packs or IMPs, are ubiquitous in military life, eaten in the field or on deployment and coming in white nine-by-seven-inch packages. Other than the main dish—chicken tetrazzini, shepherd's pie—the contents remain a mystery until the package is cracked open and stripped for the items worth carrying or consuming. An average ration pack contains approximately twelve hundred calories per meal, which hardly felt like enough to sustain us when trudging endless kilometres through Farnham, lugging heavy rucksacks and engaging in play-battle.

Also on offer with IMPs are one of two bodily responses: insane, gassy constipation or explosive, poorly timed diarrhea. Like the IMPs themselves, you never know what you're going to get; they're a veritable Kinder Egg of nutrition. They had never caused me gastric upset as a kid when Dad would bring them home for camping trips. My sister Meghan and I felt like true warriors back then, insisting that everything be cooked outside and mixing the metallic packages of drink crystals in our camping cups; regular glasses from home wouldn't do justice to the rustic experience. But, as an adult, IMPs annihilated my insides. I learned to add a travel package of wet wipes to my webbing pouch.

The morning after our arrival in the field, we went to the ablution pit to prepare for the day. I brushed my teeth while the men shaved, razors screeching against stubbled faces, hardly any of them bothering with shaving cream. Watching them scrape blades across goose-pimpled flesh, I realized I'd assumed that the daily shave routine wouldn't have applied while in the field. Then again, I'd also assumed that regulations concerning our appearance would relax, but over the course of the week several women were written up for having their buns messy and askew, something that seemed unavoidable after sleeping on the ground.

I spat my toothpaste into the pit and sealed my toothbrush back in a Ziploc bag. And then I heard it. The call to action.

"Platoon! Pick your rations!"

No other statement has ever encouraged such mania. Not a last-minute goal during NHL overtime. Not a lottery win. Arms flew in the air and items fell from hands as we flailed towards the IMP stack. I made it in time to capture a Salisbury steak, a hunk of mystery meat smothered in something resembling gravy, everything the semi-palatable texture of rice pudding. Joe arrived at my side out of breath, streaks of shaving cream smeared on his cheeks and lines of razor burn prickling with blood. There was just one IMP left.

"Fucking lung in a bag again?"

Those nearby shook their heads in sympathy. The cheese omelette, dubbed the "lung in a bag," had a truly disturbing texture that we all imagined was similar to snacking on a puffy organ.

"We can trade." I held up my steak in a loving offering, but Joe shook his head.

"What? You're crazy. I like you too much to trade this with you."

He likes me too much.

We squatted to strip the packs and fill our webbing with the main components for the day. Each IMP contained a main meal, dessert, a small loaf of bread (the bun bullet), peanut butter or honey (which usually had warnings forbidding consumption due to expiry some fifteen years earlier), condiments, powdered drinks (valued for their sugar and electrolytes), and cookies or a chocolate bar. After the breakfast and lunch packs were opened, the platoon erupted into grade-five lunchroom behaviour, with offers to trade selected items.

"Anyone want my lung in a bag?"

The rest of the platoon collectively turned away from Joe and pretended they didn't hear his plea. He tossed the meal in the garbage, saving his bun bullet and, of course, the chocolate bar.

9

The week plodded forward with painful slowness. The first few days, while we practised topography skills or how to speak on the radio, I fantasized about my civilian friends back home, who were likely sleeping off another night at the bar before their part-time jobs, their mouths still fuzzy with alcohol. My voice would crackle across the airwaves—*delta, tango, niner*—as I wished my friends and I could trade places, imagining their cozy beds with the hum of air conditioning nearby, sequined bar shirts discarded on their bedroom floors. But after several days of intense physical activity and a near total lack of sleep, there was no mental room for fantasy, and I was left to focus solely on my footsteps in the dirt. At night, for the first time in my life, my precious hours of sleep were entirely dreamless.

The third day into the field exercise, we stalked through the woods in a wobbly line, shoulders loaded with gear, and sand in our skin, hair, nails. After dinner, our platoon had been divided into sections and then loaded one group at a time into the backs of several half-ton trucks, cramming up against boxes of ration packs and wooden pallets. Joe had been separated into another section and I watched as he settled into a seat and the waxed canvas flap was lowered to keep the engine fumes out.

The vehicle pulled away, and with it went my sense of comfort. In the back of a different truck with my own section—five adults having gone days without a shower—we breathed through our noses for the first minute or so until we were impervious to our own stench. The driver seemed to tour Farnham in circles before dropping us off in the middle of the training area.

"You have three hours to find your way back to the bivouac site using the following coordinates," Gagnon said while rubbing his long chin. "You are to treat this as a stealthy mission. On your route, you will be followed by the directing staff. Should they capture you before you arrive at the biv, you have failed your mission. If you come across another section from your platoon, you are to detain them as prisoners of war and direct them to the bivouac site under your command. Understood? Synchronize watches." The section pulled back uniform sleeves to reveal sports watches resistant to the elements. "2145 hours in five, four, three, two, one." A series of digital beeps chirped.

We watched the truck chortle down the sandy laneway until the brake lights disappeared around a bend. After assessing the map, we determined the best route was to avoid the roads and instead push through the woods, which made for slower progress but offered more cover.

Darkness spread like a cloak, thick cloud smothering any moonlight, so our section moved painstakingly slowly, with one cadet leading the way. He stopped to assess his map with the red lens on his flashlight, designed to maintain night vision and prevent us from being seen by potential enemies.

"These lights are fucking useless," he said, bringing the map closer to his face. Light bounced off the laminated page with a tomato tinge. He stepped over a log, pushed through a thicket, and sent a whip of maple into my face.

"Fucking hell, watch where you're going."

"It's not like I'm going for an afternoon stroll through a meadow, is it? Christ."

I leaned forward, hands on my knees to adjust the weight of my pack. The momentary relief on my trapezoid muscles allowed for a deeper gasp of air than I'd had in two hours. Before the mission, Kelper and I had taken care to apply 2nd Skin to the blisters on our feet, followed by layers of duct tape and two pairs of socks. Next, we had taken turns sticking strips of moleskin on our hips and shoulders, where abrasions were likely to form underneath our packs. *I look like I have that flesh-eating disease*, I'd said, scratching at one of hundreds of sand flea bites. *Think of them as your war wounds*, Kelper replied as she strapped on her webbing belt. Now the moleskin bunched underneath my tunic, adhesive clinging to my T-shirt.

"We don't have time to stop," someone said, breaking the line we'd formed. "Master Corporal said three hours. We only have three hours."

"Yeah, well, we're hardly moving as fast as we should. Whiny bitches," our cadet leader muttered under his breath, gesturing towards Kelper and me, the women. Mostly me.

"Well," I said, desperately out of breath, "considering I weigh about a hundred pounds less than you but we're still carrying the same pounds of gear, I'd argue it's you who's the whiny bitch. Keep in line, man. You'll throw us off our bearing." *O is for order, not for option* was a saying I'd learned wasn't just familiar to Dad; it was a military motto. Polite niceties had been done away with in favour of efficiency, all of us having forgotten the words *please* and *thank you*. A part of me felt uneasy with this change, surprised at how quickly nineteen years of manners had been erased.

"Someone take over," our leader said, thrusting the map of the Farnham training area in the air. "I'm going cross-eyed."

Kelper snatched the map and drew her compass from her chest pocket, shot a new bearing and pointed. Topography wasn't my strong suit. I was always off the mark by about five hundred metres, left stumbling around like a child lost at the park. Kelper, however, seemed to excel at the entire military experience—everything done with confidence.

"We need to go that way." She plunged ahead, cracking twigs underfoot as she went. Her assurance settled us all into unquestioning followers, keen to go in any direction that might lead us to water and a few hours of sleep.

"And we should start being quieter now," Kelper said. "We're getting closer to the bivouac site."

As if on cue, a series of rapid gunfire bursts pierced the air and the section dropped to the prone position and readied our unloaded rifles.

It felt very real. Too real. Being hunted, no matter that I knew no actual harm would come to us, made my stomach turn. I felt the familiar flop of anxiety that was foreign to the new, slightly more confident version of myself that I had become simply by surviving IAP. *Is this what Afghanistan will feel like?* I wondered. Compared to the others, I felt alone in my terror until I caught glimpses of the whites of another cadet's eyes, the shake of Kelper's hand as she swirled her pointer finger over her head, the symbol to place us in section formation. We crept forward to spread ourselves out in a circle of protection against potential captors, breathing into the ferns around our faces. Five minutes passed without further noise before we continued on our route.

With our awkward rucksacks, first aid kits, and weapons, we stumbled, regularly deviating off route. It took two and a half hours to march three kilometres, with frustrated bearings shot every five minutes. Finally, we came upon a road lined with tire tracks. Just two hundred metres to the bivouac site, sleep, and food.

"We should stay in the ditch here," I said, pointing in our intended direction. "Keep us off of the main route."

We traipsed forward, each step taken with care, sensing humanity in the shadows. Nearby, the familiar whistle of an artillery simulator built anticipation before it exploded into the air, breaking into the sky like fireworks. We ducked into the ditch, assessed forwards and backwards for the enemy.

"Find any of them?" Petty Officer Hopper's voice crackled over a radio.

"Section B captured at 2250 hours. Section A captured by Section D and delivered to the bivouac site at 2338. Section C still on route." Bruvelle clicked the receiver of his radio and strode past my section as we crouched in the shadows, his cowboy gait recognizable even in the dark. A curl of smoke from his simulator trailed behind him like a ghost before dissipating into nothingness. Once he was out of sight, we broke into a lame jog, rucksacks bouncing like humans on horseback. We made it to the biv site twelve minutes before the deadline.

Exhaustion took over as hooch tents were pitched, and those who cared enough set up Sterno fuel tablets and metal canteen cups of water to heat uneaten ration packs.

"That shit felt real," I said, sipping at my canteen. Kelper sat next to me, leaning against an evergreen. We hadn't bothered to set up hooches. Instead we lay out our bivvy bags and cocooned ourselves, protected from the drizzle that seeped through the trees. The heat wave had finally broken and my eyes drooped with sleep.

"Can't wait until this is over. This time next week we'll be packing to go home. Can you believe it?" Kelper said, yawning wide. I showcased surprise at this unexpected glimpse of her vulnerability, now knowing that she too had wanted it to end, despite her successful soldier reputation.

"It's almost over," I acknowledged. "Finally." Once the words left my lips, I felt the rise of panic, the terror of being without her, my other platoon-mates, and the challenging structure of training life that had become comforting in its familiarity. And there would be no more Joe, no more laughs, no more late-night chats. The thought of my cozy apartment in Toronto, the home I'd pictured a thousand times—with its red paint and the barrack box turned coffee table—now seemed so far removed from what I wanted.

When I looked over, Kelper was fast asleep, water dripping from her open canteen and seeping into her uniform like an inky stain that spread with every breath.

The days in the field continued as we were tested on our small party tasks, with my score earning a pat on the back from my sergeant and a hearty "Well done, Thompson." After what felt like a culmination of IAP failures, I had ranked near the top of the platoon in organization and leadership. Finally, I had done well, had made myself proud. And I had completed my task with compassion and a dash of kindness—without yelling at people, without impatience and rudeness. After my test, the course staff called me "Padre," joking about how I'd offered too much encouragement to my troops, although they couldn't take marks away for that.

No matter. Padre was better than Robo-Thompson.

Most of us passed our small party tasks, and those who didn't failed IAP, to be re-coursed on another serial or released from the Forces. *Can't wait to go home to Saint-Jean!* someone would say, as we ate our evening IMPs on our final night in the field, and we would snap our heads in their direction and tell them to shut their fucking mouths. The Mega was home to no one.

That last night in Farnham, I knew there would be some sort of monumental physical challenge. Sure enough, when we heard the words *bug out*, our stomachs dropped.

A bug out, designed to train us for quick response in a war zone, meant packing up all gear, tearing down hooches, and marching to a new location. Considering we were leaving the next morning, it was hilariously futile, but then that was the point: to be given orders and obey them without a second thought. Dread gurgled in my gut.

Except it wasn't dread. It was my period.

We'd been told to expect our bodies to revolt against the rigours of basic training. The stress and lack of sleep meant that many of us were struggling to maintain our physical status quo—we experienced weight fluctuations, hair falling out, and out-of-whack hormonal schedules. What wasn't acknowledged was that most of these effects happened to the women. I'd been losing large fluffs of hair; my skin broke out erratically. And although I was on the pill, my period had arrived unexpectedly while standing in ranks, ruck on my back, receiving orders for our impending march.

"Excuse me, Sergeant?" I raised my hand like a child, meek and ashamed. But also, miraculously, somehow not.

"What, Thompson?"

"I really need to use the washroom, Sergeant."

"You had time for that earlier. You'll have to find a spot on the march and then catch up afterwards."

I almost laughed. I had about as much chance of "catching up" as I did keeping up in the first place. "It's important, Sergeant." He stared intensely, compassion missing from the dark discs. "Feminine-important."

Bruvelle rolled his eyes and threw his arms in the air. He pursed his lips and pushed out an exasperated puff of air. I enjoyed watching him scramble. "Fine. Hurry up." I almost felt sorry for him.

The pressure I felt was indescribable, both on my uterus and my timing as I rifled through my bag for my Ziploc of emergency tampons. Verner, my eternal shadow, lumbered behind me and shuffled awkwardly from boot to boot. The staff had a few of the two-ton trucks in operation, the lights trained on the bivouac site to make organization easier. I managed to evade the beams, ducking into the shadows.

"Stand guard, would you, Verner?"

"Yeah. Uh, yeah."

He turned his back while I dipped behind a tree, grateful for the darkness that rolled in like a wave, and I yanked down my pants and set to work. Mission completed, I squirted a gallon of Purell on my hands and stood back in ranks, wearing the stain of my womanhood like a scarlet *P*.

The march was the most rigorous I'd ever experienced. Bruvelle led the pace with his stealthy non-issued boots and quick steps that were impossible to match. As usual, I was first to fall back, my breath unable to meet the demand, my legs giving way like overcooked noodles.

"You better catch up to your platoon, Thompson." Bruvelle gestured towards my platoon-mates, who were so close but so damn far away. "I think the only way you'll learn to look after yourself is if others have to start paying the price." How this man managed a conversation considering the pace was beyond me. I could hardly think straight or see five feet in front of me, much less have a chat. "Platoon! Officer Cadet Thompson needs your help. I believe she has to be carried, don't you?"

"I don't need to be carried." I forced myself into a trot, tripping and nearly face-planting in the sand.

"Oh, but it's the only way you'll keep up, Thompson," Bruvelle said with a sneer.

My platoon-mates halted in their tracks and laced their fingers together into a makeshift bed, which I was laid across like a goddess, complete with my weighty ruck. If there had been a blanket available, I would have pulled it over my head and hidden from the people I was meant to be equal with. "I'm sorry, guys. I'm so sorry." Some didn't have the physical capacity for conversation and others jeered at me, showcasing their own exhaustion and pain.

Most everyone ended up in some kind of agony by the end of that march, and I was not the last to be carried on the human stretcher. More than three-quarters of us projectile vomited our IMPs, which we'd been forced to eat just thirty minutes before the bug out. Some people were carried back to camp on trucks (guilty as charged) and others limped into the bivouac site as though one more step might be the end of them, suffering from sprains, chafing, blisters, and shin splints. I pretended not to care when all of that effort resulted in returning to the exact same bivouac site we'd departed from, or that we had to spend an hour setting up camp all over again, only to leave the next morning.

I went to bed that night having received a warning for having messy hair while in uniform, perhaps penance for my feminine hygiene episode. I doubted the Taliban would care that I hadn't brushed my hair. All they would see was a blonde teenage girl with painted toenails who had no place in their country at all.

Before the unceremonious delivery of our graduation certificates, and leaving the first portion of basic training, there was to be an inspection of the barracks to ensure our pods were as they should be for the next serial—clean, and scrubbed of identity. I waited standing at ease in the clothes I'd only been allowed to wear on weekends, including a pair of white capri pants that could now slip over my bum without me undoing the button. Civilian clothing felt foreign; I was no longer a civilian.

Bruvelle entered the pod brusquely and I came to attention, butt cheeks squeezed tight until they stung. He silently assessed my tiny room. My kit had been packed up and sat in bags at the end of the bed, which had been stripped bare. My closet was empty, scrubbed clean until some of the white paint had chipped away, and my hair, out of militaristic habit, was pulled back into a tight bun, stark against a face and frame that was nearly twenty pounds lighter than when I arrived.

"Well, Thompson, everything looks to be in order," he said, and for the first time, his voice was calm and smooth. I wondered if there was a Mrs. Bruvelle, or children—a whole life we cadets knew nothing about. Somehow, crossing the threshold of graduation had flipped a switch to congeniality, revealing something previously under lock and key.

"Thank you, Sergeant."

"You can go now."

"That's it?"

"You want a fucking parade?"

I had actually thought there was a parade, but it turned out that wouldn't be until the next summer, when I completed phase II of hell, the Basic Officer Training Course. So I said nothing.

"So, go home, good luck. And for Christ's sake, Thompson," he said, gesturing at my body, "eat a fucking sandwich or something."

After he passed through the other rooms, Kelper approached, her smile wide. She'd scored third place on the course, the only female in the top three. I had landed somewhere in the bottom third, which came as no surprise but still stung. My success on the range and leadership skills hadn't made up for my physical weakness.

"You need to train over the year," she said, waving her course report in the air. "You have to keep up with the guys to be taken seriously as a woman."

I nodded as though I'd take her advice, but as I slung my purse over my shoulder, I wondered why I couldn't just be myself. Dad had echoed Kelper's opinion, evidenced in his fear of my potential MIR Commando status. If I wasn't the best soldier physically speaking but was great at my job as a leader and logistics officer, wasn't that good enough? Kelper had been rewarded for exhibiting the qualities the Forces valued, qualities I'd seen romanticized countless times in war books and movies. But the mission we were training for—Afghanistan—would be an entirely different kind of battle. There would be the ever-important combat arms, sure, but Afghanistan would be fought with intelligence, ingenuity—and, occasionally, from behind the desk of an operations room. The front line was a blurry concept that no longer existed as it once had, and yet maintaining that ideal was what we were encouraged to strive for. So I gave in to that, accepted it as fact, and hoped I could do something to change it. I offered a round of hugs to my podmates, a placating smile in Kelper's direction, and felt my irritation with her dissipate, making room for the empathy I prided myself on. We'd all met the requirements, and for me that felt like enough.

We filtered into the hallway to say goodbye, offer hugs and see-you-next-years. We patted one another on the back awkwardly, pretending we hadn't shared this life-altering experience, that we wouldn't go home swearing and ordering people around like it was the way society normally operated. We didn't talk about the loss of the inside jokes, how we dreaded returning to people who didn't understand what it meant to stand for more than just yourself. Although only nine weeks had passed, we had aged decades compared to our friends at home. In one summer, we'd been changed.

I found Joe in the hallway zipping a magazine into the front pocket of his messenger bag. He had been marked as one of the top students in both the written tests and the physical ones, but unlike others who made the list, cockiness was absent. *He's not like all the other pilots*, Kelper had said one night in our pod. We'd all agreed, bobbed our heads. He wasn't like the other pilots at all. Joe Shorrocks wasn't like anyone I knew.

I'd already stuffed most of my bags into my tiny car, and with a rucksack, two army duffle bags, my original luggage, and more, there was no room for anything else but me. I leaned against the cinder block walls and watched Joe say goodbye to a line of people on their way out the door, snapping photos with disposable cameras and yelling loudly as their feet hammered the metal stairs on their descent. Eventually just a few of us remained: those waiting for flights, and those in the odd position of not really wanting to leave.

"Heading to the airport soon?" I gestured at Joe's bags.

"Not yet. I fly out at nine tonight, so I've got a few hours. Figure I'll eat at the mess before I go."

"Really want that last bout of the runs, eh?"

"I'm a glutton for punishment." He laughed, his eyes squinting.

"I hope you have a safe trip."

"Thanks." He smiled wide, either avoiding my gaze or ignorant of how badly I wanted his to connect with mine. *We're meant to be together.* I willed myself to say it, and yet even acknowledging the idea with Joe standing in front of me felt childish and stupid. What did I know, even after basic training? I was still a kid. The only difference was that I didn't want my age and our distance to matter. Joe, being five years older than me, knew that it did.

"Well, Thompson," he said, pulling me close. "Until next year."

Joe hugged me tight, rubbing the ridges of ribs up my back. I breathed in Ralph Lauren cologne and a tinge of the shaving cream he used, closing my eyes and trying to fix the memory in my mind. When he held me at arm's length, hands on my shoulders, I was silent, tears tickling my eyes. He squeezed my arms, then hefted his kit bag over his shoulder and walked down the blue hall to the fire door.

"Hey," he said, spinning on his sneakered feet. "Have any bags you want me to carry down for you? Pop 'em in your car?"

I shook my head. "One man, one kit, and all that."

"Right." He smiled and waved goodbye. I knew he would understand.

I squeezed into my Beetle and drove towards home, blasting music in an attempt to drown out my confused thoughts. I didn't think of the pride Dad might be feeling or wonder if Grandpa was watching over me. Eventually, I flicked off the music and drove the remaining six hours in the quiet, paying myself a silent tribute—to effervescent personalities. To remaining kind to competitors. To occasional failures. To inexplicable heart problems and MIR visits. To painted toenails and hand cream. But above all, to coming out the other side alive, proud, and a little more confident for the experience.

PART TWO

Broken-Down Cargo Ship

Officer Cadet Thompson
May 2005-March 2006

10

My tears threatened to drown me as I returned to Saint-Jean, Quebec. I careened down Highway 401, which took me nearly the entire way from Toronto to Montreal, where I would dip south to my second phase of training. A year had passed since IAP but it felt like it had happened a decade earlier, in another lifetime, had been survived by someone else entirely.

For most of the year it had been easy to forget that I was a soldier first, a student second. Two terms at York University meant eight months of English classes, verb trees, and essays, and I'd almost managed to erase weapons training, drill, and rank structure from my mind. But now the Basic Officer Training Course, or BOTC—the second phase of basic training—loomed ahead of me like a storm cloud.

The previous night, at Trevor's farm, I'd been surrounded by teenage friends with the air of high school still clinging to them. I was in the final cohort of students requiring a fifth year of high school study if they wanted a university degree, so I plotted ahead and skipped most of grade twelve so I could graduate a year early and beat the university application rush. So while I slogged off to university and IAP a year early, Trevor and most of my classmates were just starting adulthood—destined for more schooling, summer jobs, or backpacking trips to Europe with their parents footing the bill. My bags, already packed and stashed in my trunk, sat like monuments to another life. I'd checked and rechecked my kit list, panicked I would forget something, even having nightmares about it. This time, I knew the consequences of mistakes. Push-ups. Singling-out. Reprimands. Fines. Yelling.

Early in the evening the house party had raged below me, voices collecting in Trevor's kitchen for the celebration he said was for me, although it seemed more a chance for faint acquaintances to kick off the upcoming summer. Heartburn rose up my esophagus as I applied makeup in the dim light of his bedroom, smudging eyeliner and fussing with my hair—anything to delay. I hated house parties. I'd been dating Trevor for years, and he still didn't seem to realize that. What else about me didn't he know or see? I smashed cotton candy Lip Smacker onto my lips, the same kind I'd used during IAP, now a candy-scented reminder of military life.

Joe. Joe knew I hated house parties. Joe knew what the Forces was like. Somewhere, on the other side of the country, Joe was also preparing to return to Saint-Jean for BOTC, although we'd not communicated over the past year.

A rumble of cheers and clinking glasses met me as I came down the stairs. I plastered on a smile. For a few hours I could pretend I was just like the rest of the group, that tomorrow I wouldn't be miserable in the next province over. Without the daily demands of basic training to occupy my mind, anxiety had been creeping back and inserting itself into every decision I made. And yet underneath the nerves was something else— excitement, apprehension, and some bizarre sense of longing. I nervously tugged on the strings of my halter top, the fabric patterned in sorbet civilian colours. In the coming weeks, I would wear a uniform that could never make me feel pretty.

"You going to kick ass, or what?" a friend of Trevor's said while lazily slurping a beer. The guy had never held a job. He'd be spending the foreseeable future racing horses around his family's track and sleeping with women he couldn't remember the names of come morning.

"I'm going into this year just hoping to fucking survive." My own vodka Sprite was watered down with too much ice.

"Well, hey, Trevor," the guy said, holding up his bottle, dripping with condensation. "Look on the bright side. Last year she came home thin and smoking hot, right?"

After IAP, our friends had spent weeks jokingly tugging up my shirt to reveal the new lines of muscle, and yet I never stopped them. I was weirdly proud and now used to having my worth assessed by my muscles, which—compared to the women at home—were stronger than the norm. But over the year of student life, I'd gone back to my regular size, and even though I knew the physical demands of BOTC were inevitable, I hadn't been able to bring myself to "train." On that first PT session back at the Mega, I'd regret all those nights spent sipping Pepsi and gobbling burgers with my high school friends.

It's what teenagers do. Eat stuff that's bad for them, Trevor had said when I'd aired my concerns. *But I'm not just another teenager,* I'd replied, my tone steeped in irritation. *I'm a soldier too. I'm responsible for more than just myself.* He'd rolled his eyes and I couldn't help but hate him a little for it, even when the over-dramatization of my experiences rang trite in my own ears.

"That's right," Trevor said, pulling me near and snuggling into my neck. His features blurred up close. "My own GI Jane."

I swatted at him but leaned in anyway. Growing up within military life meant regular moves and a revolving door of friends, creating a stark contrast between Trevor's childhood and mine. When Trevor laughed with friends he'd known since birth,

I hungered for the same experience—yet in the military, remaining static in one town was impossible. Trevor's family had lived in their farmhouse for generations, while mine hadn't even settled into their subdivision with a sense of permanence despite being there three years. It took months before Mom finally painted walls and bought area rugs without considering how they would work in another home.

I sipped my drink and leaned into Trevor's lips for a kiss. As the celebration gained momentum, partygoers skinny-dipped in the pool and then rushed for the trampoline, hooting and hollering. Bodies poured out into the moonlight, bewildering a cluster of cows who stumbled into the safety of the barn when the shouting and potato-gun firing startled them. Later, the alcohol made everyone drowsy. A cluster of us clung to the living room, listening quietly to hip-hop on the crackling speaker system, almost everyone asleep. I'd stopped drinking after the one watery vodka—I had to be up at five in the morning—but it seemed no one had stayed sober with me.

I observed my sleeping friends, wondering if anyone had bothered to set an alarm for work, if they had dinner plans they might have missed. Should I have been placing anyone in the recovery position lest they fall asleep and choke on their own vomit? First aid . . . what did I remember from first aid? I sipped from a glass of water and stared up at the ceiling, careful not to bump Trevor's silky-haired head from where he leaned on my shoulder. The questions I couldn't help but ask myself were the very ones that set me apart from the people who had been my friends, who were now strangers scattered around me. How could they ever really understand what I'd been through, what I was capable of, when I was no longer sure myself? In the course of a year, I'd come to feel like a grown-up, even if I had no idea what that role entailed.

I traced my finger around the tip of Trevor's freckled ear. We'd spent the summer avoiding the obvious conversation that needed to happen—our lives were heading in different directions. I checked my watch. BOTC would start in seventeen hours.

A year earlier, pulling up to the green doors of the Mega had been daunting, but preparing to do it all over for five more weeks felt unimaginable. Again, my luggage was searched. I was given a room number, a platoon, a new pod of women to compete with. We had our platoon meeting that night and I scanned the room for an absent Joe, worried he'd been assigned to a different platoon.

"One cadet hasn't yet arrived," said the new course warrant. My ears perked up and I leaned forward in my seat. "His flight's been delayed, so keep an eye out and help him get sorted before classes start in the morning. Understood?"

"Yes, Warrant." The words slipped from our mouths, a robotic and trained response, so natural that it made my skin crawl with the realization that a small part of me had missed this. The familiarity I craved existed in a life of constant change.

Later that night, I stood in the hallway punching out a text to Trevor on Mom's clunky pay-as-you-go cell.

"Thompson, is that you?"

"Joe!"

He meandered down the hallway, tugging his bags behind him, and I ran towards him like a romantic-comedy heroine, then twirling in his arms with my legs splayed behind me as though I weighed nothing at all.

"Holy shit, Thompson, you look different!"

He held me out by the shoulders to take me in like I was a child who had grown a foot taller. My hair was longer, dangling somewhere above my chest, brown instead of blonde, and my hips seemed to be softening and widening in a way that made me feel feminine, bursting with adulthood. The jump from just-turned nineteen to nearly twenty years old felt far. Joe, on the other hand, hadn't changed an iota.

"What are the odds of us being in the same platoon again? This is awesome!"

"Sixty people. A full-sized platoon this year," I said, gesturing to the cluster of cadets behind me. Again, our last names would make us allies, alphabetical order keeping us snug in the same section and lined up next to each other in ranks. I felt a sliver of hope wedge itself between my hellish BOTC expectations and the reassuring presence of Joe.

"Just like old times, eh?"

I walked Joe to his pod and gave him a hug goodnight. He still smelled like Ralph Lauren. I still wanted to marry him.

11

As opposed to IAP, BOTC focused on the finer details of being an officer; concepts I felt I might actually be able to espouse. Leadership. Duty. Loyalty. Courage. All of these words—which the military called "officer-like qualities"—were terms that felt somehow mutable, indefinable. Finally, potential to be appreciated. And BOTC was just five weeks. I had survived nine weeks at Saint-Jean the year prior. I could do five more.

Marching through the halls of the Mega, we rolled our eyes at the new IAP cadets who hadn't yet earned their cap badges or been in the field—not yet hardened, experienced cadets like we envisioned ourselves to be. It was like being a senior in high school: the knowledge of your previous position as a freshman didn't stop you from picking on them. And while IAP had seemed to forge our platoon together like steel, the shorter length of BOTC meant we were unlikely to make the same kind of connections. Besides, the rules were more relaxed—we weren't confined to barracks, we weren't yelled at as much—so, in general, we felt slightly less stressed, having been prepared for the worst. This time, my podmates—Scotdale, Trafford, Galen, and Hurley—ranged widely in age. Scotdale and I were nineteen, with Trafford and Galen in their forties, and we were amicable but distant. An added ingredient to our less intense bonds was that while civilian university students were enrolled in the entire five-week duration of the course, Royal Military College cadets were parachuted in for just four weeks, the rationale being that their military training throughout the year absolved them of requiring the "refresher week." The result was a wide chasm between Us and Them, a rift that hardly needed widening considering the pre-existing rivalry. Civilian university cadets considered RMC students to be childish and self-important— they had set bedtimes and weren't able to live off campus for several years—and they thought of us as lesser soldiers, not entrenched in military life year-round.

Tests on physical fitness and drill were in the past. Now we learned about motivating troops, operations, and military ethics. For one test, we trained in public speaking and were given a choice of any topic for a presentation. I fell back on my degree and spoke about proving a thesis in a written article, while my platoon-mates discussed military strategy, time management, or their professional futures.

Most days of BOTC passed by without streaks of colour, moments blending from one academic class to another. So when there were changes in the routine—such as physical training in the swimming pool—we perked up with interest.

I jolted a razor across my bikini line at five in the morning, nearly slicing open my femoral. Since training began, I hadn't bothered to shave a single body part, vanity left at the door of my pod, runs always done too early in the morning for anyone to notice my leg hair. I had bought a bathing suit specifically for basic training, one I felt gave the appearance of a serious swimmer who didn't care about tan lines and spaghetti straps.

It was a modest one-piece style from Roots, red with high-cut hips, like I belonged on *Baywatch*. The night before, I tried it on, standing in front of my bedroom mirror for far too long.

We were told PT would consist of pool circuit training in swimsuits. Not like IAP, when our swim test was done in full combat gear, treading water for two minutes with our uniform pockets ballooning like boat sails. After the two minutes were up, we had to swim to the opposite end of the Olympic-sized pool and heave ourselves onto a platform, unassisted, before jumping from the high diving board into the water below.

The women's locker room was a flurry of straps and snaps, furtive tugging of Lycra. We pretended not to linger on our own images in the mirror, body anxiety masked by an air of ambivalence.

"I look like a fucking whale."

Conversations echoed in the humid change room, bouncing off steamy mirrors and tiled bathroom stalls, voices belonging to everyone and no one.

"Please, look at my thighs."

"What are the odds my goddamned period comes the day of this bullshit? All I need is some string dangling from my vag. Tampon? Anyone have a tampon?"

"Think of the nicknames that could come from that."

"My tits are falling out all over the place. Anyone have an extra suit? Can't keep my ladies in."

"Oh my God, is my suit see-through on the ass? Can people see my ass?"

"No one cares about your ass. It's PT for fuck's sake."

"Please. They're a bunch of cadets. They're not fucking dead."

"Well, if that's your main concern, maybe you shouldn't be here."

"What are you saying?"

"Never mind"

"Go fuck yourself."

"After you."

Despite their harsh words, there was no anger in the voices of my female comrades. Anger had been replaced with a rough acceptance that this was who we had become, mutating into the A-type personalities the military wanted in its officers, even if outside the uniform, we were people who said "sorry" when another pedestrian ran into us on the street. The effect, however, was that I was hesitant to bond with these women, whom I was competing with in fitness, leadership, and now, thanks to the bathing suits, beauty.

I pulled up the shoulder straps of my one-piece and ensured any unruly pubic hairs were tucked before making one last pass in front of the mirror. My male comrades would see me in a swimsuit, which would either result in admiration or endless jokes, or a combination of both. My civilian, girly self wanted one thing; the professional, military version wanted another. But what if wearing a bathing suit could be my saviour? If I could offer a body worth looking at, maybe I could get a taste of worth and accomplishment. Perhaps they might like me, staff and fellow troops combined. I hated myself for that hope, for pinning my dreams on being assessed by my looks, a concept I'd been working so hard to avoid.

We took obligatory showers before stumbling into the pool area, the muggy air pungent with chlorine. The female cadets shuffled forward, toes pointed inwards, arms folded across chests and waists, confidence dissipating now that our uniform camouflage had been left behind in the change area. The men laughed and elbowed one another as they emerged from their own change room, gesturing in our direction. Some whistled and pointed while others pelvic-thrusted the air, punctuating the motion with grunts, until the course staff clomped across the floor, still in their boots on the water-laced tiling. I wrapped my arms tighter and prayed we'd be ordered into the pool, and yet I felt guilty for making my own aesthetic observations: the boys who couldn't grow chest hair; those with skinny legs and puffy bellies, back acne and ropey arms.

"Don't worry, you look amazing," said Scotdale, my new podmate.

"I'm not sure that's a good thing around here." I waved at Joe, who had tossed a pale arm in the air. His white chest, arms, and back were all dotted with tender brown spots that made him seem somehow vulnerable.

"Well," Scotdale sighed. "Boys will be boys, even when they're technically men."

The course staff settled into the bleachers while civilian PSP staff marched onto the pool deck in black shorts and red T-shirts. "Everyone in, swim a lap, and warm up," yelled a buff man in his twenties. He tooted once on his whistle, a shrill pierce of the air that I felt in the back of my teeth.

The warm-up involved swimming laps at increasing speeds, and within five minutes we were gasping for breath. A cadet who couldn't swim floundered dramatically, arms and legs akimbo, body flailing in the shallow end. Another choked and gagged chlorine water into a foamy pile in the corner. With another hefty blow of the whistle, the PSP trainer led us through a series of swim challenges. We retrieved rings from the pool floor, jumped from the dive boards, raced to the other side, hopped out and did ten push-ups on the slimy tiled floor before coursing through another lap. Self-consciousness quickly dissipated with hasty breath and flushed cheeks, ears full of water until everything echoed with bass. I flew through the drills, my swimming skills showcased. Finally. Competence. No—*physical* competence.

"Good job there, Thompson," our sergeant said casually as he passed. I nearly wept with joy.

"All right folks, that's enough for today!" the trainer hollered. "Line up in ranks and your course staff will direct you further." He disappeared around the corner as we hopped from the pool to form our lines, everyone emerging from different corners and dripping warm puddles as we walked. I snapped the wedgie from my butt and fiddled with a strap on my suit.

"Hey, Thompson."

I whipped around to face the cadet who couldn't swim, who reminded me of a rat. Despite daily shaves, he always had a bristle of shadow on his face, and his two front teeth were protruding and rodent-like. "Didn't know you had so much going on in front." He gestured from nipple to nipple, then pointed at me as I stumbled towards the rest of the waiting platoon. "We should be calling you Mount Vesuvius. Get it, guys? Her shape says it all, and then, you know, you'll make us guys blow." He laughed until the joke caught on, others laughing with him. I looked around for Joe, for someone to rise to defend my honour, but he was standing near the locker room, too far away to hear.

My face had glowed with the high of our sergeant's compliment, but the joy quickly receded, my stomach gurgling with distaste and confusion. Rat Man was still laughing, holding his belly as his head fell backwards, mouth wide and gaping. Was it weird to feel somewhat charmed to be recognized as beautiful in a place that forced me into a camouflaged background? I knew it was—and yet I swallowed, then forced a smile, refusing to allow my hands to cover myself. Until now, BOTC had felt so different from IAP, but I realized that nothing had changed at all. We were a year older, but none the wiser.

"Yes, they are pretty fantastic, aren't they?" I said, looking down at my perfect pair of breasts as I marched squarely towards my spot in ranks. I settled into my space as our warrant turned the corner of the pool and appeared in front of us.

"Three and a half minutes to change," he hollered. "And I want you out, lined up in ranks, ON TIME. You hear me?"

"YES, WARRANT."

Another unattainable deadline to meet but I couldn't find it in me to care, the heat of the confrontation with Rat Man radiating from my skin. Once under the searing spray, I went well over my allotted three minutes. Even as the course staff barked from the hallway.

Later that night at the mess, drinking vodka cranberry and French beer, "Mount Vesuvius" stuck as my new nickname for the year, men mocking my shape with exaggerated hourglass swirls of their hands, miming reaches for my chest. I never once asked any of them to stop, because I wanted to flirt, to be adored, to be accepted. My physical ineptitude in IAP still haunted me, so I couldn't also be the woman who couldn't take a joke—or worse, a perceived compliment. Staring at the bottom of an empty glass, I assured myself the moniker felt better than "Robo-Thompson," which signalled weakness. Besides, joking meant they liked me. Joking meant I fit in and was accepted. Joking, no matter how crude and crass, meant I was a soldier and that I belonged.

I tipped many tumblers of vodka down my mouth that night, trying to drown out the fear that, in taking on the identity of military officer, I was forcefully quashing others that had previously defined me. All of my labels—writer, teen, daughter, girlfriend, student—seemed at odds with the new me.

12

BOTC offered more freedom than IAP, allowing us to explore the other floors of the Mega and attend the mess whenever we saw fit. And we saw fit often. Drinking was the way to belong, to celebrate, to commiserate. And the military did all sorts of things to promote this—forced-fun events with cheap liquor costs; unwritten rules that promotions meant buying a round for the whole platoon—later wondering why a disproportionate number of soldiers and veterans ended up alcoholics. The mess was the place many of us women felt equal, if not a bit superior to our male compatriots, thanks to our ability to handle our alcohol. As a result of our antics, most of my platoon-mates spent Friday to Monday in various states of hangovers.

One Monday afternoon, the male cadets were shuttled somewhere down the hall while the females were ushered into a different training room. The sheer volume of womanhood present was almost too much to take in.

Officer Cadet Meerin sat at the front of the lecture room on a tall stool next to the dais as if she were about to make a presentation, her eyes sunken and bloodshot. Although she was a platoon-mate about my age and lived in the female pod across from mine, I barely knew her. But Meerin was a fellow female in a male world, so for that alone, we were kin. She nervously picked at her cuticles. Whatever discussion we were in for, it hadn't been on the schedule the night before, and other than in our pods, we'd never been separated from the men.

"Are we about to get a lecture on feminine hygiene in the field?" I joked with my podmates.

"That was last week, remember?" Trafford responded. Her age meant Trafford took everything in basic training with a humorous grain of salt. "Nothing like hearing some forty-year-old man directing you to clean between the folds. Couldn't even say the word *labia*, for Christ's sake."

Meerin choked out a nervous cough. Military Police officers sat next to her, and I assumed she was tired, hungover, frustrated with the whole BOTC experience, and about to be verbally flogged for over-imbibing. But a flicker of the fluorescent lights overhead revealed fingerprints on her neck—perfect circles highlighting a wide grip. Whoever it was had big hands. I flooded with compassion, tears rising to my face. We knew before we were told.

The course warrant cleared his throat, silencing us without his usual barking command. "I'm sure you've been wondering what brought you all here," he said, glancing at Meerin with a raised eyebrow. She did not lift her head to acknowledge him. "In the interest of disclosure and cadet safety here at the Canadian Forces Leadership and Recruit School, we inform our soldiers when there are issues that are pertinent to their well-being. Unfortunately, Officer Cadet Meerin was the victim of an alleged sexual assault last night in her pod."

There were no gasps of surprise. Many shook their heads or leaned towards Meerin in solidarity; she was now bright red, eyes focused on some invisible point on the floor. Tears brimmed, and she swallowed over and over like a cow chewing cud. Then she looked up from her perch and our eyes connected, for barely a moment, before we both turned away, inexplicably ashamed.

We murmured amongst ourselves, questions shooting into the air, knowing they'd go unanswered. For once, we were not hushed by the staff. Instead, the warrant watched us, his expression unchanging. I couldn't make sense of why Meerin had been ordered to sit at the front of the room, her privacy apparently not an issue. Did she want to be there? Had she been ordered to? If she had, it wouldn't have occurred to her to suggest otherwise, since we unequivocally obeyed staff orders the moment we arrived at the green doors.

"The alleged incident occurred last night at approximately 2300 hours, when as you know, after 2000 hours, members of the opposite gender are not permitted inside one another's pods." The warrant paused, as though this disobedience of the fraternization rules was the worst offence of all. Meerin stared blankly at the floor again and I found myself willing her to speak, yet also terrified of what would happen if she opened her mouth. Tears. Bizarre laughter from the strangeness of it all. Or a voice not at all her own, damaged from the hand around her throat. "Officer Cadet Meerin was followed to her pod after an evening of drinks in the Officers' Mess and was assaulted, although we won't be revealing details of the assault itself. Officer Cadet Meerin sought medical treatment this morning and proper policies are being followed that deal with situations such as these. Are there any questions?"

Assault. Investigation. Nothing to see here. Move along. All the female cadets eyed one another for strength, for resolve, for the willingness to speak. And yet two summers in a row had been dedicated to mastering the art of taking direction, listening to and executing lawful orders without question. For months we'd been encouraged to follow the pack while simultaneously leading it, to stand up for what was right by military standards, not by our own family-imposed values. I no longer knew to whom or what I pledged allegiance. I wondered if Meerin felt the same way.

A cadet in the front row raised her hand. "What's being done now, Warrant?"

Earlier in the course, we'd been given SHARP training—Standard for Harassment and Racism Prevention—taught by our course captain, who we otherwise saw little of. He was a tiny naval officer, and his delicate stature somehow made it more appropriate that he was the one teaching about sensitivity and harassment. *This guy looks totally gay*, someone muttered, the statement followed by a series of snickers. We'd joked and laughed with one another about the artsy-fartsy nature of this educational time slot—we had more important things to learn, surely. Weapons training or leadership tips. Who needs this?!—even from those of us who needed these conversations sparked oh-so-badly. *We are in a new kind of military*, the captain said. *Women make up about 12 per cent of our workplace, and we all need to learn to respect one another.* During the lecture we were shown lame videos, like the recruitment productions but without any of the sexy weapons or warfare. A boss, and the boss was usually a man, placed his 1980s suit-styled arm around a female co-worker and made untoward advances that persisted, even after the woman said no. But the woman said *no*, a word that had never left my own lips in response to unwanted touches and comments. I thought about my ass being grabbed on the obstacle course. During swim training, my body eyed hungrily like a sundae on a hot day. Meerin, here in front of us. SHARP appeared to have had little effect on our platoon and the military as a whole.

"Officer Cadet Meerin is somewhat hazy on the details of the altercation due to her alcohol consumption, but we can assure you that a full investigation is underway and the Military Police have been alerted and are probing for more details." He gestured towards one of the police officers, who looked up from his notebook and nodded for effect, red beret bobbing like an apple in water. The police presence in the information session seemed unnecessary, unless they had been sent to muzzle Meerin, ensure she didn't blame the Forces. Or perhaps the MPs were there to assure us that something was being done, procedures followed. A police officer is meant to bring comfort to people who put their faith in public service, and if we—a group of military members who technically reported to the prime minister, our ultimate boss—weren't part of that group, then who were we?

"So," continued the cadet who had posed the original question, "what exactly are the proper policies, Warrant? I mean, what's the protocol for sexual assault allegations? I'm curious how they're handled."

"We don't have the time to get into such details, but you are welcome to follow up with your directing staff to ascertain the necessary information, or consult the Harassment Handbook." We'd been provided with this document after our SHARP training, and despite being directed to consult handbooks whenever a question existed (there was, we discovered, a handbook for everything, all styled in confusing bureaucratic language), the policies themselves served as nothing other than generators of further concern—meanings and solutions tied up in upper-level language and legal military jargon.

I weighed Meerin's options as I imagined she herself had done after waking, her mouth papery and body sore: speak up for what was right, or stay quiet and accept that making noise would only draw the wrong kind of attention—the kind of attention that the military didn't seem to want us women to draw. The protocol of a handbook seemed comically out of place next to Meerin's cracking exterior, her bruises, her shame.

"Any other questions?" the warrant asked, as though he didn't really want an answer.

My hand shot up into the air. "Excuse me, Warrant, are you saying that the guy is still out there? Do we need to be on the lookout for someone in particular?"

"Again, all protocols are in place, Officer Cadet Thompson, and your safety is of prime importance."

"But not even a description so we can protect ourselves? Meerin, you don't know who it was? Was he in our platoon?" I asked her, but she didn't look up, my cheeks burning with regret for having put her on the spot.

"Questions will not be directed at Officer Cadet Meerin," the warrant boomed, his teeth clenched.

"Didn't exactly answer the question, did he?" Trafford whispered.

"What I can tell you," our warrant continued, "considering this is an active investigation and we do not want to manipulate the process, is that the padre is here should any of you like to seek counsel or have experienced similar situations at any point in your lives. Occasionally, these kinds of events can serve as triggers." His voice was robotic and practised, and I tried to keep my eyes from rolling. The padre? Really? He was a nice man in his fifties, and we welcomed his presence because he was the only Saint-Jean staff member who smiled and asked how we were coping. But still, he was a man. An officer. A higher rank. What good was all that to this room and this audience?

I briefly considered sharing my own harassment scenarios, openly discussing stories of unwanted touching and comments we'd experienced in our limited weeks of soldierhood—and civilian life before that, too—but then what would be the point, when even assault didn't seem to warrant further action? The responses from those in charge were why so many of us didn't speak up. *What's the point?* a fellow cadet had mumbled once. *It never changes.*

Back in IAP, one woman had claimed that one of her course staff had harassed her. When she submitted an official complaint, the male staff member came around to us, his cadets— the people whose careers he could end before they started—and asked if any of us were willing to write him memos of support, since, you know, we knew of his character, that he would never harass someone. I didn't know shit about his character or the facts about the charge, other than the reality that I couldn't imagine how hard it had been for her to come forward, knowing the backlash she'd receive, the isolation from her platoonmates and the coinciding reputation for whining. But I wrote a memo of support for the male staff member, signed my name below words I didn't mean.

"Officer Cadet Meerin, do you have anything to add?"

Meerin looked up and straightened her spine as if calling herself to attention. She could barely open her eyes, though whether that was because of her nasty hangover or the situation at hand, it was hard to say. "Just that, um, it was really scary, and I'm sorry that it happened."

"You don't have to be sorry," someone said from the front. One of her roommates. "You didn't do anything wrong." We collectively nodded, murmured our assent, but Meerin looked back down at her boots. I felt sick to my stomach, that same anxious feeling I'd nurtured since childhood but which had been dissipating with my newfound military confidence. I pressed my fingers together in a steeple and flexed them back and forth, my leg bouncing with jitters.

"I don't know what I was thinking. I shouldn't have . . ." She trailed off, eyes to the ceiling. I wondered if the perpetrator was currently in a room surrounded by male cadets, having to atone. I ran through the known list of males in my head. Or maybe it was someone else from another platoon? I pictured the faces that had sneered at me, the eyes that had assessed my shape, the hands that had touched. It could have been nearly any one of them, and yet we were expected to trust these men with our lives.

"In the meantime," injected the warrant. "I'd like all female cadets to be extra vigilant in looking out for one another and to ensure that drinking activities are curtailed to a minimum, as this puts you at increased risk for being made a target."

Perhaps it was his rank, or the reality that making waves would do nothing but highlight the troublemakers, but we let him—this man with arm muscles larger than my thigh—tell us that our actions were the cause for assault, for being vulnerable. Or perhaps no one argued with his victim-blaming because it all seemed to make sense, that drinking plus a hyper-masculine environment equalled a wanton woman begging to be taught a lesson. Whichever it was, the room of female cadets sat wide-eyed and blinking, accepting that our gender was to be the source of our own undoing. My mess-hall meal did somersaults up my throat.

"That will be all," the warrant barked. "Dismissed."

The warrant and MPs left the room and we burst into hurried discussion. I sat temporarily frozen, hands clenched.

"Well"—Trafford mimed checking her watch—"that had to have been done in record time. Now, ladies, don't go breaking any rules and getting raped tonight." She wagged a finger, then regarded her whole hand with disgust. "Makes you wonder what we're in for, eh? A career of this bullshit?"

My podmates and I looked at each other, Trafford's statement hanging weighty in the air. Scotdale bit her lip and squeezed my leg under the table. I shook her off and crossed my legs in the other direction. In that moment, all touch felt wrong, even the compassionate kind.

"I wonder what tale was spun for the guys while we listened to this," Scotdale said, unable to tear her eyes from Meerin, who was now surrounded by a collection of mourners. She'd broken into tears, her hands shaking. Those of us who didn't know her well looked away, fiddled with loose threads or uneven name-tags on our uniforms.

"Likely, to wear protection and make sure they don't get caught," I said.

"That isn't funny."

"Oh, I'm sorry," I spat. "Who said I was joking?"

We were led back to the common room to meet up with our male counterparts, who were already seated as though they'd been lingering a while, waiting on us to finish up. I assessed eyes for shadiness or for heads bent low, but everyone looked bleak-faced. Joe sat next to me, resting one ankle on his other knee, hips splayed wide.

"So, did you guys get more information than us?" he asked. "Poor Meerin." He shook his head.

"What'd they tell you?"

"That Meerin was assaulted last night. That's about it."

"No details?" To our left, a cluster of men slapped each other on the shoulders, laughing over some cracked joke, the discussion in the training room apparently already forgotten. My mouth felt acidic and slimy. "They didn't say, 'Hey guys, if this was you, come forward. Respect women.' Nothing like that?"

"Nope," Joe said, shaking his head solemnly. "My guess? They already know who did it. They're likely just trying to figure out how to handle it, and handle it quietly."

I twisted my beret in my hands and tugged at my bun. "Everyone protecting the fucker instead of the person who needs protecting. Would be nice to know who it was and if they've been kicked off the course. We haven't heard of anyone being taken off course or charged, have we?"

"No," Joe said, settling into a moment of silence. "No, we haven't heard anything like that." We leaned back in our chairs, anger burning until I felt sick and lightheaded despite the spring air that blew through the curtains.

"This is going to be brushed under the rug, isn't it?"

Joe patted my leg and stood to fill his canteen at the fountain.

I went to bed but slept fitfully. After that day, we didn't ask Meerin about who had attacked her. Either we didn't want to know, or we were somehow aware that the answer was moot. The Forces' method for rectifying the situation was clearly already in motion—or at least, that's what we'd been assured. Toying with the woollen blanket between my fingers, I wondered how women could confidently slot themselves into a male-dominated field when the people they're meant to trust most are also the most likely to betray them. The wars we would fight could be right at home, not only on the doorstep of faraway countries.

The next time our platoon visited the mess, we slurped back highballs and shots as though they were water, every liquid taking on the same oily sheen until they were indistinguishable from one another, our reprimand long forgotten. Joe and I sang Queen's "Bohemian Rhapsody" at the top of our lungs, swung around pillars with rosy cheeks.

So I didn't notice when a male cadet followed me to my pod, the warrant's warning apparently lost on both of us. I didn't notice when he crept up the stairs behind me, or maybe he didn't creep at all, maybe I was just too off on rum that my wits were focused on steadying myself up the stairs, not the potential for danger. I'd been flirting, after all. Flirting all night with shameless, wild abandon because I trusted most of these men, and those I didn't, the alcohol convinced me I did. So I also didn't notice that Joe and another platoon-mate noticed this, and their noticing led to them following me too, ensuring I got safely to my pod behind the locked door. The other male cadet had asserted that he was just going to bed, that me being there was a coincidence, since we were in the same platoon, after all, living on the same floor, and no, he hadn't realized he was being so very quiet. And maybe we all felt this was a somewhat reasonable explanation, since Meerin's experience had made us take stock of our separate roles in keeping the peace. *It's not a big deal,* I insisted later. *He was probably just going to bed.* I told Joe not to worry about telling the staff; ignoring the icy feeling that crept across my skin whenever that male platoon-mate approached me throughout the rest of the course.

Joe ushered him back downstairs before he could make any mistakes. Meerin's assault was never spoken of for the remainder of BOTC. We were already learning the importance of keeping our country's secrets.

13

We had just spent days in first aid training, making arm slings with uniform scraps and pointless fabric donuts for eye protrusions. I lobbied to be Joe's partner, hoping CPR was to be performed on live people instead of the blue-chested dummies we were given. The training had been a nice break from the refresher days on how to give orders for small party tasks, in preparation for our BOTC field work. Outside the training rooms, warmed by the Quebec sun, we ran through pretend tasking scenarios, taking turns as the leader who planned and executed the whole thing. My confidence was slowly building, with the occasional wane—the field meant fitness, and I feared it was the one task I wasn't up to.

We were days away from our second-last week of the course, which would take us back to the dreaded Farnham, and to ease the mounting dread, my female platoon-mates and I sat in the sparse common room of our pod, our voices resonating in the cement block structure. Curtains had been pushed back to let in the last of the warm evening sun.

Unaccustomed to sitting idle, we occupied ourselves as we chatted, everyone engaged in various tasks: weapons cleaning, boot shining, ironing and folding, packing. I polished my boots until my fingertips were raw, chamois wrapped around my pointer and middle fingers, which I dipped in water, rubbed into the black paste, then used to shine the leather until my reflection appeared in the toe box.

As a kid I'd spent hours watching Dad polish his boots, basking in the routine of them being laid out on the kitchen table, ghostlike without feet to fill them, like orderly soldiers. He didn't put the television on, didn't have music, the ritual of polishing all he needed. When I was little, I chalked up this absolute focus to a need for concentration. As a teen, I'd wondered if it wasn't obsession. As an adult polishing my own, I realized the act was a distraction from the frightening internal noise of all the places those boots had been. I had the urge to call Dad and ask about it, confirm my suspicions, then thought better of it. I had assumed, or maybe hoped, that my own military service would break the ice between family and Forces, and he might finally feel free to unload some of the secrets he carried from his two Golan deployments in the seventies. Because I could finally understand at a level no one else in the family could.

When this ideal fizzled out with the reality that none of us could ever unpack that baggage for him, I found it harder and harder to hide my disappointment. So I didn't leave the pod to call my Dad. In fact, throughout BOTC I hardly bothered to call my family or Trevor. What I needed, where my focus was required, was there at Saint-Jean.

I was in a good mood, surrounded by these women. The level of competition I'd felt with Kelper was less intense this time around, and I now bloomed with a feeling of belonging as I learned to admire the skills I brought to the military table. I was smart. I was kind. I worked hard. I hoped that would be enough.

I didn't know much about my female podmates. Didn't

know their origin stories or about what they hoped for in life. But I knew the qualities that seemed to matter at the time: their dedication, their drive, their wit. We let the get-to-know-yous end there, content that we understood parts of one another that might not matter in another job. We either trusted one another with our lives or we didn't, and when it came to the women, I'd come to prefer one of them in my corner than almost any man.

Trafford, whose age seemed to permit a breaking of the rules, had snuck a bottle of red into the pod, and opened it by pressing the cork in with the stem of her pen. Pieces of cork bobbed along the surface of the inky liquid like tiny people on a life raft. We passed the wine around and took greedy gulps straight from the bottle.

"Don't hog the goods," Trafford said, her teeth stained with Bordeaux, motioning for it to be passed. "Oh my God. That's so good."

"It's good because it's technically not allowed," Scotdale said.

"I can live with that," Trafford responded as she sealed her lips to the bottle and took a large swig. "I'm so tired I could just curl up in a ball with my bevy of cleaning supplies and sleep until next Monday."

"I hear you on that," I said, unsuccessfully stifling a yawn. "I think I clean and work out here more than I sleep. Speaking of which, do you think we're just absorbing all this stuff through our skin?" I held up the tin of polish. It smelled of earth combined with acetone, some bastardized scent of my childhood. "Not to mention the CLP oil. Every time I clean my rifle, I get carbon glued to my cuticles. For all these chemicals, I'll probably have three kinds of cancer before I finish this stupid course."

"So is this a vanity question or a scientific one?" Scotdale asked with a smirk as she tested the heat on the iron. It sizzled with readiness. She spread out the collar of her uniform and pressed the button to release a spurt of steam that puffed her dark hair into a mushroom.

"Bit of both."

"I can't stand the smell of it either," said Trafford, who sat on the floor with a toothbrush, scrubbing at non-existent dirt stuck in the corner, preparing for inspection. We were always preparing, hovering on the edge of not caring and caring too much. "I go to sleep reeking of army stink. But hey, the whole world is made of carbon, so a little extra under your nails isn't something to get worked up over."

I took my turn with the wine, surreptitiously peeking around the pod to ensure course staff weren't lurking about. I hated wine, red in particular, but I let the lukewarm liquid spread down my throat, coat my mouth, and leave a dry tang on my tongue. I regarded my comrades—Trafford scrubbing dirt, Scotdale ironing, Galen breaking down her weapon for cleaning—and nearly laughed at the scene of domesticity within such an absurdly masculinized life.

After a few gulps of wine—added to over-exhaustion and a touch of heatstroke from that morning's run—our tongues loosened. We talked about our boyfriends, Trafford the only one with a military partner, having already learned the lesson that it's hard to find a man willing to follow a woman, even in the new millennium. I told them about Trevor, how we rarely talked, since he was often combining fields until late at night, and when we did speak there was nothing to share, no experience I felt he would understand. Instead, he and I discussed the weather or the latest bar he'd visited. I was growing up and I'd left Trevor somewhere in the dust, uncertain of how to set him free.

"What about Joe Shorrocks? You two seem pretty tight." Trafford smiled, baring her red-stained teeth.

"What about him?" I stared down into my shoes. My perfect, shiny shoes.

"There's nothing between you two? No little romance late in the night?"

"Here?" I scoffed. Too forced. Too fast. Too everything. "How can anyone have romance here?"

"Hey," Trafford said, producing another bottle from her purse and waving it in the air like a racing flag. "Sometimes, you just click. Age, geography—hell, even basic training . . . none of that matters. Call me crazy, but as soon as a guy opens a door for me, I'm hooked. Potential for chivalry and I'm undone, and Mr. Shorrocks there, he's got the chivalry thing down."

"Shouldn't we not care about chivalry?" said Scotdale, glancing up from her ironing. "Shouldn't we refuse to perpetuate those kinds of male-female stereotypes when we're here, trying to prove we can handle everything the men can?"

"I may be an officer in the Forces, but I still don't mind being treated like a lady." I said the words quietly, worried I'd upset some tender balance of feminism. Was I allowed to want chivalry? The room was silent, just metal on metal, toothbrush on linoleum, chamois on leather.

"I don't know about you," said Trafford, breaking the silence. "But I don't have anything to prove to anyone. He can hold my door any day." We laughed so hard at the concept of a female soldier having nothing to prove. *Ha!* It was an instance of lightness, a moment so cherished and accepting that my whole body shook.

We were busy laughing, so when a dark blob careened past the window, I turned back to my boots, thinking perhaps it was a shadow, a passing bird. But Trafford jumped up to press her face against the glass just in time to hear the thud through the open sliding window. Ten floors below, a body lay in an unnatural position, shoulder out of socket and arm wrapped disturbingly around his back—or her back. In uniform, we all looked the same. A puddle of red seeped from underneath the body like a creeping shadow.

"Holy shit. Someone fucking jumped." Trafford clutched the bottle to her chest like it was a newborn, straining her body against the window to catch the right angle. We hopped up to see, pressed greasy faces to the glass, leaving smudges of sunscreen and makeup, our panic a tangible residue smeared across the pane.

My heart thumped in my throat. Suicides belonged on crime dramas and warning posters, not here, and so I half expected the soldier to pop up and proclaim it was one big joke, then execute some drill commands, although their saluting arm was disturbingly out of joint.

We had been fooled, in some respect, because we'd not been warned that the intensity of basic training would only exacerbate existing mental health issues. A mere hint of nerves could quickly turn into a weight too heavy to carry. I'd never wanted to die during training, but I'd certainly had moments where I felt I couldn't keep going—then I'd shaken the thought from my head because quitting felt like failure.

So I hadn't witnessed a suicide, surely, because the reality of life in the Forces wasn't supposed to exist in the Mega. Here, everything was pretend—preparation for military life, for Afghanistan, for the wars that would follow. Death was not supposed to start here.

From slow to fast forward, everything fell into sharp focus. A swarm of cadets filtering towards the body. Grass the colour of key limes growing in mangled tufts around the Mega perimeter. Birds diving through the newly sprouted maple leaves. Combat boots clomping on the floor, in the hall, outside—like a drum leading the charge. The treasured wine placed on the floor, then accidentally spilled with the clatter of glass on linoleum. Yelling in the hallways, people trying to ascertain if help had been called, all of us trained in first aid, which appeared useless. We'd been taught to ask the injured person for permission to administer our clunky training. A nod of the head, an acquiescence. I doubted this cadet would be giving consent to anything.

From our bird's-eye view, we watched as someone dropped to their knees and reached out to check for a pulse. It occurred to me that I was looking at a dead body. Unequivocally dead. But I did not look away. What I couldn't handle was the soldier's beret, still in place. Removing that damn hat was the highlight of my day, my bun set free from the unforgiving wool with a sigh, and I would massage my aching scalp with the tips of my fingers. My beret had become an idol of suffering, and yet this cadet had ensured their hat was on straight before flinging themselves out a window. Dress and deportment were cornerstones to soldiering. So I might be right on the money; perhaps they had regarded that hat as their own symbol of suffering.

"Who is it?" Scotdale asked, no one with an answer. Crowds pushed closer. There were doctors coming. Directional staff. People who would know what to do, and I felt an eerie calm. There would be a family to notify, a funeral to arrange, debriefings to inform us of how to feel. Procedures and handbooks.

"Some guy. Definitely male. Hairy-looking."

I had to concentrate on staying in place to remove myself from the experience. How many of us had felt pushed to the limit, unable to go any further? Just the night before, I had cried until I couldn't catch my breath, filling my journal with details of the inspection where course staff had poked at my insecurities until I was certain my weakness had become the glaring reason I couldn't succeed. *Do you wonder if your fellow troops see you as weak, Thompson? Do you feel shame about not keeping up with your platoon? Do you?* All of that strife over a scratch in the paint of my closet, a closet that surely hadn't been repainted in years. When the sergeant left, I'd had to swallow tears, unwilling to surrender to the anxiety. Some days, I felt a cozy acceptance of my new military life. Other times I was so laden with emotion that I could barely wake for PT, crying as I laced my sneakers. But I kept going. I wasn't always sure why.

My hands shook with nerves, but we avoided touching or offering hugs. Scotdale sucked on her bottom lip to keep from crying, while Trafford climbed onto the windowsill to crane her neck.

"He's dead," Trafford said, matter of fact. "Poor fucker."

"I wonder why he . . ." Scotdale started, then stopped, pressing a hand to the glass.

Doctors appeared and began to corral the crowd, those standing by ordered back to their pods. The last of the sunlight wavered as emergency vehicles arrived, the whole compound shuddering with engine vibrations and reverberating sirens.

"Some people just can't handle the pressure." Trafford said out loud what we'd all been thinking, words spoken without judgment, full of understanding. It might have sounded harsh to someone outside our concertina-wired perimeter, but we watched, dry-eyed and blank, licking lips and fidgeting. Who hadn't been berated, failed a test, or stumbled on a ruck march and worried that they would never quite match up? How many times had I gone to sleep praying for a deviation from the exercise-eat-inspection-train-eat-sleep routine, crossed my fingers for a reprieve from more challenges my body and brain weren't up to? I regarded the victim below, wondered about his dreams of military life, a career he was proud of. All of that now dissipated into dust.

"Well, I guess we should get to bed, am I right? PT at five."
Trafford checked her watch to punctuate her point.

"Shouldn't we do something?" Scotdale bit her lip until I
thought it might bleed. "I don't know . . . go down and offer
some help or something?"

"Honey," Trafford squeezed Scotdale's arm in a motherly
gesture. "No one can help that guy. At least, not now." If not
now, then when? How much earlier would someone have had
to intervene to save the soldier's life? "Nothing for us to do but
get some sleep and make sure none of us reach the point of hurl-
ing themselves from the Mega. No one is going to be scraping
my body from the grounds of this shithole, that I can assure you."

Trafford took great care to wipe up the spilled Bordeaux, no
one mentioning the similarity to the spread of maroon around
the corpse of our comrade. We shuffled back to our individual
rooms, the warm feeling of our alcohol buzz quickly fading.

I lay in bed shivering, pulled my scratchy blanket up to my
chin, sneezed as the wool met my face. Trafford was right: all
we could do was look after one another, and yet my platoon-
mates were also the people to whom I felt shame for showing
weakness, surely the same failing that had led that cadet to the
pavement. We could not, would not, be seen as weak: a soldier's
refrain. And then again, the need to call Dad, to ask about his
time in the Golan. How many times since leaving the Sinai had
Dad wished to slip closer to dreaming and never wake? If my
soldier father hadn't seen emotion as a failure, perhaps he would
still have a military career ahead of him. Or maybe he would be
able to laugh and make jokes, and maybe, just maybe, I would
catch glimpses of who he used to be.

As a kid, with Dad serving as a commanding officer at several units, he was occasionally called out in the middle of the
night. I would answer the phone, voice meek and nervous, to

hear the authoritative tone of the Military Police asking for Major Thompson, and I would pass the phone over obediently. Dad would listen through the receiver, eyebrows meeting in the divot between his eyes, and then he would leave in a hurry, coat tossed over hunched shoulders, and return hours later. He would discuss limited details with Mom when he came home, their voices harsh whispers from their bedroom, unaware of me hovering silently outside. *Who knows how long he's been hanging there*, Dad whispered once. *Poor bastard*. Someone, one of Dad's troops, had been found hanging from his neck in the shacks. Another time, an overdose. A few others made the effort without achieving their goal. And while Dad looked weary from the experiences of supporting families and coordinating care during those late evenings, more than anything he looked ashamed that he hadn't stopped these suicides, not noticing that the armour these soldiers had projected to the world was the same army-issue my father possessed. But each morning, he would still wake his daughters gently, sometimes brushing my hair before school, a smile all the defence he needed.

Later that night, journal out, I slammed it closed again and thrust it under my mattress. I slipped on socks and tiptoed down the silent halls and then tapped on Joe's pod door, which was answered by a sleepy cadet. He rubbed his eyes with his knuckles.

"Shorrocks," he called over his shoulder. "Thompson is here to see you. Again."

Joe was silent when he met me in the stairwell. I sat down and leaned against him wordlessly, lips quivering but never allowing the tears to break, until eleven o'clock neared and the staff would be making the bed-check rounds. When I stood, he told me to get some rest and disappeared back into his own pod.

I went to sleep angry, alcohol burps infusing my breath, dreaming of wine, tall buildings, and Joe, and the haunting knowledge that some histories would repeat themselves. As much as we would continue to fight wars, we would continue to struggle to cope with the weight of that work. We would continue in our silence.

14

It was time to return to the fields of Farnham, and like in IAP, passing or failing BOTC came down to the small party tasks. All of the other tests that came before—drill, weapons, obstacle courses, knot-tying, and public speaking—were meant to contribute to our ability to apply this knowledge in giving orders to be obeyed, not just followed. The mission of the Farnham experience was to highlight that we weren't just logistics officers or engineers or air traffic controllers—whatever our military occupation may be. First and foremost, we were leaders.

To execute the tests, we would be separated into sections of eight troops. When it was a cadet's turn to be tested, they would be given a geographical location in Farnham and a set of orders—build a rope bridge over a ravine to save a pretend stranded family, construct a structure to provide shelter to troops—and then the cadet would relay the location and an expected arrival time to the rest of the section, before setting off on a thirty-minute advance reconnaissance to prepare his or her plan before the rest of the section followed. The taskings were more complicated than those in IAP, with the added element of topography skills.

Don't question yourself, Joe had said as we prepared for our final inspection. I was doing his ironing and he was scrubbing my floors, a trading of skills mixed with social time. *Positive thinking goes a long way. We'll both do great.* I squirted a blast of steam into the back of his shirt, pressing sharp creases with military precision.

This time around, we didn't have to march to our Farnham bivouac; instead, we were dropped off, bags and all, in the middle of the site. We sombrely set up camp and revelled in eating our IMPs warmed instead of cold, which we knew, considering the intended pace in the days to come, would be how we'd have to eat them for the rest of the week.

Another year had done nothing to stifle the humidity of Quebec, which was experiencing a wild heat wave for the end of spring. We sat to the side of another nameless sandy road, nibbling on the contents of our ration packs during a luxurious five-minute break. The bun bullet hadn't changed either, and I squirted a packet of overly sweet jam across the carbs, and chewed and chewed and chewed, willing saliva to soften it.

I was nearly out of the small ration of Tylenol that I'd stashed in my tunic, pain swarming my knee until I could hardly tolerate walking without feeling sick to my stomach, having woken that day in agony. It was nothing, I told myself, just the usual aches and pains, although nothing about the look and feel of the joint felt routine. But I was only a few days into field week—hell, I hadn't even had my chance at a small party task. The first two days had mostly been spent marching around the training area, practising map skills and looping through the in-field obstacle course, the twelve-foot wall nearly killing me since it demanded a straight vertical rope climb. Then last night had been spent on the range, our first night shoot, with our bullets lighting the air like fireflies, the feeling of war a little too realistic. But those two days felt anticipatory, like we were kill-ing time. Clearly, BOTC's week in the field was dedicated to the small party task and nothing else. I couldn't quit now, not when I was so close, no matter the pain.

So I stuffed Tylenol into my mouth and chewed them with the bun bullet that now frothed with pinkish jam paste. I ate my medicated sandwich in silence and prayed someone else had brought painkillers and was willing to share.

Heat aside, basic training made the best and shittiest parts of ourselves more prevalent. Those who would have been friendly acquaintances in university became my closest companions in a miserable existence; Joe as an example. People I would normally dislike in civilian life, I hated with fiery passion. Rubino, a member of my eight-person section, fell into the latter category. He was all bravado and arrogance, loud talking and hip swaggering.

"Rubino, you're up." Our sergeant wiggled a finger at Rubino, who hopped to. I sipped from my canteen while he received his orders, eyeing him for signs of stress, signs I desper-ately wanted to see—something I secretly admonished myself for. He came trotting back to us and relayed the location where he'd been assigned to complete his task. He took off after giving us the coordinates, and we languished in our short break.

"When is it ever not a million degrees in this province?" a cadet muttered, likely someone from a moderate climate like British Columbia or Nova Scotia.

"What, you expected it to be a cushy ride?"

"I didn't say that."

"Fuck, enough already. We should get going."

Someone shot the bearing with their compass and marked the route with a grease pencil on the laminated Farnham map. Three kilometres—not bad as far as distances went, and yet I wasn't confident my knee could handle it.

After forty minutes of slogging through the sand, we arrived at Rubino's site to find him scribbling on a field notepad, his pencil making streaky lines as we fanned out on our stomachs in a protective circle, weapons pointed, giving him time to finish. My body clunked to the ground, knee giving up, metal magazines pressing into my ribs, as we trained eyes on an unseen enemy that, according to the rules of field engagement, was continuously and mysteriously lurking in the woods.

"On me!" Rubino cried once he finished writing, tapping his head for effect. Our section stood and circled him with our rifles slung across our chests.

"Situation," he barked. SMESC, or "five paragraph order," is the series of steps taken to deliver operational orders to troops while offering all pertinent information to complete the task. The acronym stands for Situation, Mission, Execution, Service/Support, and Command and Control. No more, no less. In the weeks of practising and preparing, I often went to sleep dreaming of my life in terms of SMESC:

SITUATION: Officer Cadet Thompson is miserable in basic training and will not make it. She is a completely shit soldier.

MISSION: To make Officer Cadet Thompson pass the fucking course so that she may actually make someone proud someday.

EXECUTION: Pass small party task through miracle of God. Somehow convince everyone she is not a gigantic screw-up.

SERVICE/SUPPORT: Food is supplied by ration packs and combat pockets full of beef jerky and M&Ms. Sand will permeate every meal.

COMMAND AND CONTROL: Commanding officer is father, Major Bill Thompson, Canadian Forces Base Borden.

Rubino coughed twice and snapped me back to the muggy day, my sticky clothes, and my canteen that did not seem to contain enough water.

"I repeat. Situation: There has been a nuclear, chemical, radiological, and biological spill in this area to measure fifteen metres south"—he pointed into the woods—"ten metres east, and back to this point. Mission: We are to cordon off the area to protect unaware civilians, using metal posts and paracord, while ensuring proper CBRN warfare protections are in place at all times."

If our sergeant had been standing closer, he would have heard our united moan. *Chemical. Biological. Radiological. Nuclear.* All these words, even in this pretend scenario, were associated with the gas masks that hung forgotten from our webbing in protective pouches, the rubbery rain gear that didn't let perspiration evaporate, plus heavy leather gloves and the inability to drink water without having to fuck about with the temperamental mask safety straw. The effect would be a full body steam that no one wanted to experience after days without a shower in an intense heat wave. More often than not, when a random GAS, GAS, GAS! attack was called, I threw my mask on in record time, only to find it full of sand because the Velcro case would not stay closed, and Farnham had a way of sneaking in. I'd cough and choke while the course staff hovered in front of me and dared me to take it off, even as I gagged on grains of finely weathered rock. *Take that thing off and you'll be fucking dead, Thompson. DEAD.*

Rubino's orders went on to tell us how we would execute his mission using metal stakes and the thumper, a circular metal tube with handles—designed to hammer the stakes into the earth—that had magically been left on site and weighed about forty pounds. He then outlined the separate tasks for each cadet. I was usually assigned to sentry duty, apparently capable of nothing other than standing around with my weapon to challenge anyone who might pass with the code word. I was routinely embarrassed by this job because it seemed somehow beneath me, and yet if I was honest I had to admit that 90 per cent of my fellow troops were more physically capable than I was. I could accept that fact and focus on being one hell of an assertive sentry, or I could pretend to physically manage things I couldn't, especially with the pain in my leg. Sentry duty won out, nearly every damn time.

"Thompson," Rubino shouted more loudly than he needed to. "You will follow Officer Cadet Firth, who will carry the metal stakes, and you will employ the thumper to ensure they are in the ground."

I almost laughed. In fact, half the section smirked, as if they too wondered what in the hell Rubino was thinking. Me and the forty-pound thumper? Really? It was close to a third of my body weight. But speaking up, saying anything, would validate what everyone thought of me, not to mention what the men thought of all female troops. In this, I was certain: I would carry that thumper like my life depended on it. And the reality was, on an actual deployment, my life and those of my fellow troops actually might.

Once he finished assigning tasks to the rest of the section, Rubino clapped his hands together in front of him, dispersing us like dust. "And don't forget, everyone is to wear their gas mask and gloves at all times, and since we don't have access to CBRN suits, we will wear our rain gear, which will provide added protection." I almost laughed aloud at the idea of rain gear protecting us from nuclear chemicals. We might as well have been told to wear garbage bags over our heads.

"Ensure the wrists are cinched tight. Understand?" Rubino pointed to his wrists and motioned opening and closing the wrist strap. "All right, get to work, troops. And you, Thompson." He leaned in close, a finger raised to my nose. "Welcome to real work."

With a last look of longing at a sliver of shade under a scrawny maple, I donned my gas mask and rain gear and tugged on my leather gloves like the rest of the section, before plunging into the woods, dragging the thumper through the sand like a child's doll and wincing whenever it bonked my sore leg. Voices were stifled as we shouted to one another across the fifteen-by-ten-metre-square space, our bodies blending into our surroundings as they were designed to.

I awkwardly lumbered after Firth, pulling the thumper in the soil behind me, dragging up a trail of leaves and dirt, while two other troops followed us with loops of cording to lash onto the stakes to mark the imagined spill. Firth managed to plunge the first few stakes into the soft earth with little to no effort, making my work with the thumper unrequired. But the further we plodded into the woods, the denser the ground became. I would approach the stake, squat to retrieve the thumper, and raise it over my head to cap the metal post, then pound it up and down until I could hardly breathe, hammering the stake a foot deep. Half the time I required Firth's help to get the thumper up and into place before conducting the dull symphony of metal on metal. My teeth ached each time it connected—but, job complete, I would heave with all my might and tug the tool to the next marker Firth had placed. Five. Seven. Nine stakes. How many to go? I had to finish. Had to. If I couldn't, what hope was there for me on an overseas deployment? How could I protect others when I couldn't do this one simple thing?

"You need help with that?" Firth asked as he pushed through the bush with his sleeve and held the branches back from my face as I snuck underneath.

"I'm good." Puff. Wheeze. "All good." I wasn't good at all, sweat falling in sheets down my thighs and breasts and face, pooling in the canister space of my mask. Drowning in my own sweat seemed an unappealing way to go.

My tongue smacked dry against the roof of my mouth, and I chewed gritty sand between my molars to take my mind off the increasingly unbearable heat. The uniform that was melting into my skin. The water in the canteen that I could not drink with my gas mask on. Sun broke between the leaves in a hazy filter of dust and I saw heaven, maybe, or perhaps it was hell, and yet I'd never read the Bible so what would I know?

There was something about wearing the gas mask in the field that was simultaneously comical and stressful. On the one hand, I knew this piece of gear could save my life. On the other, combined with the awkward weight and size of webbing, rifles, and a forty-pound thumper, we looked totally ridiculous. I couldn't stop laughing to myself, snorting away in the rubber-scented void. Firth mumbled something from his goggled eyes and I nodded without really hearing him. *God, is that you? Joe?* I couldn't stop laughing until I couldn't stop sweating. And then I couldn't stop swallowing down my own heatstroke-induced vomit.

I'd not admitted to anyone on course that I had a lifelong, all-consuming fear of vomit, diagnosed as emetophobia. Nothing had the power to make me cower in a corner with fear more than a night of food poisoning or the stomach flu. But this decision to push through overgrown ferns and moist fallen logs in thirty-eight-degree heat was beyond my control. I had no choice but to swallow repeatedly until an acidic burp of bile made it into my mask, and just like that, I was undone.

I pulled up the mask and barfed in a liquid pile at my feet. Puke splashed onto my combat boots and Firth offered a glint of sympathy as he stuffed another metal spike into the ground. My body shook and yet I had never felt so relieved. The rush of fresh air, no matter how sticky, was akin to sex, to a mojito on a Mexican beach, to a bed with Egyptian cotton sheets far away from Farnham. One more retch, plop, cough, spit was followed by gasps of fresh air.

"Thompson, what the fuck?" Rubino tromped towards me, combat boots squashing branches underfoot. I took a swig from my canteen, rinsed, spat again. "Are you directly disobeying an order of safety? Get your fucking mask on before the sergeant sees and you make me fail because you fucking fake-died of chemical warfare."

"Yeah, I'm fine, thanks for asking." I gave him a mock, irritated salute and tugged my mask back onto my face, adjusting it on my slippery skin that hadn't been washed in days, like putting makeup on a balloon. Firth was motioning with his gloved hand at his latest spike, moving his palm up and down in case I wasn't aware of the purpose of the thumper and my role in its operation. The thirty-eight-degree heat would not subside, and I found myself shaking each time I lifted the thumper until Rubino declared me too slow and had another cadet take over, his point made. Forty-five minutes later, we collectively collapsed on the ground, puffing, wheezing, and gagging. Another of our comrades stumbled to the tree line and barfed his IMP into the woods.

Rubino failed his small party task, which I hoped was due in large part to a lack of concern for the health of his troops— not enough breaks and rest in the heat. We knew he'd failed the moment the sergeant delivered the post-task brief in hushed tones and with knitted eyebrows. Rubino sulked all day, and bitched at anyone who came close to him while looking like he might perpetually break into tears. Once, our eyes met and he gave me the finger, as though my throwing up had been the cause of all his hardship, although he felt bold enough to ask me for some gummy bears later that night. A slice of beef jerky, perhaps? I only had one slice left. I shoved the whole thing in my mouth and chewed with my mouth open. I wasn't going to let all that fresh air go to waste.

15

It was the day after Rubino's tasking, four days into the field exercise, and I had long since run out of analgesics. Now my knee ached so badly that I wondered if this second-last week in basic would finally be my undoing.

"Don't go," Scotdale said, cautioning against the field MIR. "If you complain too much, they'll haul you back to Saint-Jean and make you re-course." Since Meerin's assault, women had no longer been allowed to partner with men as fire buddies, so thanks to an odd number of women in our platoon, three of us were assigned to one another like awkward musketeers, our three ground sheets woven together into a hooch so big we called it the Palace. My hoochmates and I had settled into our sleeping bags for a blessed few hours of sleep. Four at the most, and I was on sentry duty from three to four in the morning. Snoring already echoed from various corners of the biv.

"She won't have to re-course," said our other hoochmate. "Not if she passes her tasking."

"No, I'm serious," Scotdale said, grasping for my hand, which was buried in the sleeping bag, rubbing my sore leg. "A friend of mine got re-coursed when she missed a full twenty-four hours in the field. They call it 'incomplete.'" When pressed,

Scotdale's knowledge of this loose rule was the result of a military game of telephone, like most of our knowledge of the inner workings of basic.

The course staff had refused to answer me when I asked what the ramifications of going to the MIR would be, like they were testing my willingness to put up with the pain, as if that were the real test of the week. *It's up to you*, they'd say, shrugging their shoulders, a hint of a smile. *If you think it's bad enough.*

"How'd you hurt it?" Scotdale asked, wiping camouflage off her face with a baby wipe. We had just returned from an evening exercise spent marching around Farnham—which was what we'd done all day too.

"No idea." I couldn't mark the exact moment my knee had started to ache. I only knew that the sharp pain was beyond the usual shit we'd come to expect—the blisters and bruises, bites and aches. Inexplicably worse.

"Here," Scotdale said, dropping some ibuprofen in my hand. "I brought it for my period, but you use it."

"You're a goddess, you know that?" I swallowed them dry but struggled to sleep, even as my hoochmates were out within seconds. When I was woken by a fellow cadet for sentry duty, I stumbled through the woods and took my post at the head of the biv, weapon at the ready. At 4 a.m., my shift technically over, the pain was so intense I offered to stay at my post, just to avoid walking back to my hooch. Sleep, I knew, would evade me.

The next morning, my small party task involved setting up a rope bridge across a deep stream. The test went off without a hitch and I scored one of the best marks in the platoon for leadership, just like in IAP, and my assessor stared at me with an element of shock that would have been offensive if my mind hadn't been so focused on my knee. But I couldn't celebrate. As soon as I was given my passing mark, I asked to be taken to the MIR, collapsing into an embarrassing heap. The sergeant rolled his eyes and told me to get into the half-ton truck, and we drove in complete silence through the maze of sandy roads before he dropped me off at the Farnham-based MIR, which was nothing but a stationary trailer.

I knocked on the door and pushed my way through when no one answered. "Hello?"

I peeked my head in and then stepped fully into blissful comfort, the air conditioning blowing across my skin and making me shiver.

"Can we help you, Officer Cadet?" The stern voice belonged to a medic sporting a white smock over his uniform, bleached and crisp. My body stiffened and I snapped to.

"Officer Cadet Thompson, 898," I said, trying my best to sound tough. *Do. Not. Fucking. Cry.* "I think I've hurt my knee."

"You think or you know, Officer Cadet?" The medic held a clipboard as a barrier between us, assessing me with raised eyebrows. The small MIR consisted of a cluster of three work-stations and two exam tables at the back, both covered in rolls of crinkly paper and guarded by privacy curtains. Nearby was a corporal taking inventory of a medical cabinet, counting and recounting on her fingers.

"I know, Master Corporal. It's pretty painful."

"Fill this out and go over to the exam area." He handed me a medical chit where I filled in my details: Service number. Name. Platoon number. Nature of injury. I scribbled my information and handed the clipboard back before stumbling to the exam table. Surrounded by wipes, antibacterial wash, and generic cleanliness, I felt overly aware of my Farnham-brewed, fetid stench. When I pushed a finger against my skin, a slump of dirt slid underneath my fingernail.

"So," the medic said, reading hastily through my chit. "Your leg hurts."

"Yes. Right at the knee joint."

"What caused the injury?" His words were spat out like he sensed I might be malingering, trying to get out of something.

"Not sure exactly. It just started aching really bad and now the pain is getting sharp and stabby." I made a knife-poking gesture with my finger for effect. "I feel like it's pretty serious."

"Let us be the judge of that, eh?" He sounded bored and annoyed, like my presence was taking him away from the more important task of medical supply inventory or playing games of solitaire at his desk. "Take off your boot and roll up your pant leg."

I did as instructed. My toenails were bare; I'd learned that lesson the summer prior. A blotchy bruise had spread across the inside of my knee and it was wildly swollen—round and shiny where the edema pushed at my human seams. The medic poked and prodded until I cried out, and he gave me another exaggerated eye roll, his patience apparently extended to its limit. Then he bent my leg in several awkward and painful directions before stepping back and placing his hands on his hips.

"Just as I thought. Tendonitis."

"No way." I stared at my knee, uncertain, shaking my head. He had to be wrong. There was no way tendonitis could feel this bad. "You're kidding."

"Do I look like I'm kidding?"

"It's just, how do you . . . I mean, I guess I'm wondering how you know that without any imaging or anything." I was nervous in challenging the authority that came with his training, especially after months of learning to obey orders at all costs.

"Take a look," the medic said, waving his hand in the air. "I don't have an X-ray machine just lying around here. Besides, you don't need it. Like I said, tendonitis."

"Okay." My whole body sagged, deflated, as I started putting my boot back on, wincing as I went. How could I stretch out this moment in an air-conditioned room with a running mini fridge that likely housed cold drinks and maybe even a limp bologna sandwich? And yet, even as the thought entered my head, I admonished myself for it, for craving acknowledgement of my pain in a world where I wasn't to be taken seriously because of . . . what? Age? Gender? Rank? Injury?

The medic was already at a workstation hammering details into his computer database, my presence forgotten. As I wrestled on my footwear, I noticed I was wearing Dad's combat boots, labelled with his name and service number. Maybe we'd accidentally switched them when I last visited, or perhaps after polishing I'd grabbed the wrong ones, considering we wore the same size. Staring at his initials and the digits of his service number written on the interior of the leather in black Sharpie, I felt emotional, and so very tired. Had Dad ever said he was hurting, out loud, to someone who would have cared? Sure, I was only surrounded by the sand of my own country, but was it so different from the dirt in Egypt, where Dad had hurt himself beyond repair? I couldn't help it then, tears lurching up through my whole body until I was vibrating. *It's just exhaustion. You're injured and have barely slept in days. Deep breaths.*

The medic turned from his computer and took a deep breath himself. "Listen," he said, his voice betraying a hint of sympathy. "I can give you these." He dropped a few coated pills into my hand.

"What are they?"

"Ibuprofen."

I laughed openly while the medic looked unimpressed. Advil. I felt like my leg might fall off and he was giving me Advil.

"So that's it? I just go back out there?"

"Oh, that's what this is about." He threw his arms up in the air and eyed me like he'd finally gotten my proverbial number. "You want out of the field work, am I right?"

"I don't want out of anything. I just hoped maybe I could get a ride with the staff between tasking sites or something." Even saying it out loud, I knew the idea of chauffeured hustles to small party tasking sites—while my platoon-mates lumbered there on foot—was a fantasy, one I wasn't sure I wanted in reality. Pain or pride. It seemed there was only one option, and like our platoon T-shirts said: *pain is temporary*. Without another word, I popped the Advil, requested a few more for my pocket and waited on the front steps of the trailer for the staff.

"Well, Officer Cadet?" I didn't recognize the master corporal who was picking me up; course staff for another one of the platoons. I hauled open the door of the truck and used only my left leg to swing up onto the tall chassis.

"Tendonitis."

"Ah." A silence fell over the truck, everything muted by the growling engine.

"What do I do now?" I called over the noise.

"What now?" The man chuckled as he shifted gears. "Now you soldier on, Cadet."

"What?"

"Soldier on. You suck it up and keep going. Or you can quit. Just say you can't do it and you'll be free."

I gripped the handle of the door, pressed against the cool steel, and closed my eyes a moment, thinking of everything I'd done to prove I wanted to be a soldier when it seemed the person who needed the most convincing was myself. Now I felt hopelessly stuck between the wanting and the hating, the disdain and the love—all for a career that seemed not to want me. I'd come so far, had even had some successes, and yet this injury could unravel it all. I kept looking from my leg to the sandy roads rumbling past the window, then back again.

"Well, here you are." The master corporal pointed to where my section was slurping from canteens and nibbling on ration packs at a new tasking site. One of our course staff members, Sergeant Pike, stood nearby with a clipboard, pen at the ready for marking. "Last chance if you want to throw in the towel."

I didn't make eye contact, scared of what would happen if I did, and hopped one-legged from the truck. I was dropped off just as Rubino was about to begin his second attempt at the small party task. Setting up a communications tower? Arranging a command post? I couldn't see him for the circle of troops that surrounded him.

"Hey, Thompson." Someone shuffled over to make room for me in the group. "How did it go?"

"Tendonitis, apparently."

"Shit, join the club," someone else muttered. We were all experiencing our own forms of pain. Tendonitis was low on the seriousness ladder and I felt the judgment seeping from their pores.

"I'm pretty sure it's something else though," I said, like I needed to rationalize my choice to seek help. *Don't be a* MIR *Commando.* Dad's words hung like a thought bubble over my head.

"Platoon, on me," Rubino called. We jumped to our feet, break time now over. He gave his SMESC orders calmly and sternly, less cocky this time.

"Thompson. You're in charge of lacing the mod tents for the main structure. Think you can handle *that*?" As much as I disliked Rubino, I wanted him to pass. Failure had the same effect on all of us, and no matter how hard he tried to hide it, desperation was evident on his face. When he finished giving his orders, I bustled over to where the modular tent sections lay like a pile of dirty clothes, and my nimble fingers made quick work of my task.

"Done over here!" I hollered. The troops in charge of hoisting the poles for the tent stepped in behind me to right the tent.

"Thompson," Rubino barked. "There's another section to be laced over there."

I moved quickly, full of assurance. If only my leg had received the memo that this was not the time for giving up. Upon reaching the next section of tenting material, fingers at the ready, my right knee gave way. When I fell forward, my kneecap clattered against a rock and I couldn't help but cry out sharply, hissing air through my teeth and clutching my knee to my chest in the fetal position.

"Thompson, shit, you okay? Rubino! Sergeant!" Everyone came running, hovering over my head. I knew they were there, but I couldn't open my eyes. Just rolled back and forth on the ridge of my spine, waiting for the stabbing sensation to subside. When my eyes finally cracked open, Rubino had his hands on his hips, eyebrows knitted in annoyance. But he'd learned his lesson. He had to look after his troops.

"Thompson, you sit to the side and rest. Firth, take over lacing."

"Rubino, I'm sorry." From the ground I grasped for his sleeve like a lost child as he pulled away, ignoring me. This time, he passed with flying colours—the assessing staff member, Sergeant Pike, exhibiting his positive result with a thumbs up.

"All right, back to the biv everyone," Pike hollered. She was a small woman who moved quickly and with efficiency.

She directed us to collect the various items from the task site and load them onto a half-ton truck that had materialized. I lingered behind, nursing my leg, now on fire, the swelling worse with each passing moment while my section lined up on the side of the road and prepared to march.

"Sergeant Pike?" I approached while my section took their last sips of water before the trek, adjusting their packs. "I'm desperate. Please. Can I have a ride back to the biv?" What no one knew—not the staff, not my fellow troops, and certainly not Rubino—was that the simple act of asking for help was one of the bravest moves I could make. *I can't do this* is the hardest phrase for a soldier to utter. And Pike knew it. Looking at my face, my unbecoming trembling bottom lip, my clenched fists—she knew that without a small act of kindness, I would give up even though there was only one more night and we would be back in Saint-Jean. Just one night. Surrender was written all over me.

"Get in." She nodded to the truck bed. "But don't talk to anyone about this, understand?"

I nodded hastily and tried to slip away from my section without them noticing. They noticed, of course, when they arrived at the bivouac site and found me already at my hooch, pouring cold water over my knee like it was an overheated radiator.

Hours later, after dinner, my platoon stumbled along a sandy road plunked in Quebec's backwoods, my moist camouflage uniform clinging to my skin like I'd been dunked in honey.

I knew then, despite the opinion of the crusty medic, that I'd broken my leg somewhere in the dusty field while schlepping that seventy-pound rucksack and my C7 rifle slung around my neck. Its cause was uncertain—apparently just a stress fracture,

I found out months later, damaged further by too much marching while carrying too much weight for my one-hundred-and-thirty-five-pound frame. *You should have stopped marching once it started to hurt*, the civilian doctor would say. I laughed at this preposterous idea.

For our final night in the field, our section was on a mini exercise, the point of which seemed obscure to all of us. March from point A to point B. Set up camp. Shoot at potential enemies. We took shelter amongst the pine trees, affording the opportunity to rehydrate and change damp socks. I nestled in a ditch with Joe and gnawed on my contraband beef jerky, then offered Joe a piece and sensed he understood the importance of this gift. In the field and at war, calories and protein are to soldiers what cocaine is to an addict.

I pulled the sand trap from my combat boot to assess the damage, rolling the fabric up to my thigh. My knee looked like it had swallowed a basketball, and the blotchy, purple bruise had continued to spread like spilled milk.

"Your leg looks like shit. You sure you can keep going?" Joe asked.

"Do I have a choice?"

Joe cocked his head sympathetically, his blue eyes catching the last of the sunlight. He hardly appeared to be sweating in the sticky heat, nor did he seem tired or to be covered in sand flea bites. Joe was the kind of guy who made basic training seem easy, but it was impossible to hate him for it.

I turned my palms up and brought my shoulders to my ears. "I've got to 'soldier on,' right?" I chewed my jerky pensively as I leaned against my ruck and stared up into the sky, stars emerging through the ebbing light.

"Give me your rucksack. I'll carry it back to camp," Joe said.

"I'm fine. I'll be fine," I said, waving him off.

As our platoon packed up, Joe reached out a hand to heave me vertical. Somewhere in the distance, an artillery simulator went off, the sound of mechanical gunfire automatically directing my trigger finger to my rifle's safety switch, my body at the ready. The simulator painted the sky with artificial white light that highlighted our faces hidden in the trees. Collectively, we paused, waited. No more gunfire. We could keep moving.

I hefted my bag onto my shoulders and winced as I meandered onto the road. I could barely see the end of the sandy route ahead, symbolically informing me that I could not—or would not—reach the end, no matter where it led. Joe adjusted his rucksack so it was on his chest and squatted in front of me.

"Hop on. I'll piggy-back you to camp."

"You can't be serious. It's three fucking kilometres! Between me and my bag, that's over two hundred fucking pounds."

The whole scenario seemed ridiculous, but so did the idea of hobbling back to camp myself. I shimmied my bag onto the ground, where it landed with a thud, a plume of sand making us both cough. I rested my hands on Joe's broad shoulders and closed my eyes to fight off a wave of pain-induced nausea. He smelled like Tide laundry detergent; a miracle considering our surroundings.

Once I was on his back, Joe lumbered steadily as a tugboat while I clung to him, a broken-down cargo ship. He carried me the entire way, my rucksack dragging in the dust behind us, like a mitten on a string.

That night I slept under the stars in nothing but a bivvy bag, shivering even though I wasn't cold. And the next morning it was over. BOTC. We had passed, emerged on the other side, with just a week of parade practice and paperwork standing in the way of home.

When we arrived back at the Mega, smelling like garbage and in various states of disrepair, we lay in the sunlight, rucks at our side, until we were cleared to go up to the pods and take turns fighting for the shower.

"You're the only injured chick who made it." One of my platoon-mates gestured at me with a nod of his head, referring to me being the only one of four injured women who had chosen to stay in the field and not return early. This cadet was in his late thirties, a former infantryman who had already been to Afghanistan as a corporal and was training to become an officer. "That's something to be proud of. You took it like a man."

Like a man. I pictured a wartime propaganda poster restyled for this millennium's Afghanistan, some Canadianized version of Uncle Sam's "We Want You." The image would depict pixelated desert camouflage, drones dropping bombs in the background, and a freshly shaven face grimacing at the viewer. The fine print, in minuscule type at the bottom of the poster, would read: *Girls Need Not Apply.*

I rolled up my pant leg again for a cursory inspection, and both the colour and size of my kneecap drew significant attention. For once, I basked in the knowledge that I was a real soldier. All I'd needed to do was break my leg and march, never stopping.

16

We practised for the BOTC graduation parade for most of our final week, the mood jovial in light of our impending freedom. We joked during breaks after sweaty loops of the parade square in the sweltering heat, alternating sips of water and squats to get blood moving in our toes after half an hour at attention. At night, we prepared our dress uniforms for the big day—ironed, steamed, washed our temporary-issue white belts and gloves—this being the first time we would wear them.

Since I'd enrolled in the Forces, I'd pictured this parade as the culmination of my family's generational military pride, so caught up in the ideal that the physical implications—considering my knee injury—of the week of drill practice didn't occur to me. I kept slipping into the bathroom to gag, pain swelling up in my belly, before lifting the sand trap of my pants to splash cold water on my fiery skin. Besides, the medics had assured me that the tendonitis would heal once I was home, and no damage would be done. I had already spoken out about the pain once, and having felt the judgment from the staff and my platoon-mates for doing so, especially when my medical assessment didn't highlight any major issues, I didn't intend to again.

"Thompson, why are you wobbling all over the fucking place?" the warrant hollered from his stance in front of our platoon. We'd just completed another round of practice, all of us hazy with exhaustion. He kicked me out of the front line, burying my apparent drill ineptitude in the middle row of the ranks. "Don't you fuck up my parade, Thompson!"

While some kids enjoyed the Macy's Thanksgiving balloon extravaganza or Toronto's Santa Claus Parade, my idea of a parade was soldiers lined in ranks on the tarmac, tricoloured heads forming orderly rows like a packet of matches. I used to watch Dad lead his troops, officer sword slicing the air, overwhelmed with a sense of duty before I understood the definition of the word. Dad explained that longer parades were hard on the body, especially in heat. It's easy to lose consciousness while at attention due to the required body tension and being unable to shift weight in the unnatural pose. Options for coping with said dizziness were slim: 1) Take a knee. This, of course, was the less honourable approach; the one that led to ribbing and jokes in the mess later on. Phrases like *Can't hack it* and *What a pansy* would abound. But this option, although resulting in ridicule, literally saved face, preventing contact with the crude cement of the parade square. Or: 2) Faint. It would hurt like hell upon waking, but there was honour in a face smashed to a pulp. As a child, I saw a female soldier pass out in a change of command parade held in the middle of an August heat wave. She woke up without eight of her teeth and needed two jaw surgeries to correct the breaks. She never looked the same and couldn't chew steak anymore, but she wore her new dentures like a badge of honour. She was routinely commended for her dedication to deportment.

—

"So this is where you sleep?"

Mom, Dad, Meghan, and Trevor had arrived in Saint-Jean the night before my graduation parade and stayed at a local hotel. After taking me out to dinner, Meghan said she wanted to help me pack and would take a taxi back to the hotel, so I'd snuck my sister into my room, where she now sat on my bed, feet tucked up to her bottom so her body formed a tiny ball.

Until that moment, my military sphere was personal, reserved for me only. *Home* and *military* felt as separate as night and day. Now, having my sister in my barracks pod—a woman who was six inches shorter than me, and frail, somehow—I felt comparatively strong, full of useful knowledge. Meghan, meanwhile, was living with a drug-obsessed boyfriend and was addicted to some kind of poison herself—a topic we didn't discuss because we had mostly detached from one another as we aged. It was the Meghans of the world that I realized I wanted to protect.

"This is the palace of sleeping arrangements, yeah."

"The blanket feels like sandpaper."

"Try sleeping with it."

I fussed with my woollen air force uniform. To remove traces of lint, I'd tapped the material with a hand-wrap of duct tape, and I'd ironed it three times until each crease was sharp. Even if I wasn't the perfect soldier, my uniform let me pretend it was possible.

"What the hell is this for?" She held up my clear plastic ruler to the fluorescent light. It lay permanently on the fold of my bedding, even when I slept.

"For measuring my sheets. Have to make sure the fold of the blanket is exactly one foot from the top of the bed."

"Well, that's fucking pointless."

I shrugged, remembering when I too had thought it was pointless. More than once, after being reprimanded for shoddy bed-making skills, I'd return to my room at the end of the day to find the course staff had wedged my twin mattress so it dangled from the frame of my window. Now, as I packed up the T-shirt measuring card, the balled-up socks, the pristine soap dish, preparing my belongings for inspection felt like the most ordinary thing in my world.

"Think our army Dad will admit you belong to him tomorrow if you're wearing an air force uniform?"

"Don't think he'll have a choice. Name tags will kind of give our relationship away."

Meghan looked around the room, her bluish-green eyes a perfect match to my own. She smelled of cheap body spray and fruity shampoo; I smelled like deodorant, if that. I probably smelled like army.

"I'm really proud of you. You know that, right?" She fingered a corner of the blanket, looking impossibly small. "I can't believe you actually did basic training."

I didn't know how to tell her that she should be ashamed. I was a MIR Commando. I had openly admitted weakness. Hell, I'd been driven back to the biv. I wasn't worthy of admiration at all. And yet I couldn't stand to dispel the charade because I cherished the new way she looked at me. And I was, despite my IAP failures that now felt like a distant memory, feeling a bit proud of myself.

"It wasn't that bad. I made some great friends." I tugged my civilian clothes from their hangers and stuffed them into my duffle. "Kind of learned what I was capable of too, you know? And hey, maybe one day I'll actually help someone else." On the other side of the experience, my previous reasoning of enrolling for a free education had disintegrated like paper reduced to ash. Fighting to succeed in this job had highlighted how badly I needed the Canadian Forces—and I hoped, somewhere in the world, how I was needed too. I wanted to be good at my job. I wanted to know it was possible for me to be a soldier, not a de facto version at the bottom of the pack.

Meghan smiled and passed my toiletry kit to be buried in the bag. "Was it all worth it then?"

In the hallway, laughter reverberated as my platoon-mates celebrated. I thought of the exhaustion, the workouts, the gas hut, the rappel tower, the obstacle course, the inspections, the food, and, of course, my throbbing, aching knee. I tried to forget the harassment, the assaults, the death; all of it present and future like a map of my career. And then I thought of pride and accomplishment. Of personal strength and perseverance. Of the glorious achievement in proving I could do it. I thought of Joe.

"Yes. Absolutely."

The next morning, graduation day, when Mom, Dad, Trevor, and Meghan pulled up outside the Mega and got out of their car, I felt like an adult for the first time in the company of the people who had raised me. Petite Mom fanning herself in the summer heat; Dad's uniform prim and ironed; Meghan looking out of place in a revealing sundress; Trevor a tangible reminder of home.

To add to the poetic appeal of the parade, my graduation marked Dad's last day in uniform after thirty-five years of service, his career ending just as mine began. He looked completely lost and miserable. Soldiers meandered past, saluting the bars on his arm, and Dad would salute in response before retreating into himself, ever watchful of his surroundings. I wanted to take his hand and hold it in mine, to tell him that even though I'd only finished basic training, I understood to some meagre extent and that his medical release was not a stamp of shame. But saying this would make him angry. Over the years, each family member had felt some semblance of responsibility for his mental health, although it was a war thirty years earlier that owed its apologies for his suffering.

"Hi again." I hugged the members of my family in awkward succession, then shifted back onto my heels and rolled forward, trying to ease pressure on my right leg. My gym shorts dusted my bum cheeks and my air force T-shirt hung loose around my chest, water still dripping from my hair.

"Look at your hands," Dad said. I held them up in the air for inspection and, indeed, they looked like they didn't belong to me, cracked and bleeding, eczema irritated by weapon cleaning oil and daily rituals of pod scrubbing and boot polishing. "Heels too, Jesus." It looked like rabid animals had attacked the backs of my feet where countless kilometres had been logged. Other than his routine observations, Dad put a hand on my shoulder and squeezed in acknowledgement, pride spreading like the warmth of his palm.

Trevor eyed me in a way that made it impossible to tell if he was attracted to my new muscular body or if I was now too tomboyish for his liking. Seeing him at Saint-Jean, with his hair stuffed under a backwards baseball cap and a button-up shirt tucked into khakis, I instantly wondered what we were doing together—the soldier and the farmer. I gave him an awkward kiss on the cheek, feeling detached. Nearby, Joe stood in a cluster of our fellow troops, laughing, his mouth wide and head thrown back. By the end of summer, Joe would leave, be on a flight back to Calgary, provinces away from me.

"You guys are supposed to go over there," I said, pointing at the drill hall. "I have to go finish getting ready."

I shuttled off to my room. The rest of my platoon would be staying behind at Saint-Jean for a summer of French training, so our barracks had been rearranged according to language proficiency. With several courses under my belt, I'd already obtained the necessary language skills to be exempted from the training, so I was the only one leaving, left behind in a pod as everyone moved to their new sleeping arrangements. For the first time, I realized I didn't want to go.

The uniform was donned slowly, a relished ritual. Bra, underwear, tall black socks. Robin's-egg blue shirt, stiff with starch. Pants, tunic with the golden buttons, all name tags and badges attached precisely the night before. And, finally, the white sword belt. I stood in front of the mirror in my pod and shot a slick of hairspray across my French braid, which dried into a crispy sheen as I tugged on my white gloves, stark against the air force blues. I smoothed on my wedge cap, tilted gently to the right, then peered at the reflection, blinking to garner the same response from my doppelgänger.

Outside the drill hall I lined up into formation, Joe behind me with a presence that made my skin itch.

"All ready for this?"

"As much as I'll ever be." I smiled, swallowed a groan of loss. In hours, no more Joe.

"How's the leg?"

"Same. Bruised and swollen as all hell. Attractive, above all."

"Well," Joe said, straightening his rifle against his side, "I figured that went without saying."

The parade was about an hour long, punctuated by static crackling through oversized speakers, each of the hundreds of graduates' names read slowly through a microphone. Scanning the bleachers with my head not moving, I watched as Meghan swayed to "O Canada" as though it were a bar anthem, her sundress swinging from side to side, Trevor swatting at her to stand still. With Dad's senior officer status, Mom and Dad had been moved to the VIP section for the march past, in which dignitaries were saluted. No matter how hard I strained my eyes, I couldn't see them from my perch at attention.

A command was called and we snapped to, rifles held tightly at the butt and eyes forward. The march past was impressive, four platoons comprising sixty cadets each, the monotonous clunk of boots on floor like the rhythmic clap of hands. As our platoon approached the VIPs, I found Dad's face in the crowd, his reddish-grey moustache tightly trimmed, and Mom at his side, her grip fierce on his arm as she dabbed at her nose with a tissue.

"This is it," Joe said over the sound of the band, careful not to move his head. I could hardly make out his voice over the thunder of our feet, his uniform nothing but a blue blur. "That's your dad there. Look how proud he is."

"PARADE. EYES RIGHT!"

We marched past, my eyes connecting with Dad's icy blues, bloodshot and tired with emotion. When mutual tears slipped down our cheeks, we waited until they blended into our faces, dried instantly in the hot weather. Even long after the parade, we did not speak of the crack of soldier exterior, of the worries of Afghanistan, the pain of wars passed. We did not acknowledge how much that moment had hurt, how good it felt despite that broken leg, how bizarre this propulsion into adulthood was. We never said a word. Thompsons are soldiers, after all.

We crowded into a different mess, a room none of us had seen before, saved for celebrations involving civilians. Officer cadets hovered in swarms, smears of air force blue, army green, and inky navy black moving in coloured cliques. Caps, wedges, and berets were left on tables, strewn in corners, tucked in pockets, the noise ratcheting up several decibels as people barked for the bartender. Our course staff hovered over a bar-height polished table, hunched into one another like they were mid-plot in a conspiracy, the relief of collective responsibility finally being offloaded from their shoulders. Sergeant Pike's small body was buried underneath the weight of a row of medals on her chest, indicating she'd already been to Afghanistan and several other places too.

"Excuse me, Sergeant Pike?" She didn't turn, and yet I couldn't will myself to tap her on the shoulder, out of respect. "Sergeant Pike?" I yelled between cupped palms, and she wheeled on her heel to face me.

"Officer Cadet Thompson. Congratulations on your graduation." She shook my hand firmly while the rest of the staff watched on.

"Thanks," I said, blushing. "I just wanted to thank you for that day in the field. You know, driving me back to the biv." I whispered this last bit. "I was in a lot of pain and I just . . ." Behind Sergeant Pike, the course warrant folded his thick arms across his chest and smirked like he was enjoying the exchange. "I just appreciate you noticing that."

"My pleasure." She, too, whispered. It struck me that she was somehow ashamed as well, that we'd colluded in empathy. I pressed my left hand to cup hers like a politician, then turned on my heel and refused to thank the rest of the staff—out of what? Hatred? They were just doing their jobs, after all. Ambivalence? Hardly . . . I'd come to care more than I wanted. Anger, perhaps, because I wanted to hold my black and blue knee to their faces and ask if it looked like I was fucking faking it. But even as I walked away in search of my platoon, I knew that even saying nothing at all was the confirmation they needed that I harboured too much emotion for a business that made emotion moot.

"Thompson! Over here!" Fellow troops waved me over to a corner of the mess to pose for photos. I stood with them and smiled while I eyed my parents, sister, and Trevor, huddled at one of the folding tables set up to accommodate the extra bodies. Dad was slumped over a tepid beer, face on like he was at a funeral. Mom was vibrant, chatting to another parent, while Meghan and Trevor sat together saying nothing.

"Your Dad must be proud, eh?" said a fellow cadet, his arm slung around my neck while his mom, a woman peering from behind a large Canon, asked us to say cheese. She swiped away tears and clicked several times in a row.

"My dad?" Dad's eyes were now wider than when I'd looked just seconds ago. A deer in headlights. Desperation in uniform. "Yeah, he must be." He was. He'd told me many times, but now I needed to hear the words again. And again.

"Here he comes. Introduce us!"

Dad grabbed his beret from the table as he stood, and he strode over to us with purpose. He wasn't tall, but there was an elegance and presence that shut us up as he took the fifteen steps in our direction. "Okay, Kelly, we're going to get going. Get your things, eh?"

"Dad, these are my friends . . . Champion, Struthers, and—"

"I said, go get your things."

We all went quiet. Dad did not look at my friends, and I couldn't seem to either. With a corner of his gold-braided sleeve in my hand, I pulled him a few steps away and leaned to his ear. Years of mechanic work in thrumming tank engines had significantly damaged his hearing. He refused to get a hearing aid.

"Can't we stay a bit? I really want to spend some time with my friends before I go."

"We're all tired. You've had the whole summer with them. Your mother and I are tired. It's been a long day." Looking to

Mom laughing wide, Meghan eyeing my male platoon-mates, Trevor and his hat, which was now strewn on the table, Dad appeared the only one who was tired, with sacks of chubby skin languishing below his eyes.

"It's kind of a special day, Dad. Just half an hour?"

"I thought your knee hurt," he said, gesturing at my wounded limb with a rough flail of his hand. Then he leaned closer, eyebrows high and tight, words spoken between clenched teeth. "This is hard for me." I examined his face, uncertain. I didn't want to end up sad like him, and yet professionally, I wanted to be his mirror image—both desires twisted together like tree roots. I wondered in that moment about the basis of that sadness, whether or not it was about his own past, or fear for my future.

Dad pulled back suddenly, his voice terse and loud. "Let's go. We'll wait for you in the car, okay? Meet us with your kit outside the green doors in five minutes. We'll bring the car around."

"Can I at least have fifteen?" I could hardly speak, already looking for Joe, then overwhelmed by guilt for delaying my dad's comfort. "Fifteen minutes?"

"Ten."

I hung my head and gave in to the demands of not only a higher rank, but also my Dad who I loved, his major's stripes scratching my palm as he whipped his sleeve from my hand. I felt dizzy, like being at the top of the rappel tower, everything flipping upside down and sideways.

"Has anyone seen Joe?" I called out to no one and everyone. "Who?"

"Joe. Joe Shorrocks." My voice was panicky as I tugged on the shoulders of my friends and also complete strangers—anyone wearing air force blue with a trim waist and little-to-no blond hair. I searched wildly, but since they had all been assigned different rooms the night before, I had no idea where to find him. I tore out of the mess, leaving my wedge hat behind. But I didn't go back for it. Instead, I searched the near-empty halls, checking and rechecking my watch that I'd failed to synchronize with Dad. How much time did I have left? Two minutes? Twelve seconds? Not enough time.

I was crying as I unlocked the door to my temporary room, loaded my kit bags onto each shoulder, and took the damn elevator like I was a god. Then I dropped my key off and burst into the sunlight without my wedge—against the rules—because it was back somewhere in the mess with all the happy people. With Joe, perhaps.

I walked towards my waiting family, who sat in their car, in varying states of annoyance, waiting for me to follow them in my Beetle. It was hot. The parade had been long. And I was shaken about a career that was a lifestyle, a partner I wanted but couldn't have, and an injury that no one believed. Almost twenty years old and a soldier, officer, girlfriend, student, writer. In order to fit into some of those roles, I'd have to shed the others.

17

After completing my summer training, I had a year left at York to finish my Professional Writing degree. Upon graduation, I'd be promoted to second lieutenant, commissioned, and posted to my first unit.

Once back in Toronto, nestled in my apartment in a shitty part of the city, I immediately launched into weeks of physiotherapy for my apparent tendonitis, until the doctor held my MRI report in the air and confirmed my self-diagnosis: a broken tibia in the knee joint. They immobilized me in a huge leg brace and I spent the rest of the summer splayed across the sofa. Even though my platoon wasn't around to see, I felt gloriously validated. Not a MIR Commando.

The tolls of basic training were emotional too. Joe and I kept in touch by email, flirting back and forth throughout his remaining time at Saint-Jean. Eventually, emboldened by my newfound officer confidence, I typed him a simple email. *I like you*, I wrote. Bold. I pressed Send before I could change my mind. There was a maddening two-day wait before his response indicated he liked me as well, but his tone was moderated by age and realism. He pointed out our physical distance. Our ages.

I wasn't to be deterred. After a trip to La Senza for a thong so tiny it could have been used as a slingshot, I visited Joe at the Mega before he returned to Calgary. I arrived having only just shed my leg brace, and that night a group of us danced in a dark bar where we stumbled through beer orders in poorly executed French. When we returned to the Mega, Joe slunk into the room we shared and lay himself chastely on the twin bed when I said it wasn't necessary for him to sleep on the floor.

"I'll turn around while you get into bed," he said, eying my fully clothed body.

Before he could look away, I started to disrobe. First the halter top, which I undid while watching him, tugging it slowly over my strapless bra, down over my stomach. Then my pants, revealing my happy yellow thong and, if all went well, the painful wax I'd received to make the underwear worthwhile. Never before had I seduced anyone, but then, never before had I wanted such adulthood, such commitment, something I sensed Joe was able to offer. A summer earlier, I would have had my hands wrapped abashedly around my soft middle, eyes on the ground, shame written across my face.

"Do you ever think . . ." I swallowed. Once. Twice. I was a brave officer. I would lead. Conquer. ". . . that you might like to kiss me?"

Joe's palms tightened around the sheets as he turned and faced the ceiling. "It's not that I don't think of it. I like you—a lot, actually. It's just that I'm not sure it's a good idea. We live far apart. We're young. And I don't want to take advantage, you know."

We're young. The statement hung in the humid air, swelling and taking on more meaning as the moments passed. We were undoubtedly young, and yet old enough for war. Old enough to leave home and protect others. Old enough to be soldiers. How much older did we have to be?

"Well," I said, unsure of where to look, where to place my awkward hands. I rolled onto my side in my unshed thong and went to sleep, knowing my first planned mission in the Forces had failed.

When I left the next morning, Joe insisted on carrying my bag to escort me to my car. "I know this weekend didn't turn out how you expected." He blinked in the sun, hand still on the frame of my car door. "But I care about you a lot."

"I care about you too," I squeaked.

"Well, I guess I'll see you sometime."

I wanted to know when. I wanted a date, a time, a battle plan. I wanted answers. Instead I nodded and reached up on my tiptoes to hug him goodbye, and I let him tuck me into my car like a fragile package. I sobbed so uncontrollably that the Tim Hortons cashier gave me a free donut and insisted nothing could be worth such upset as she passed me a steaming cup of tea. She didn't grasp that I'd left behind something epic, and I lacked the topography skills to find it on any map. She didn't understand at all.

Most people approach their final year of university with job hunt anticipation after four years slogging through academia. My future, however, was already mapped out, and so my final year felt like Frosh Week in reverse, before imposed military structure and my posting to my first unit. But my career balance felt tenuous considering my knee, which despite the clean bill of health given by the orthopedic specialist, continued to ache. I tried to pay it no mind, having learned soldiers were designed for suffering.

Meanwhile, Dad's medical release continued to sink him further into depression. His teary moments were increasing, bursts of inexplicable anger not abating since he'd left military life. So in February, three months before I was to graduate, the doctor recommended a stint of hospitalization to wean him off old medications and start with a clean slate. Dad heartily agreed to anything he thought might make him better. *I just want to be fixed*, he said, as though a wand or pill would erase a war, reset the clock. The best location, the doctor said, was the Centre for Addiction and Mental Health, or CAMH, in Toronto, so that's where he went.

On my first visit, just days after his arrival, I inched through rush hour, resulting in an hour to get to downtown Toronto, where I edged my Beetle into a too-tight parking space. From the outside—and, as it turned out, from the inside as well—the hospital seemed a place people went to die, to be forgotten, to be miserable, to be alone. I paid for parking with my already maxed-out credit card, and said a little prayer when the machine spat out a sliver of a receipt giving me precisely one hour for an exorbitant fee.

Clutching my purse to my chest, I approached the building, my eyes set firm on the entrance. Nearby were several patients, one with a colostomy bag dangling precariously from a strap around his waist. Inside the bag, soupy brown liquid sloshed each time he wobbled unsteadily on his feet, and he dragged on a cigarette until his cheeks caved in on one another. Two guards, both wearing white scrubs, stood beside him with their arms looped casually across their chests.

"I just need . . . I'm here to . . ." I cleared my throat. "I'm here to visit my dad."

"In through there, doll," said one of the guards, or perhaps he was a nurse or doctor. An orderly? He was handsome in a comforting way. "Who you looking for?"

"Bill Thompson."

"Hey, the Major!" The man smiled wide, as though my father's name was the password to enter. "Yup, he's on the sixth floor. They'll have to buzz you in, but don't be alarmed. All totally normal."

I stepped into the hospital, and after acquiring some directions I made my way to the sixth floor. The windows were saturated with dust, while staff in scrubs lingered with patients in various states of distress. Everywhere around me, doors clanked, buzzed, and alarmed. Voices moaned through the hallways as though the patients were permanently aching. Metal snapped against metal until it felt like the whole building was rattling in my ears, a drumbeat that couldn't or wouldn't subside. I approached the nurse's station and handed over my driver's licence, then said the name of the patient I intended to visit.

"First visitor for Mr. Thompson," said the woman, her eyes focused on my ID. She unbolted a door and I made my way into the locked unit. The woman sent someone to fetch Dad while I lingered at the entrance.

"My family doesn't live in Toronto," I said, like I had something to explain. "He has lots of people who love him."

The common room was bright with sunlight and overhead fluorescent bulbs, everything an eerie white. Chairs lined the room haphazardly, with patients slumped against the backs as though the ridges of upholstery were all that held them up, their eyes trained on the television that was blaring some cartoon or another, although the room was full of adults. I flipped a limp, unreturned wave of my hand, and felt I'd entered a scene from *One Flew Over the Cuckoo's Nest*.

"Hi, Moo."

Dad shuffled forward with his eyes trained on the floor, his sneakers squeaking across the linoleum. He wore loose jeans and a Harley-Davidson T-shirt, hair neatly combed and glasses perched on his face, although he rarely wore them at home. He had just showered, still smelled of soap and bleached towels.

"Dad!" I hugged him tight but his arms formed a loose circle around my shoulders, his whole body non-committal.

"Isn't that nice, Mr. Thompson. A visitor!" The woman who had gone to fetch him from his room all but clapped her hands together, her fingers clasped tightly in front of her.

"Do you want to sit?" I gestured to the chairs, the non-verbal chatter of Roadrunner chirping overhead.

"Not here," Dad said, taking me by the arm down the hall-way towards his room. The space looked out onto busy Queen Street, with a lone twin bed, an armoire-styled locker where his meagre things hung in a uniform row, and a desk and chair. If it weren't for the moaning of disturbed patients, I could have sworn I was back in basic training's dorm-style living, except there I had gone willingly and no one had locked me in.

"It isn't much." Dad still refused to make eye contact with me. I plopped on his bed and bounced for effect while he sat politely in the chair, vinyl crunching underneath him. In the bright light that came through the window, his skin looked grey and slack on his thinner frame, and his face was full of new wrinkles and worry lines around his eyebrows. And for the first time I could remember, he was unshaven, as though the delicate balance of his military and personal selves had started to morph into something new and uncertain.

"Hey, at least it's sunny. Any nice neighbours?"

"You kidding? I had to tear into some bastard who thought emptying his colostomy bag in the bathroom sink was appropriate and sanitary. Woman down the hall cries all night. Some guys talk to themselves. Hard to sleep with all that going on."

He seemed embarrassed by the company he was keeping, but I was overwhelmed with pride that he was trying so damn hard to get well. My father—leader of troops, organizer of events, militant document-keeper, fastidious home repairman. All of these titles remained true, just as the self-defined identities endured for the other patients down the hall.

"Besides," he said, leaning in. "No one here really gets it." *It.* The military. PTSD. War. If there was a sentiment that would be imbedded in the minds of the older generations of suffering soldiers, it would be that their treatment providers didn't understand them. Couldn't understand, unless they too had lived the life. I liked the conspiratorial tone Dad used, as though I understood "it," and just by letting me in on the secret, we were cementing our bond further. *It.*

"I brought you something." I jangled the bakery box in my hand like I was teasing a kitten. "Lemon-filled donuts from the Portuguese bakery."

He almost smiled but not quite, then took the package from me and ate all four of them, each one weighing in at nearly a quarter pound. I watched in silence, dumbfounded but delighted.

"Thanks, Moo, I needed that," he said, licking lemon curd from his fingers. "Food isn't too good around here."

I had glanced at the menu on his desk, each patient allowed to choose certain items as though staying at a high-end hotel. Cereal. Yogurt. Hard-boiled eggs. Juice (prune juice high on the list for all those constipating medications). Dad had not checked anything off as his selection.

"But then, could just be the medication. Treatment."

Treatment. That's what they were calling the electric shock therapy he was undergoing twice weekly. He was under anesthetic each time, and as a family we had been assured it was an alternative to his continued emotional torture. Doctors claimed it was more advanced in the new millennium, that people were no longer left mute shells of themselves who could only drool and stare listlessly like in the 1950s. But I could only picture the process in its early stages, with leather strap-downs and pieces of wood clenched between pained teeth.

"Well, it's not that you don't have an appetite," I said, gesturing at the crumbs left from the donuts. We laughed together, and a bird outside his barred window chirped from the nearby tree. Bars on the windows, like prison. Dad put his hands over his eyes to shield them from the sun, as though the joviality of the bird had been too much to bear.

"Moo, I hate to say it, but do you mind leaving? I'm so tired."

I'd been there all of ten minutes. I'd driven an hour in rush-hour traffic to get there. But his face. His skin. His surroundings.

"Of course I don't mind, Dad. You just focus on resting up."

He walked with me back to the entrance, where the guard from earlier was jotting notes on a clipboard.

"Hey, Major T. This your daughter? Met her downstairs."

"Yes, Mike, this is Kelly, my youngest, the one in the military. Mike is one of the nurses here." I could tell he liked Mike, and it probably had something to do with the fact that the nurse's tone was not condescending. He spoke to the patients like the adults they were—a refreshing concept, I would later discover.

I shook Mike's hand, which swallowed mine whole. He smiled wide as he clapped his hand on my dad's back, holding all of us awkwardly close.

"So nice to meet you. Major T here, he's earned some mad respect. We kind of defer to him for answers and organization, although I gather he's used to that. Looks like you will be too, carrying on in his footsteps and everything." Even in the hospital, the flock still turned to Dad for shepherding. Mike turned back to his paperwork and I brought Dad in for a final hug.

"You'll come back tomorrow?" Dad's voice turned up at the end, pained and questioning like a child.

"I can't come for the next two days, Dad. I have midterms. These marks really count for my final grades." Midterms. Real life that continued. Without these marks I would not graduate, would not be posted, and in all likelihood would garner some serious shit from my university liaison officer at the Toronto Area Support Unit, a string-bean sergeant with a red moustache that bristled at all us young punks in the Forces. "But I'll be back in three days. I'll bring you some slippers and anything else you need. I'll bring you something to eat."

He nodded sternly, his best means of keeping both of our emotions at bay. I squeezed Dad's arm and kissed his cheek, then Mike buzzed me out with a cheerful wave. I did not look back through the tiny glass window to watch Dad disappear. If I turned around, I would give in to everything: to sadness, to pain, to a feeling of hopeless resignation. But I returned the next day despite my midterms. And the day after that. Then the day after that, until all forty-two days of his treatment had passed, each time staying for the ten minutes for which Dad could stand my company, before repeating the agonizing process over again. I barely passed my midterms.

When he was cleared to go home, I arrived to drive Dad back to Barrie, where Mom and Meghan waited. When I showed up at the door, he looked lost, clutching a small bag of belongings with hair askew and white whiskers dotting his face. With Dad having spent my lifetime in the Forces, in which he'd been required to shave on a daily basis, this new, flustered version of my father made me want to cry.

"Jeez, Dad. You need a haircut."

"Not exactly finding barber shops in there." He gestured with his head towards the hospital but couldn't bear to look at it.

"Mom won't like seeing you like this." I didn't say, *I don't like seeing you like this.* "We should stop first." We folded ourselves into my Beetle.

"I just want to get home." Dad leaned back in his seat. We'd accepted early on in my visits that I wouldn't interrogate him about life on the ward. An unspoken ceasefire. "I'm tired, Moo. Just take me home."

"Come on," I said, turning right onto Queen Street to go further downtown instead of home. "It'll make you feel better. Like when you're sick and then you shower and feel like a million bucks."

"I am sick." He whispered the words into the window, fogging up the glass in the cold March air. But he didn't argue as I pulled up to the Aveda hair salon and turned off the ignition.

Inside, we were assaulted by deliciously scented air, a hint of mint and vanilla spilling from a diffuser on a shelf. Stylists and customers milled nearby, appearing to have emerged from between the covers of *Vogue*, with skinny-legged pants, piercings, and neon lipstick. Dad was the only male.

"Seriously, Kelly. Not here. Isn't there a barber or something?" He turned to leave, re-buttoning his coat.

"Dad, come on. It's the only place we saw that was open. Besides, it's my treat."

The receptionist was in her early twenties, and I approached before he could say another word. "Hi, do you have any openings for a men's haircut?"

"Well now, let me just check the books here," she said, assessing Dad and revealing a row of perfect teeth. "Oh yup, look at this. Debbie can see you right away."

"How much is it?" Dad inquired.

"Eighty dollars, sir."

"For a haircut?" Dad's jaw hung slack and I rushed in to fill the void.

"It's totally fine. He needs a bit of pampering . . . right, Dad?"

"Oh, he's your dad?" The woman beamed like we were a Norman Rockwell painting. "I love father-daughter days!" After asking for his name, the receptionist put Dad in a nylon cape, which he somehow deigned to wear, before bringing him over to the sinks to have his hair washed. I sat on the sidelines and chatted with the stylist so that Dad wouldn't have to, knowing the small talk might be too much for him to handle. Energy bubbled under my skin, nervous that he would start to panic or get emotional, and I plotted how I would cover that up for him, but within minutes he leaned back into the spray from the nozzle and dozed during the essential-oil scalp massage. Then, after him sitting for a record forty-minute haircut, the stylist spun around the chair and fluffed his thick strands with a pinch of pomade.

"What do you think, Bill?"

Dad regarded himself in the mirror as though looking at a stranger, while I held my breath. "I think it's the best damn haircut I've ever had in my life." And then he actually smiled. I'd forgotten that when Dad smiled, his moustache bunched under his nose and his eyes crinkled, and even though the hairdresser couldn't understand the impact, Dad's and my eyes connected in the mirror before we looked away. My face next to his, I regarded my own hair, which I'd spent the year growing so it would easily slip into a bun for my upcoming posting just as the military demanded of me. Full-time military life. I'd taught my strands to assimilate to the military dress regulations, relegating high school's blonde pixie cut to my old civilian life.

I paid and left an exorbitant tip, grateful for the hour of bliss they'd provided my dad. Back in the car and careening towards home, towards freedom and rest and food and an end of the electric shock therapy, Dad kept pulling down the sun visor to inspect his new style in the warped mirror.

"Not bad for an old war vet, eh, Moo?"

"It looks great. Back to your officer self." I slammed on the horn to bleat my road rage at a speeder in his souped-up Civic. "I know it's been hard—the hospital and everything, and leaving the military." *Military*. It was like a code word between us, and for the first time, looking at his haircut that was not a brush cut with a number three clipper, I understood that. "But you'll come out of this the better for it, you know that—right, Dad?"

He said nothing for a long time before reaching over and patting my hand. "So will you, Mooster. So will you."

PART THREE

Duty Bound

Second Lieutenant Thompson to Captain Thompson
April 2006–September 2011

18

"This is just the beginning," Dad said, holding up my posting message on a crisp piece of paper fresh from the printer, smearing an inky stain across the expanse of white with his fingers. *This is just the beginning.* It felt like a horrible, accurate cliché, a literary faux pas I'd spent four years of university trying to erase from my vocabulary.

The message had arrived by email, informing me I would be posted to the Canadian Forces School of Military Intelligence (CFSMI) in Kingston, Ontario, as their administration officer, my first logistics role. The message itself was a series of staccato numbers followed by sparse sentences full of acronyms I didn't understand. Service number, rank, title, position—everything in unintentional code, jargon that Dad had to decipher for me.

Dad had only been home from the hospital for a few weeks, his mind hazy after the weeks of electric shock therapy, bags hanging beneath his eyes like overfilled water balloons. But once presented with the posting message, his irises turned bright and shining, because this was a piece of paper he understood. I watched him from my perch on the couch, remembering. The time he picked me up from school in an armoured personnel carrier. The times he spent polishing boots in rhythmic swirls. The times he'd been coursing through the back fields of countless training areas to lead troops in war exercises, returning to us dirty and exhausted and yet happily in his element.

Mom sat next to me and launched into the metal bowl of potato chips that sat between us on the couch, giving my hand a firm squeeze with the hand not smothered in grease. If she was pleased or disappointed that I was moving to Kingston, three hours away, she said nothing, and I wondered if she—an artist who became a nurse because her mother had insisted art wasn't a practical career—felt I was selling out after my own arts degree. In one month I would graduate from York University and become a fully fledged military officer with a job, a desk, a platoon. *This is just the beginning.*

"Kingston. Wow. Not your average first posting, eh?" Dad flipped the page over like he expected a line of information on the other side; finding nothing, he flipped it back. I'd done the same thing.

"Yeah, they said I'd be going somewhere less desirable, so it's a shocker." I stared at the paper in Dad's hand blankly. Since BOTC ten months earlier, I'd had nothing to do with the military other than contact with my university liaison officer, and anxiousness had found a way to creep back into my subconscious, dismantling the confidence I'd spent the previous two summers building. Everything felt uncertain, especially my soldiering abilities. What if I forgot the ranks, forgot who to salute, forgot the organization of the Forces as a whole? What about my leg, which I wasn't even certain had healed?

"Well, you've impressed someone." Dad smacked the paper with his hand for emphasis. "Or you wouldn't have gotten this."

I couldn't help but roll my eyes, which instantly irked him. He sat straighter in his seat, preparing for battle.

"Dad, I ranked in the bottom third of my basic training. I don't think I impressed anyone."

"You did well on the range." And then, as an afterthought: "And your small party tasks, in IAP and BOTC. That's where it really matters. Leadership and weapons skills win wars." It was like he had cemented my course reports in his memory. And it was true: where it counted, I had done well in my training. And yet looking at my comrades from that time, it felt that without athlete-level fitness and an A-type personality, I was viewed as less than.

"Yeah. I guess."

"No, no, none of that. You have to assert yourself if you're going to be an officer."

"Dad, I'll be the kind of officer I'm going to be. I just have to accept I might not be the typical gung-ho, pushy, army kind."

Dad had his way of soldiering, one honed by thousands of years of masculinity, and in his mind, I was to follow that path, not carve my own route to success through some feminist credo. Generational military history is often like this—a soldier talks to their parent about some element of their work, complaining perhaps. *Oh, it doesn't work like that, not when I served*, the parent says dismissively, falling back on their personal experience, which is now dated by the passage of time. Dad and Grandpa T had waged the same argument, Grandpa's knowledge based on serving in Korea in the fifties, and Dad relying on knowledge from the Golan in the seventies, with decades of advancement between them. But wars change, militaries change, policies change. It was for this reason that Dad had promised to be merely an observer of my career, a peacekeeper. And yet peacemaking habits die hard.

"No, I mean it," he said, standing now, his face gone red and his jaw clenched firm. A finger waggled pointedly near my face. "Don't walk in there admitting where you failed, or your troops will eat you alive." When Mom and I sat passive, watching, he threw his arms in the air, then slapped his sides. "Why do I even bother?" He stormed out of the room, mumbling on his way out the patio doors, to go haul rapid inhales on a cigarette.

Once he was outside, Mom allowed a gentle huff of air to escape her pursed lips. Lately, being in Dad's company was a tense balancing act, any perceived slight leading to anger, the reasoning behind the emotion generally lost on us. Mom and I had learned to form our own army in silent solidarity.

In May, I arrived at CFSMI sporting my dress blue air force uniform, customary for a first day at a new unit, a starched crease breaking atop shiny shoes. Having only settled into my new Kingston apartment four days earlier, I was fifteen minutes early to ensure I wouldn't be snared in traffic, but as I eased into the parking lot, I rediscovered a military mantra from my childhood: fifteen minutes early means you're barely arriving on time. I parked and choked down a beer-scented burp. The night before, I'd sat on my skinny apartment balcony and sipped at a bottle of lager the previous tenant had left in my fridge. I hated beer, but I was starting a new job and I was an officer and I was twenty-one and I was fretting over whether or not my Blistex lip balm would be too glossy for my first day on the job. Instead of having the anxiety-soothing effect I'd hoped for, the drink made me feel sick.

CFSMI was housed in a large white building with high, skinny windows that let in slivers of sunshine. There was a guard hut at the entrance, and a perimeter of chain-link fencing boasted concertina wire looped along the top like silvery ringlets. The commissionaire sat inside the booth reading a paperback, but stirred at my approach.

"Hi there." I waved, then brought my hand down to my side. An officer, certainly, would not wildly wave their arms about in greeting. "I'm here for my first day of work. Here. I work here."

"This building is restricted access, so you require a security pass."

"How do I get one of those?"

"You should have a sponsor." His face softened and he flicked the book's pages with a thumb, the sound like a kitten's purr. "Someone assigned to meet you at the gate."

"Right. I'm here to see"—I ruffled through my pockets for the old receipt I'd written the name on—"Captain Murphy. Do you know her?"

"Oh, yes. I'll call the security section and have someone escort you to her office. You can get your pass later today."

A quick phone call later, my escort stumbled towards the gatehouse. After being issued a temporary pass, I followed him through several coded security doors before arriving at Captain Murphy's office, a small room off the main corridor. I expected someone to scan my fingerprint like I was a Bond girl.

"Captain Murphy's office, at your service." He flourished a hand towards the door, behind which I could hear the sound of determined typing. "Good luck, and welcome, Ma'am."

After a deep, steadying breath, I knocked on the door, coming to attention as I'd been taught. "Officer Cadet Thompson, Ma'am." I stuck out my hand to shake that of my new boss, but she didn't return the gesture and my hand fell limp. She assessed me, then stood.

"Welcome to CFSMI," Captain Murphy said. She reached her hand out then, as though I hadn't anticipated the proper moment thirty seconds earlier, and pumped mine vigorously like we were in a strength competition, the skin of my hand buckling under the pressure. I squeezed back and maintained eye contact.

Papers were tacked up all over the walls: years of business plans, Julian calendars, standard operating procedures, and fire orders. It was a tiny space, no window, like they'd piled her into the broom closet, with no knick-knacks or trinkets hinting at a life led, just a photo of two cats peering innocently from within the border of a picture frame. Only moments together, and I gathered that Captain Murphy liked rules and rarely strayed from them. I also gathered that Captain Murphy really liked her cats.

"Nice to meet you, Ma'am."

Linda Murphy was average height and build, somewhere in her fifties, with a length of brownish hair pulled into the regulatory bun.

"Likewise. Did your furniture and effects arrive safely?"

"Yes, Ma'am. I'm just up on Bath Road. Got a nice apartment there." Within a day of my final exam at York, movers had come to my sketchy Toronto apartment, looking around the scratched parquet, into the cockroach-infested kitchen, at the bathroom tile covered in mould, and questioned aloud how I could afford movers when I couldn't afford an exterminator.

"So," she said, clapping her hands together, "I'm sure there's lots of change for you, coming straight out of university. Your degree is in what now?" Before I could answer, she flipped open a folder and snapped it shut again. "Ah, Professional Writing." Her eyebrows knitted. "It says here with a specialty in books? What does that mean?"

"There were three streams, Ma'am. Technical writing, books, and magazines or periodicals. I studied the book side of writing."

"And what does that entail in terms of study?" The words came out slowly, questioningly.

"Lots of editing, grammar, that kind of thing."

"Ah, grammar. Well, that's my area as well. Your generation didn't learn proper grammar in grade school." I didn't know how to respond so I just nodded in agreement. "But what I don't understand is why you studied writing if you were going to be in the military. Books especially."

I fidgeted with the ring on my middle finger, sensing our first meeting wasn't going as well as I'd hoped. "I believe writing skills are vital in all workplaces."

She nodded, seemingly pleased with my answer. "Indeed they are. Well, down to business. I am the platoon commander of the support platoon and, essentially, our jobs are to support the training of intelligence officers and operators through whatever means necessary. Business planning, accommodation booking, organizing events and graduations, and administratively managing student records and documents. As Admin O, you fall under me but in a sense will be in charge of the orderly room with three staff members. There's also the collation cell, which deals with the tech side of things and managing our digital assets."

"Got it," I said, even though I hadn't. I'd have to look up *collation cell* another time.

"I'll walk you down and introduce you to your staff, but just a reminder that ultimately they work for me. You understand the concept of the chain of command, right?" She showed me the organizational chart, my position box hovering underneath hers with three staff members branching out underneath me. She stood and gestured to the door, then paused. "One more thing. When we spoke last week, you mentioned you were just finishing treatment for a broken leg. All healed up? Is that a situation that needs to be managed?"

A situation that needs to be managed. Her eyes darted to my legs to assess their seaworthiness. Approaching the unit, I had tried to hide my limp and the fact that my knee still hurt like hell. The doctor said my X-ray was clear so I was healed, waving me off when I said it had taken an MRI to locate the break in the first place. And if I'd learned anything in my few years of service, it was that admitting weakness the moment I arrived at my first unit would be akin to professional sabotage. Dad had encouraged my vow of knee silence. *Sometimes you just have to deal with a bit of pain.*

"I'm sure it's on the mend, Ma'am."

"Good. Happy to hear it. Because"—she spun on her heel—"you don't want an injury getting in the way of your career progression. Just to be sure, book an appointment at the MIR to get it checked out, yes? Inform me of any progress." I was unclear if Captain Murphy was entitled to know my medical diagnoses, but I said nothing and followed as she briskly moved down the hallway, answering her many questions while we walked. *Yes, family nearby. No, I don't have a spouse but I do have a boyfriend. No, I don't want kids.* I never got a chance to ask any back.

Murphy led me behind the main building to a trailer within the fenced CFSMI compound, connected by a rickety plastic annex that fluttered in the breeze. Inside, the trailer was bright and humming, fluorescent lights highlighting the workstations and a conference room in the back. It was clear that those who worked in the orderly room were the outcasts of CFSMI, the people not in charge of the actual intelligence training but necessary to the smooth functioning behind the scenes. We were the wallflowers of the military education system.

Captain Murphy introduced me to my new staff members: Sergeant Zaph, a master corporal, and a corporal—all women, a fact that only briefly resonated with me. They were friendly, offering their help if I had questions, smiling before quickly returning to their work. Military folks are used to the comings and goings of new arrivals. I was a blip on the radar.

"And you'll be setting up here," Captain Murphy said, pointing to a workstation in the middle of the room—a corner desk and coordinating ergonomic set-up. I let my fingers drag across the shelving and fingered the air-filled wrist rest that was now my very own.

"I'm really excited to work with everyone," I said with a burp of nervous laughter. *God, Kelly, no fucking giggling.* The nearest in rank to me, Sergeant Zaph, was more than twenty years my senior. How in the hell was she supposed to answer to me?

"We're looking forward to it too," said Murphy, on behalf of everyone. "We'll let you get set up at your station here, and then come to my office in an hour to discuss your role."

"Will do, Ma'am." I immediately set to work, proudly placing a framed photo of me at my Forces enrolment with Dad standing at attention beside me. "That's a rather revealing dress you wore for your enrolment, isn't it?" said Captain Murphy as she inspected the image that afternoon. That night I took the photo home and replaced it with a new one.

The rest of my first day involved a steady stream of strangers rolling in to meet the new girl, and I quickly learned that I wasn't just the youngest person in the orderly room, but in the whole unit.

Later that afternoon, Bob, the civilian tech guy, called me down to his office where he sat punching keys on his computer. "Let's set up your first and only military email address," he said, waving at the screen. He patted a seat next to his while I offered my middle name, role, phone extension. He typed everything in on his keyboard, filling the white space line by line.

"All you gotta do to win 'em over," said Bob, "is keep that candy bowl flowing." He was referencing the empty plastic dish left behind by my predecessor, currently collecting dust on my desk. "Works every time." He winked at me and then ribbed my arm with his elbow. "Isn't that right, kiddo?"

In the following weeks, I dutifully put out more sweets than I could afford, and the warrants flittered by under the pretence of form signatures as they scooped entire handfuls of Werther's Originals into their camouflaged pockets.

"So," Bob said, leaning in. "Just a heads-up. Dealing with Captain Murphy isn't going to be easy."

"Pardon?" I felt trapped between shared commiseration and loyalty to the boss I'd only just met. And yet I sensed Bob was a relatively good judge of character, and not one to take anyone's bullshit. He was in his sixties. He was a veteran. His workspace was plastered with photos of chubby grandkids offering gummy smiles to the camera, and those demotivational posters I'd seen on the internet.

"I'm just saying, she doesn't take kindly to anyone, really. Much less other female officers. Your age is gonna work against you."

"I think my bubbliness might be more of a challenge than years," I said as Bob scribbled my new email address on a piece of paper and handed it to me.

He clapped me on the back in solidarity, as if he too was young and female. "Nothing wrong with a little femininity," he said. "Fuck knows we could use some of that around here."

Within a week of my arrival at CFSMI, I'd earned the title of "Kiddo" from the civilians and the necessary "Ma'am" from the troops who worked for me. A twenty-one-year-old "Ma'am." The term was always said with a question mark, like they too wondered about my ability to lead troops into a minefield of paperwork, much less an actual battle.

19

After a month, every day at CFSMI was painted the same colour, everything shades of brown and grey, and devoid of any interest. I was promoted to second lieutenant once my university transcript proved I'd graduated, but the rank change was considered minor in terms of the respect attached to it. Meanwhile, I tried to learn how to do my job without actual logistics training, eventually mastering our financial software, managing staff, and answering questions by searching through military directives. I figured out my role through trial and error, emphasis on the error.

A few months into my posting, Captain Murphy called me into her office to discuss the latest email that I'd sent unit-wide, seeking section input for the business plan. The email, she explained, didn't have the right tone, or perhaps something was missing from my signature block, or she didn't like a word I'd used. The week prior, Murphy had plopped binders of business plan examples on my desk, but after a few minutes staring at graphs and pie charts, numbers and terms, the documents might as well have been written in Russian. I had slammed one of the binders shut, willing a course message to arrive in my inbox that would officially load me onto logistics officer training, making my work less of a jigsaw puzzle.

The rickety visitor's chair in Captain Murphy's office—essentially, my chair—had no arm rests and was always adjusted to be at least six inches lower than her seat. For the first month at CFSMI, I had adjusted it upwards with each office visit so that my knees didn't hover somewhere near my armpits. Each time I returned, it was lowered again. This instance was no different, the chair creaking under my weight. She'd printed out the email, highlighted the pertinent errors.

"Kelly, don't you think this word would be better?"

I stared at the clock. Ten to twelve. Almost lunch. Nearly freedom.

"Kelly, do you think this email needed to go unit-wide, or could you have narrowed your addressing scope slightly?"

Oh, look. She'd changed her cat photo to a more recent snap of the female, pawing at a toy.

"Kelly, are we going to need to discuss memorandum format again?"

There was no point. No matter how thoroughly my work was dissected, I'd slipped into mental survival mode. I crossed off days on the calendar, pondering just how long I could take it. One year? Two? Captain Murphy's constant criticism resulted in me being unable to send an email in under an hour, reading and rereading, editing, adjusting, adding BCCs and CCs. Even my own name looked marred and improper. Did I spell Kelly Sara with an *h*, or without? I had nightmares about Murphy standing over my bed, cracking an actual whip, a hoard of cats snaking out from her uniform. Sometimes, in these dreams, she gripped my contract in her hand, proof I couldn't escape the military even if I wanted to—not without paying back three years of university and my military salary. I was duty-bound to complete a certain amount of service: two months for every month of schooling they'd paid for, meaning I owed four years before I could be released penalty-free. And anyway, to leave now would mean donning the label of failure I'd been working so hard to shed. So I waited. I waited for the chance to execute a task that would result in praise from my boss. It had been months, but still, I hoped.

"Well, I think I've given you a lot to think about, don't you?" She snapped shut the folder containing the highlighted email, crossed her long legs, and foisted the document into my hand. "Why don't you take this and see if you can't find the other places you went wrong." I took the folder from her, but like someone handing over a hefty cheque, she couldn't seem to part with it. "I do this for your own good. You know that, right? As your mentor, all I want is to see you succeed."

She was earnest. I could see it in her eyes, the upturn of her groomed eyebrows, that she hoped she was doing good, teaching me the tools of the logistics trade. But the urge to laugh at her comment was quickly replaced with an overwhelming urge to cry. Professionally, I was desperate to align myself with my female boss, a potential ally, and yet each meeting in the beige office tempered my ideals. I still had no friends at the unit, or civilian ones. Other than small talk with the women in my section, I was painfully lonely. And I could not, judging by Murphy's assessments, do anything well. "Yes, Ma'am."

She leaned forward, elbows on her knees, as though taking pity on me. "So, I spoke to your career manager." Then she leaned back in her seat, pleased with the offering.

"Log training? I'm going on course?" I was excited, suddenly pert in the stunted chair.

"Well, it was a possibility and she did load you, yes, but considering your knee, I think you need more time. I asked that you be removed from the course and considered for an alternate serial at a later date."

Unconsciously, my hand covered my kneecap, heat radiating through the fabric. The location of the break still ached and throbbed, but military doctors at the MIR had shrugged their shoulders and said I should be fine. I was awaiting some further testing, but as usual the military and its medical staff seemed underwhelmed by my pain. "I'd be fine, Ma'am. It's a desk-based course. Exactly what I do here."

"But there may be field-based elements to it, carrying a rucksack and that kind of thing." My silence said what we both knew: there were no field elements to the course. "Until we know more about your medical situation, I think we should hold back. Besides, you're not ready for the course anyway."

"I'm not ready to learn how to do my job?" I was unable to hide the snide tone from my voice.

"Like I said." Her voice was firmer, irritated. "We should hold back. That's my decision."

We. When did Captain Murphy and I become *we*? "I should get back to work," I said, resigned.

"Don't forget to look over your email again for errors." She turned her back before I left the room.

I wheeled out of Captain Murphy's office deflated, too exhausted to be angry. On particularly hard days, after executing her various orders, I would take to email, open the nationwide address search key and type in one name. *Shorrocks.* Joe's email address and coordinating information would pop up, revealing that he was on training in the Prairies. Through our sparse communication of occasional one-line emails, we pretended the night of my revealed panties had never happened. Instead, I followed the trajectory of his career, imagining how ours would intersect.

"Interested in some celebratory lunch, Ma'am?" I blinked, finding myself standing stiffly outside the air force intelligence training cell, where the staff of five diligently hammered away at their keyboards. One of the sergeants was signing a course report, a new platoon of recruits having graduated earlier that morning. "Wrapping up the course here, so we're going out for a bite. Saigon Delights off Division, you know it? All the spring rolls you can eat. Spicy as all shit."

"Sure," I said, trying to sound casual. Trying to sound like being invited into the inner sanctum hadn't made me feel like I'd finally proved my efficacy after months of effort. "I'll go grab my wallet."

"We'll meet you outside," said the sergeant, who flipped his raincoat over his shoulder.

"Second Lieutenant Thompson, is that you again?" Captain Murphy called from her office like a saintly aunt. *Yoo hoo!* I begrudgingly reappeared in her doorway. "Going somewhere?"

"I've just been invited to lunch, Ma'am. I shouldn't go over my usual hour, so I'll be back in plenty of time."

"Well," she said dryly, locking her computer and gathering her things. "I know they probably just wanted to invite the young, pretty officer, but Saigon Delights is actually one of my favourite restaurants. Can I join you?"

It was not a request. I followed her out the gates and obligingly sat beside her in her clunky Acura. At the restaurant, we sat at the end of the long table by ourselves, the other troops eyeing me like I was a traitor, and I found myself wondering if Captain Murphy had been right all along and my invite was attached to my appearance, not work performance. It was a long time before they would invite me out again.

Captain Murphy was an embedded part of my life both on duty and off, partly because she was also my neighbour. In fact, I could almost see her house from mine, nothing but a residential street and a park between us.

Neighbours should have tea together, no? she said one day.

I arrived at her house on a Saturday afternoon at precisely two o'clock, as instructed, carrying a bouquet of Gerbera daisies for her and a bag of Whiskas Temptations for her cats. I shook the metallic package like I'd seen them do on the television commercials and a loose-bellied tabby arrived pertly at my feet, nose scrunching in the air as she backed onto her hind legs.

"Where did you get those?" Captain Murphy asked while stirring cocoa on the stove. Despite being in her private home, she had not invited me to call her by her first name. I'd never known anyone who made cocoa instead of hot chocolate, with rich Mexican powder instead of two heaped teaspoons of Nesquik. She poured it into two mugs and dusted the tops with fresh nutmeg grated on a small Microplane.

"PetSmart?" I held the treat in the air with a hand-in-the-cookie-jar expression.

"I don't give them generic foods like that. But thanks for the thought."

My eyes connected with the cat, to which I tried to offer compassion with raised shoulders and turned-up palms, the animal and I both under the thumb of Captain Murphy. She gestured for me to sit at a kitchen island stool, slicing me a piece of coffee cake that was drizzled with a thin line of crystalized caramel. "I only make it twice a year. It's not very good for you. Too much butter and fat."

Pierced with my fork, the cake crumbled dryly, but the flavour was good. It had sat on the counter for more than a week, I guessed, constantly hacked at, sliver by sliver, a daily indulgence doled out in measured iotas. As we ate, Murphy launched into a series of complaints: about the tittering of laughter from children on the swing set in the park behind her home (must they squeal like that?), the irritation of her neighbours and their noisy shutting of the hot tub lid (didn't they know she was sleeping?), the derelict owners who didn't keep their lawns as trim as hers (she mowed it every Sunday). She talked about doing her own home repairs to save money, and aggressively paying down her mortgage before she reached the compulsory military retirement age of sixty. *Save, save, save for the future.* But as I looked around her modest home, at her shoddily performed home repairs, her week-old, twice-a-year cake, I began to wonder if Linda Murphy ever bothered actually living or if everything was conserved for delayed enjoyment.

"Is there a partner in your life?" I asked, although I already knew she was single—wearing that fact like a medal she'd earned simply for not needing a man.

"I was married once. Didn't work out and we divorced twenty years ago. When we got married he said he didn't want kids. Turns out, he did. Whole brood of them now."

I nodded and sipped my drink. It was the best cocoa I'd ever had. "No one since then?"

"There was someone." She looked out into the backyard, distant. A squirrel darted past the window, flicking his tail in a tease while the cat salivated on this side of the glass. "But that didn't work out either." I sat silent, hoping it would encourage her to speak more. As I ate my cake, I realized how desperate I was for her to like me, how much I wanted to form a bond with another woman in the Forces. If Captain Murphy accepted me, then it might mean that I could be a professional success, not simmering in the bottom third of military officers. It might mean the idea of a military career wasn't so fucking bleak. "We were very different. For one, he didn't see the point in recycling."

I almost choked on my liquid chocolate. For anyone else, shucking a partner for not tossing a can in the blue bin would seem over the top. For Captain Murphy, it made eerie sense. "That isn't to say men haven't tried though. Back in my earlier years, they tried." When I didn't respond, she smoothed back her hair and cleared her throat. It was the first time she had ever revealed intimate details about herself, and I found I was curious to know more about who she was and where she was from. I wanted to know what had formed Linda Murphy's hard shell, which I suspected hid something gentler underneath. Sipping from her mug, she looked beautiful, cheeks pinked from the heat of the drink.

"I like living alone though. I like to do my own thing and concentrate on what interests me. My home projects." Evidence of her home projects was to be seen all over, from the honeyed maple cabinets and floral valances to the blind-covered windows designed to hold back the heat and save money on air conditioning. Hers was a single life, one that—taking in her surroundings—I suspected she was as attached to as she claimed. And in that moment, I absolutely adored her; her independence was a quality I could relate to.

"How long have you been in the Forces?" I asked, unable to think of anything else to say.

"Oh," she said, swatting the air as if her career were nothing worth chatting about, "I joined the Reg Force in the seventies, then retired and re-enrolled as a reservist later on." Her head dropped and her jaw set into a firm line. I wanted to take her hand and give it a squeeze of understanding. A woman. In the military. In the seventies. Even my hard-army Dad had shown compassion for women who were flung into military roles without the men being educated on how to appreciate what females brought to the professional table. This would have been especially so when Murphy joined, when women didn't comprise the now 12 per cent of the military population, but rather were anomalies. Screw the front lines; Murphy's battle would have been right at home, in her unit, trying to prove herself to any man who wondered if her good looks and willingness to enrol in the Forces weren't an invitation to assault. I thought of Murphy's highlighted emails, her disdain for my youth, her condescension, and considered that maybe she was simply a product of female military life a few generations before me. To be taken seriously, she had to be without fault, and therefore so did I. I watched her now, in her home, thirty-odd years after her enrolment, fussing about with grated nutmeg. It was like seeing a lion prowl through the Arctic—completely out of its element.

"So," she said, sharing moment over. "Your window was open at three a.m. when I went for a run. Do you always keep them open like that?"

And then:

"So, tell me about this boyfriend of yours."

And then:

"Last Tuesday you didn't have blue bins out. Don't you recycle?"

And then:

"Your guests last week were parked on the sidewalk. That's illegal, you know."

I danced around each question like an aged Rockette, expert yet sloppy, no fight left in me. Captain Murphy tucked into her cake, staring straight ahead and chewing slowly, the light filtering in from the patio doors making her look younger and spirited. I regarded her as she ate, finally coming into a less hazy focus. I took another bite of cake and told her it was delicious. My relationship with Captain Murphy confused even me. To be liked or to be respected—I suppose I would have settled for either.

20

For me, the intrigue and excitement of CFSMI lay with the human intelligence (HUMINT) platoon, and though it was housed on a separate property, it still fell organizationally under CFSMI. The HUMINT folks trained soldiers to garner information from informants, a task expanding in importance as Canada's role in Afghanistan continued.

My first visit to the HUMINT trailers was to pay out petty cash claims for student exercises. I slogged my heavy cash box down the street, and flung open the trailer door to be met with a crew of men mostly in their mid to late forties, clapped-out on sofas in the break area with coffees in hand. At two in the afternoon.

"Ma'am, thanks for coming over." A short, thin man approached and held out his hand, which I pumped up and down while making eye contact—assertive, professional. The warrant and I had met briefly at the unit welcome dinner but I hadn't seen him since.

"My pleasure," I chirped, far too enthusiastically. "I'm Second Lieutenant Thompson. Nice to see you again."

"Warrant Paul Livingston, Ma'am. Your first time over to this side of the battlegrounds, right?" He had a kind smile that scrunched up his nose, and rosy cheeks on otherwise pale skin that matched his towhead.

"That's right. Where should I set up?" I jingled the cash box, change rattling like a bell.

"The students are just finishing up a lecture," he said, gesturing to a classroom off the main break area. "Why don't you come meet everyone in the shop?"

I was introduced to the all-male platoon, pausing when a sergeant stopped to share a joke he was in the middle of telling. I can't remember the punch line—but we all laughed. I hadn't been excluded. In fact, I'd been welcomed.

"This is our platoon commander, Captain Matt Harvey," said Paul. An attractive man strode towards me with confidence, muscling himself between Paul and me.

"Good to meet you. Kelly, right?"

"That's right, Sir." I blushed. I had no idea why I was blushing.

"Christ, call me Matt. We're a little less formal around here, aren't we, Paul." Paul nodded. "Hearing good things about you already, Kelly. You're making an impression."

"And who is this?" The voice came from a man in the corner. The corners of his lips curled into a smile as he approached.

"That's Warrant Ray O'Neill, at your service," answered Paul wryly.

"Nice to meet you, Kelly," Ray said.

"Calling the ma'am here by her first name, right off the bat, Ray?" Paul said jokingly.

"God, I'd love to hear my real name once in a while," I said. "Kelly is fine."

The friendships came naturally. From then on, I unconsciously reserved all of my free time for Paul and Ray. We toured Kingston's quirkiest restaurants, visited festivals, went to movies. At home, all my meals were prepared for three, because one or both of them would inevitably show up at my door for a cup of tea or a bite to eat. We were inseparable, a bizarre trio comprising two war-seasoned warrants in their mid-forties and a blonde, bubbly officer in her early twenties with three years of service. But for anyone who challenged our friendship and didn't understand it—which was most of our unit and my friends back home—it was within the walls of the HUMINT trailers that I finally felt like I belonged in the military, with people who didn't treat me like an outsider. It was with Paul and Ray that I learned what it meant to be willing to protect my fellow soldiers with my life, a concept instilled in basic training but only actualized in daily service.

My section and I had just returned from lunch with Captain Murphy, who had wanted the orderly room to share a meal before the preparation for the next serial of intelligence operators arrived for their courses in September. She called it "team building" but we called it forced fun. We ended up at her favourite Thai place because none of us could cope with her disinterest in our suggested locations. We spent the meal choking out rough bursts of conversation through bites of green curry.

I had settled into my desk when the email appeared at the top of my inbox, pinging with an Outlook chirp.

SUBJECT: I Saw You
Are you coming back from a long slow boozy lunch?

Matt

I read the message and blushed, resisting the urge to print and edit for punctuation. Captain Murphy wouldn't like that—me correcting a captain—no matter that I was right. No matter that Matt flirted whenever he was in the orderly room, and he didn't wear a wedding ring. My fingers hovered over my keyboard, uncertain.

SUBJECT: Re: I Saw You
Long: sort of. Boozy: absolutely not. I don't think Capt Murphy would want me sloshed after lunch. Ate too many spring rolls and spilled soy sauce all over my uniform. Thank God for CADPAT camouflage.

Kelly

Ping.

SUBJECT: Re: Re: I Saw You
Good thing CADPAT uniforms hide all sins! Well, you were laughing and looked rosy-cheeked. Happy.

Matt

When he came into the orderly room trailer later to sign some paperwork, we shared a secret flirtatious smile before I returned to my computer.

"Kelly, could you please join me in the conference room?" a voice called out into the orderly room. In the conference room behind my workstation, a female officer, who was on the brink of a posting out of the unit, sat waiting with her hands folded neatly in her lap. We barely knew each other but she seemed to consider herself one of my mentors. A crucifix hung from her neck, disappearing underneath her uniform T-shirt. Still, I knew it was there; had seen her rub it like a talisman between her thumb and pointer finger. She gestured for me to shut the door.

"Kelly, have a seat."

Nerves burned hot on my face. Was I in trouble for something? God, what had I done that was so bad Captain Murphy wasn't addressing it directly? I sat obediently at the table as the air conditioning hummed along with the fluorescent lights. I could hear the buzz of the orderly room, my staff clicking keyboard keys and ruffling papers. The sounds of efficiency.

"So, Kelly, I'll be honest. Captain Murphy and I are a little concerned."

"Oh?" What the hell did I do? I ran through several scenarios in my head, panic squeezing at my chest.

"We've noticed that Captain Harvey has been showing you an awful lot of attention lately. Attention that could lead to something you don't want." She leaned into the conference table, taking up more visual space. A blotchy flush rose to her cheeks.

"I'm not sure I understand." But I did. I knew exactly what she meant. My hands were clammy, my breath a hoarse whisper. Dad had warned me about the slippery slope of female military members dating within the Forces, because they faced judgment that, like it or not, wouldn't impact the man in the relationship. He didn't say whether he felt that judgment was warranted or not. Hell, even I'd criticized female comrades who seemed to line up a parade of partners, and then been angry at myself for doing so.

"Is something going on between you two?" the officer said, leaning forward as though her body language conveyed concern for my well-being, not the need to save my soul from a slight against God. "Captain Murphy and I are worried about how this will make you look. Your career is just getting started."

I swung from anger to anxiety and back again. It seemed to me then that everyone was concerned with how I looked, acted, existed, breathed, and yet who was assessing Matt's motives and behaviour? But this was the military world I knew, had been raised in, had seen romanticized on screens and in books. The men fought the wars we saw on television, and the women, it seemed, were to wage those same wars, along with other battles all their own.

The officer fiddled with the cross underneath her shirt, looking embarrassed to be having this conversation, and I softened towards this seasoned female captain—and the other one sitting in her office, judging from afar—who was just looking out for me, surely, having seen young women preyed upon in her career. I hoped so badly—even though something told me this hope was futile—that she only wanted to protect me.

"Nothing is going on, Ma'am." And it wasn't, other than some shameless flirting. I hadn't ever seen him outside of work. And then, to cement it both in my own mind and hers: "There's absolutely nothing to worry about."

She smiled, not unkindly, but the expression was tinged with tolerance, or like she'd swallowed something sour. "Well, that's good, because you have a boyfriend to think about, right?" I nodded, silent. My relationship with Trevor still limped forward, neither of us wanting to hurt the other by doing the inevitable and ending things. "Kelly, you have a way with people, and that way should be celebrated, to an extent, but you have to be careful about who you show too much affection for, understand?"

"Too much affection?"

"Flirting." *You flirt with everyone*, Captain Murphy said to me once with a placating smile, as though she intended it to be some shared joke and not a reprimand, and I found myself wondering why I could not be bubbly and still be good at my job. *I don't flirt*, I'd replied. *I'm just friendly.*

Ah, she said, fingers tenting into a steeple. *But they're the same thing.* And maybe they were. The possibility kept me up at night, wondering if everything I knew about myself and my character was tinted by burgeoning feminism, not by reality.

"I appreciate your concern, but I am who I am, Ma'am." But I didn't appreciate the concern. I didn't appreciate it one iota. "I'm friendly, but I do my job and I work hard." I stared down into my lap, where I prayed a normal response would materialize. Angry tears threatened but I willed them away.

"No one is saying you're bad at your job, Kelly. But I don't want you falling into this trap that many young military women do. No one will take you seriously if you're cavorting with married men or half of the unit."

"Cavorting with half of the unit?"

"Well, not you, per se, but the reason will stand with some." She didn't need to elaborate. As a woman in the Forces, she knew that a relationship with a fellow military member, married especially, came with a label of being easy, slutty, whorish, and a bunch of other descriptors that made me feel sick. "Captain Harvey is charming, and he seems to be spending a lot of time around here. That's my main concern."

I wondered if the young male officers joining the unit were offered the same sage advice, but decided against asking and instead accepted—or, at least, tolerated—this invasion into my non-existent personal life. "We're not involved with one another," I said emphatically. "I'm just being friendly. I think he is too. He's never indicated otherwise."

She nodded solemnly, still fingering the necklace, the points of the cross digging into her thumb pad. "And then there's the situation with Warrants O'Neill and Livingston." My friendships with Paul and Ray were deemed a *situation*, and I stifled a smile. We'd be laughing about this at dinner tonight. "You should focus on making friends with other female officers. Other young people. Why don't you ever go to the mess to network? It's not right, spending all your time with two men my age."

I must have raised my eyebrow and gestured around me, because the ludicrousness of her statement struck us both temporarily silent. I was the youngest person at the unit by at least fifteen years, and the only other female officer—present company excluded—was Captain Murphy, and I sure as hell wasn't planning a mani-pedi bonding afternoon with her. And the one time I'd gone to the Officers' Mess, hoping to meet colleagues and make friends, I'd spent the entire time fighting off unwanted advances, returning home after one drink to sip ginger ale in the tub, alone. I'd barely bothered to maintain friendships with any of my female basic training comrades either—what was the point when I didn't feel a lot of common ground with them? We'd spent so much time competing with one another, unwilling to stand next to one another's weaknesses and successes, that we hadn't formed the intense bonds I'd imagined we would.

"They're my friends, Ma'am. That's all. Warrants O'Neill and Livingston are the only people at the unit who have made an effort to welcome me. Who invite me to lunch or talk to me like I'm not an idiot." I hoped this explained everything, with my meaning subtle between the lines.

"Well," she said, now standing over me, tossing her arms in resignation. "Be careful. I just wanted you to go into this with your eyes wide open. You don't want an unwanted name for yourself."

Dismissed, I returned to my desk like a chastened child. I couldn't say I hadn't been warned, but about my own actions or Matt's, I wasn't sure.

21

A few months later, I primped for an hour and a half for my excursion to Starbucks. My bob was tucked behind my ears— I'd cut my shoulder-length hair a month into working at CFSMI, unable to handle the headaches from the tight bun released from my beret each night.

I placed my tea order and plopped into a chair at the back. Matt entered and waved energetically, and upon grabbing his mug of medium roast, sat with legs splayed wide and a shit-eating grin on his face. "I'm really glad you could come," he said. His inky eyes blinked back at me, set deep and crinkled around the edges.

I wanted not to like the attention. I also wanted not to like him, because a) he was married, and b) although he seemed like-able, the charm was also somehow off-putting in its assumption of my submission. But I'd acquiesced to the military in so many ways that I could feel myself shattering like a dropped vase.

"We can't do this," I said in a hurry. But why was I there, then? "You're married and I have a boyfriend." On that point, Trevor and I barely talked anymore, the phone line haunted by our ambivalence towards our seemingly un-united future.

Matt took a gulp of steaming coffee and brushed his small hand over my knee. "I get it. There's no pressure or anything.

You know that, right?" At this, his voice softened with concern in a way that told me I was his in my complicity.

"I'm just . . . I'm not this person." I watched as a woman manoeuvred a double stroller through the tight doorway while her husband ordered. He went over to where she sat, balancing a tray, and gave her shoulder a kiss. Somewhere, in this very city, Matt had that—a family with someone—while I was a walking cliché—the Other Woman. "I'm only twenty-two. I mean, seriously, I turned twenty-two just a few months ago. You know that, right?"

"I do."

"And you're how old?"

"Thirty-nine."

"With a kid."

"A daughter. Yes."

"So, is it that I'm young? Do you do this a lot?"

"I have been with other women who aren't my wife, yes. But no, your age isn't what attracts me to you. It's you."

His candour was simultaneously disturbing and refreshing, but all I really heard was that my age, this anvil that had been dangling from my neck since my arrival at CFSMI, was for the first time not the definitive marker of my character. He liked me.

"I wanted to give you this." He reached into his coat pocket and pulled out a CD in a cheap plastic case, burned from home, offering it to me.

"Seriously?" I'd stopped making mixtapes for boyfriends when I was still in high school, which wasn't all that long ago. He frowned when it appeared I didn't appreciate the gesture. "You made me a CD?"

"I wanted you to be able to listen to it and know how I feel about you."

"That's sweet, thanks."

"Make sure you listen to the whole thing." He smiled warmly and I stared at his lips. Not the wrinkles around his eyes, although I found those inexplicably attractive. Not the nerdy squint of his nose whenever he laughed.

"I'm headed to see my family today, so I'll play it on the way down." I still missed home achingly, and while I usually turned feelings into creative writing work, I hadn't written a thing since I arrived in Kingston except work emails, memos, and business plans. Since I began full-time work in the Forces, even my journal had been abandoned, which left me feeling uncertain of who I was. If I wasn't a writer, if I wasn't creative, and if I was willing to cross this stark line with Matt, then who was I?

"I wanted to give you this too." Matt pressed a piece of paper into my hand, with an email address scrawled in blue pen. "Since you can't really call me, because, well, you know . . ." His wife. "We can communicate this way."

I had to swallow a few times and plaster on the smile I reserved for dealing with difficult staff members at the unit. Holding the piece of paper in my hand, the magnitude of the upcoming deception wasn't lost on me, nor was the fact he'd never spoken his wife's name in front of me. I'd met her once at a work function. She was skinnier than me, beautiful, and I liked her. They seemed a dynamic couple, although he assured me it was an act. I dropped the paper and the CD into my purse.

"I should get going." I could feel my nerves rising like a tide. What the fuck was I doing?

"Already?" He looked disappointed, a big crease appearing between his brows. Matt craned his neck to crack it, and the tattoo on his shoulder became visible, blurred with age and shitty handiwork.

"Yeah." This wasn't me. I followed rules, and always heeded them. "I promised my parents I'd cook for them tonight."

"That's nice of you. Well, if you're sure you have to go."

I grabbed my coat and swung my bag over my shoulder. He gave me a long hug as I tried to squeeze past him, his hands rubbing up and down my spine until I thought it might melt into his skin.

"I'll see you Monday, at work," he whispered into my ear, kissing the tip with a juicy smack.

Trevor and I eventually broke up, parting with a gentle kiss on the porch. The day after, I called him and we chatted like we'd been best friends for the last few years, not boyfriend and girlfriend, the transition a smooth coast into adulthood. Shaking off a former life was as easy as changing my clothes.

I listened to only one song on Matt's disc before pressing Eject, a smile on my face. But I should have listened to all the music on the CD, to the tinny recordings of New Order and Journey. Because if I had listened, I would have realized that I saw those songs as someone else's youth. To him, the music—a blast of eighties rock—represented when he had felt his most virile, and I should have recognized how, in this impending relationship, I would be the one to blame when this all went to shit. If I had listened to the songs, to the voice in my head, to the female officer at my unit, and to her and Captain Murphy's archaic patriarchal views, I would have crushed the CD under the toe of my combat boot.

We moved fast. For his birthday, I presented Matt with a key to my place in a velvet box with a card that read *To my love*, because those words made the affair palatable somehow.

Thursday nights were ours. He breezed in the front door while I chopped vegetables in my tiny galley kitchen. When I moved in, Mom and I had scrubbed the counters and cabinet doors, which were the colour of baby poop. *What a shitty kitchen*, we had said, giggling. But the kitchen was mine; a stepping stone on my route to Grown-Up Land.

"Hi," I called, feeling comfortable yet nervous in our performance of Boyfriend and Girlfriend. Boyfriend comes home to Girlfriend cooking dinner. All normal. It was the one day of the week we allowed ourselves the indulgence of pretending.

"What're you cooking?" Matt approached and grazed the back of my neck with a kiss. His lips were cold from the winter air that rattled my elderly windows in their frames.

"Pasta of some kind or another." I swirled the pan of onions and chicken breast, then added some garlic until it was steaming and fragrant.

"You following a recipe?"

"Nope."

"Hmm." He popped a piece of chopped red pepper into his mouth, neither condoning nor actively disapproving of my cooking methods. "I should make you my famous pasta sometime. My bacon chicken pesto."

"Sounds tasty."

"Well, I use a jarred pesto and those precooked bacon strips, so it's easy." He snatched a piece of chicken from the pan and popped it into his mouth, and I swatted his hand with the spatula. He picked up the knife I was using and inspected it. "You know, I'm going to get you some non-shit knives as a present." He dangled one of the offending utensils in the air like it was host to the plague. The knives and their cracked plastic handles were indeed awful, since most of my home furnishings were castoffs, gifts, or from discount department stores.

"You've never actually bought me a present, so I'd suggest starting with something more romantic than knives." I grabbed the peppers, sprinkled them over the meat, and added a splash of white wine, which evaporated to steam.

"What?" He looked incredulous, hand on heart. "I've bought you gifts. Surely I have."

He hadn't. Not that I wanted stuff—somehow being showered with goods felt like being paid for services rendered—but I wanted a gift simply because it meant he'd made an effort.

Matt leaned against the sink while I put a pot of water on to boil and salted it. I hoped Ray and Paul wouldn't show up unannounced for dinner or a movie. *I told them I was busy, right?*

"You don't add oil to your water?"

"That's actually a bad idea. Means your sauce won't stick to the noodles."

"Never heard that." He drizzled some in anyway, avoiding my eyes as the oil produced slick bubbles.

I reached around his waist and kissed his neck while dropping a spoon into the sink, and he rubbernecked at the clatter of metal on ceramic. There was a stack of dishes left sitting, some of them for longer than I cared to admit, a haze of greenish fur lining the moist edges. "God, I love this about you." The words were said with a hint of disdain. "That you don't really care about housekeeping." He poked around in the mess and caused a small avalanche of glasses and plates.

"What's your problem today? It's like you're picking everything apart."

"Nothing. Why?" He eyed a particularly scuzzy plate. Leftover potato salad, the chunk of Yukon Gold now a soft puff of grass. "You still live sort of like a university student."

"That could be because, until quite recently, I *was* a university student."

He bristled. "I was just joking."

"Somehow," I turned around with a spatula in my hand, wielding it like a conductor's baton, "your jokes always seem like exactly what you really mean to say. So, here's the thing: I'm younger than you; therefore, less well-off than you." I gestured between our chests, where our rank badges sat, both of us still in our uniforms from the day. Two thick bars on his chest to my one. Two ranks between us, the power and balance firmly weighted against me. "I don't have children to cook for all the time, so I don't always do my fucking dishes. I don't follow recipes because I like to experiment. My knives are crap because I can't afford new ones. I'm twenty-two, for Christ's sake." I couldn't discern if Matt's jokes irked me because they were truths, or if it was because it was the same attitude I faced each day at CFSMI from people who didn't profess to love me. But I couldn't shake the concern—a concern I pressed under the weight of that rank badge and ignored in the following months— that Matt was using his HUMINT techniques, the skills that allowed him to endear himself to subjects who had valuable war-related intelligence to provide, to keep me in his arms.

Tears burned hot behind my eyes as his locked on mine. When I cried, he always said my red eyes looked beautiful, so I turned away, not wanting to allow him access to this part of myself or to consider why he saw me cry so often in the first place.

"Oh, I'm sorry. I didn't mean to upset you." He took my face in his hands and I gave in, always, always surrendering my own righteousness, and I melted as he gently tugged my body towards him, leading me like a horse to water. He ran delicate fingertips down my shoulders as he kissed at my collarbone, and I acquiesced as we stumbled into the bedroom, dinner left to burn. I did so much of that back then: ate burnt meals alone after the deed was done.

—

The day before—Thursday, always Thursday—I'd spent a sweaty evening in bed with Matt, drunk on Appleton Estate rum that he kept stashed in my freezer. Now I languished with a glass of wine with my best friend, Nikki, splayed on her couch as she took in the news of my affair. Nikki, it seemed, didn't share the same judgment that I'd been harbouring towards myself. But I couldn't stop replaying a conversation I'd had with Joe the week prior, him in the middle of pilot training in the Prairies. I'd told him about Matt, God knows why, and he'd only said, *Oh, Kelly,* in a way that was so full of disappointment that I still couldn't get the bad taste out of my mouth.

"Oh, what's the big deal?" Nikki waved an arm in the air dismissively, then poured me a refill of wine until the liquid jiggled at the brim. "Now's the time for fun like this, while you're young. Is he hot?" She'd been with her boyfriend for three years, a guy who resembled a *GQ* model. They owned a house together. They were talking marriage. I was having an affair and my place sported Ikea furniture and shitty knives that matched my fucked-up choices.

I shrugged. "He's almost forty for Christ's sake, Nik. *Forty.*"

A year earlier, if I'd been told I'd be sleeping with a married man, I would have responded that this kind of thing wasn't in my nature. I had goals to achieve. Checklists to complete. But as my affair continued, I'd lost my sense of purpose in the Forces and in life. At work, products of the war in Afghanistan piled up: meetings about pushing out more students to meet requirements overseas; dead colleagues from battles, IEDs, and suicide; and a tangible pain that emanated from those who returned home. Co-workers sprang in and out of the unit before they deployed. We attended strained and protocol-based military funerals. We said countless goodbyes to people who died, people who deployed, people who were medically released after struggling with the after-effects of said deployments. The days of death were harder and harder to avoid, and bringing the black mourning bands out of the unit storage closet and donning them became another part of the routine. Each death felt like a reminder of my own military mortality.

"Sex good?"

Another shrug. Nikki looked disappointed. The sex *had* been good, back when it was adventurous and taboo, when my experience totalled two partners who had been too young to explore. But now I left our encounters feeling like exactly what I was: the Other Woman. That realization stopped all orgasms dead in their tracks, although faking it had become a talent for which I felt a bizarre sense of pride.

"Do you love him?"

I probably said yes, if only to make myself feel like on the balance sheet of okayness I was slightly further into the black. Nikki leaned in closer, squeezed my shoulder, but knew me well enough not to fuss.

"So, if he's not super hot and you kinda-maybe-don't-really love him and he's not awesome in bed, what's the point?"

"Excellent fucking question." I gulped back the entire glass of wine and held my hand out for more.

22

Are you back from vacation yet?

Facebook, a relatively new phenomenon, advertised that I had a new message from Sonja Harvey, Matt's wife. The two sentences glowed on the backlit computer screen.

Matt missed you.

She knew.

My fingers shook over the keyboard and I swallowed arid Caribbean air. I was attending a friend's wedding in the Dominican Republic, and I'd spent the entire week sipping watered-down mojitos while floating in the pool.

It had been months since Matt and I had been together, the affair ending a year after it started, all without any real conversation or discussion. There was no monumental argument or demand for him to leave his wife, but rather the knowledge that neither of us seemed to care about the outcome of our relationship, letting it fall into the void of wherever failed relationships mire themselves. I had started dating someone else, and Matt had dropped away from my existence with shocking ease.

Staring at the Facebook message in the resort's business centre, I broke into a sweat, gagging into the wastebasket with a sign overhead: PAPER ONLY. Bursting along the palm-lined walkways, I reached my room and fumbled with the phone until my boyfriend, Ben, picked up the line.

"Ididntmeanitandididntmeantohurtyouandimsorrythisis allcomingoutandihopeyouarentembarrassedtobewithmeand imsosorry." All in one breath, choking on ragged sobs.

"It's okay, babe," he said. "We all make mistakes." I exhaled a desperate sigh of relief as I paced the pastel-themed room. A collection of ants milled in the corner, crowding the daiquiri slush I'd spilled the night before.

I hung up and reached for rum from the mini fridge. It was only recently at CFSMI that I'd begun to feel like I was making a difference, doing my job effectively and gaining a reputation for being an officer who would complete whatever task was assigned with a smile on my face, a smile that I felt I had tempered into a Captain Murphy-approved version, absent of flirting. All of that hard work would be buried under an avalanche of assumptions. I was about to be the unit joke; one that had been told about every woman who ever dared to have a sex life in the Forces.

"Ma'am, how was your vacation?"

My three staff members smiled as I entered the orderly room and moved quickly to my desk. Clearly, they had no idea. Yet. I wanted to take a photo of their welcoming gestures and smiling faces—mentally snapshot the feeling of teamwork we'd managed to create despite Captain Murphy's rigid rule. For once, I wanted nothing at CFSMI to change.

"It was fine." I could barely smile. "Got a tan and all that."

"We can see that!" The master corporal sat with resignation at her workstation when I didn't engage in my usual banter, too busy eyeing the blinking red light on my phone. Messages.

I dialled in to my voicemail and heard Captain Murphy's terse voice. *Kelly, come up to my office as soon as you arrive.* I gripped the armrests of my office chair and choked back panic. I would present myself, my uniform pristine, and do what countless soldiers before me had done at war: attempt bravery in the face of conflict.

I came to attention in Captain Murphy's doorway. "You wanted to see me, Ma'am?"

"Sit down, Kelly." I sat across from her in the too-short chair that skittered, nearly toppling me onto the floor. Murphy sat on her chair as if it were a throne, hands folded neatly in her lap, the multi-coloured wheel of her screensaver performing its digital dance.

"Major Harvey came in to speak to the CO on Friday. I'm sure you know what about." *Major Harvey.* His recent promotion grated; mental road rash. She paused, leaned back in her chair, and assessed me with squinting eyes. "You know, Kelly, you should be ashamed of yourself. We all saw where this was headed, and you just let it happen." I swallowed over and over, desperate to disappear into myself like those snakes that eat their own tails. "Don't you have anything to say for yourself?"

"I'm not here to justify what I did." A squeak. A whisper that barely registered. I was a meek, subservient mouse because I couldn't bear the weight of my guilt.

"I just can't understand this at all, or what would make you engage in such a tryst." Her voice bordered on shrill.

"I wouldn't exactly call a year together a tryst."

"Oh, you wouldn't, would you? You're kidding yourself, Kelly. Did you think it would all work out for you in the end?" Her long fingers curled into her palms.

"I don't know what I thought, exactly. I don't think I thought enough about it, to be honest, or I never would have done it."

"God, *you think*? He's telling people you pursued him, of course." It wasn't clear if she meant *of course he's blaming you because you went after him*, or if she meant *he's being a typical man and making you take the fall*. I gathered it was the former.

"That's completely untrue. I have proof, actually." I was emboldened by this fact, that I had kept all of Matt's and my emails in a special inbox folder. But then I immediately hunched my back, as seemed the proper pose for contrition.

"I was relieved, at least, to hear it wasn't just about sex," Captain Murphy said, inspecting her fingernails. For the life of me, I couldn't figure out why she cared. "Major Harvey did admit that there was love between you."

"I'm not sure how that's relevant, Ma'am."

Murphy recoiled from my grasp for dignity. "Well, I bet you were happy when he was promoted. Someone to help you get somewhere," she said. The look on her face, one of such judgment and contempt, made me want to wheel over in the rickety chair and slap her.

"He's hardly a shining professional star for me to attach myself to, Ma'am." Matt's career was average at best, and since he'd been posted to a new unit, we no longer had anything to do with one another, professionally or personally. Somehow, I expected better from my female boss, something other than the perpetuation of gender stereotypes and the outdated concept of sleeping your way to the top.

"As if that matters!" She threw her hands in the air, then stood and paced under the lights, casting a Murphy-shaped shadow. "Your colleagues now have their own perceptions, and at this point, none of them will be viewing you in a very admirable light. We've seen this scenario countless times with so many other women, Kelly." At this, her voice softened a little. I left it unsaid that if countless other women had behaved like me, then by the very necessity of math, countless other men had also played Matt's role, although the males were not sitting in their boss's office being chided. "Do Warrant Officers O'Neill and Livingston know about this?"

"Paul and Ray?" This is when the tears started in earnest. I had already told Ray, who was about to return from a deployment to Afghanistan and had made it clear that he wanted nothing to do with me when he got home. Paul had made me grovel slightly, then welcomed me back as a friend, albeit tentatively. I could handle looking like an idiot at work, but the fallout within those friendships was a wounding loss. "I've spoken to them both, yes."

"I assume they're furious."

"Yes." But in the case of Paul and Ray, the anger felt justified. I'd lied to them for nearly a year.

"O'Neill has always had eyes for you. You know that, right? This probably killed him. Especially while he's deployed." Although he'd never breathed a word of his affection to me, Ray had, in countless small ways, shown that he loved me, and I felt such painful guilt over it that, each morning over the coming weeks, when I logged into Hotmail and hoped for an email of forgiveness, the absence of correspondence from him made me cry. Murphy seemed to sense that my friendship with Ray was the proper button to press, the best way to make me hate myself. I pulled balled-up tissues from my pocket and blew my dripping nose. "You know, Kelly, we're going to have to think about the ramifications here for your career."

"Ramifications?"

"You had an affair with someone at your unit." Captain Murphy glared at me like I was a moron, making it clear that I hadn't just done something morally wrong, but that my actions also reflected poorly upon her, as though my sex life correlated with her supervisory skills. She had warned me—through the delegate female officer, in the conference room. I imagine she wanted to say, *I tried to make you see sense!* And my resulting affair meant Captain Murphy could tell herself that she'd tried to protect me, had read my flirtatious ways like a book. And yet I'd disobeyed. "So, we'll have to decide what kind of administrative action will be taken."

I was quiet, breathing in through my nose and out through my mouth. I'd been a semi-logistics officer for eighteen months, and in the absence of training I'd done exactly what Captain Murphy had directed me to—dedicated myself to perusing the Queen's Regulations and Orders, the Defence Administrative Orders and Directives, the Dress Instructions, and any other blandly worded military directive I could find. All those hours spent staring at bureaucratic language had confirmed that, morally, I was an asshole. Professionally, I'd made myself look like an idiot, but I sure as hell hadn't broken any rules or laws. And she knew this. "He's not in my chain of command, Ma'am. He doesn't even work here anymore."

Her irritation sprang into incredulity. "And? What difference does that make?"

"Well." Did I dare go any further? I'd never challenged Captain Murphy before, much less while I was busy staging my own act of mea culpa. "Matt and I aren't in the same chain of command, so I didn't do anything wrong as per military guidelines. I realize I acted stupidly, but I also don't feel like this relationship is anyone's business other than our own."

Murphy's eyes went wide as she blew out a puff of air that fluttered her fringe, resigned and angry. She knew I was right. After a year and a half of these morning meetings, we were adept at reading each other's mind. But Linda Murphy was not one to be taken down with logic. I sat for the next thirty minutes while she reasserted herself, words slipping past me on a current. At twenty-three, I didn't know how to defend my honour—nor did I feel capable of it. Captain Murphy said Sonja had told Matt that if he wanted to stay married, he was to inform everyone of our dirty little secret before I arrived home from vacation. All of our shared friends. My staff in the orderly room. My boss. Our commanding officer. "So, people are talking," she said. A different boss would have quelled the discussion amongst the troops before it even took root.

I decided that the only solution was to make my personality as diminutive as possible, while giving every ounce of myself to my work. In the coming months, I hardly looked up from my computer unless I was asked a direct question, I worked late to avoid leaving at the same time as everyone else, I didn't chat about my weekends.

I worked. Went home. Ate. Slept. I did everything to snuff out the spotlight of interrogation, although it occurred to me that I had been flooded by that same red glow the moment I arrived at the unit, simply for being young and female. No matter how hard I scrubbed at my skin in the shower, I was forever blushed and silenced.

A few weeks after the affair was revealed, Paul and I sat in the local Tex-Mex chain restaurant, engaging in our monthly all-you-can-eat fajita challenge. Between us, a plate of sizzling peppers, onions, and beef spat juices onto the table while I smeared guacamole onto yet another wrap. I was at seven fajitas to Paul's four. Nearby, our server, who had some ridiculous cowboy name like "Wild Eddie," leaned against the tortilla machine, gaping in awe at my appetite. Ray was noticeably absent. He'd returned from overseas but still wasn't speaking to me.

"You hardly put anything in them," I said, gesturing at Paul's anemic wrap, three strips of steak limp on the plate. "That doesn't count as a fair battle. Not that it matters, since I'm basically lapping you at this point."

"Listen there, heifer. Not all of us want to eat half the cow."

We laughed together but I felt sick—from the meal or my tenuous friendships, I wasn't sure. The HUMINT trailers no longer felt like home, and when I had to go over there for work, I said hello to Paul, performed whatever task was asked of me, then made haste for the door. The witty banter was gone. Shared jokes just a memory. Clearly, the HUMINT guys had taken sides in the battle, and Paul was the only one even remotely in Camp Kelly.

Despite the time that had passed, Captain Murphy continued to lord my mistake over me. *Just so you know, they're still talking about it*, she would say, gesturing to the hallways where my co-workers went about their business. I was never sure if she was lying, but I was certain that the glassy eyes and reddened cheeks her comment elicited in me were exactly the result she wanted.

"I actually think I'm going to be sick." I put my fajita down on the plate and resisted the urge to gag.

"A sure sign to throw in the towel."

We sipped our Cokes and I fidgeted awkwardly with my napkin. "Thanks for meeting me. Didn't think you'd be wanting to carry on the fajita tradition."

"Like I said, doesn't mean I condone what you've done."

I hung my head. "I get that."

I left it there. Didn't bring up the fact that, decades earlier, he'd had an affair with a colleague, one his wife discovered but later forgave him for. I also failed to mention Paul's late-night email from several months earlier, in which he'd professed to having feelings for me, never acknowledging it again after I squashed that hope. Because sitting there, discussing my sex life over fresh tortillas, it seemed he'd developed amnesia, a disorder spreading rapidly throughout CFSMI.

"I just really want to apologize. For lying to you guys and everything. I don't have an excuse."

"Well, I appreciate the apology." He dabbed at his face with a paper napkin. "Then again, we always knew Matt was screwing somebody."

"You did?" I slurped more Coke, hoping the carbonation would help with the nausea.

"Please. You know what he's like. Always flirting." Paul took another bite and shook his head. I wondered who else Matt had been flirting and sleeping with throughout his life and career, and if those relationships had broken military rules. I didn't know what he was capable of, and clearly, considering Ray and Paul's shock over my affair, we didn't really know what anyone was capable of behind bedroom doors. But there were some certainties. The way I was treated by my co-workers showcased how the old boys' club rallied in support of one another, their moral fabric disintegrated like Jell-O.

"Just in his nature then? You never talked to him about the way he acts?" I eyed the fajita. Felt sicker.

"What good would that have done?" Paul looked up from his plate like he genuinely wanted to know. Matt's actions were deemed excusable because he was led about by his dick and the military had been a man's world long before I entered the scene. And I, flirting young seductress, was meant to have withstood his advances and remained chaste. It occurred to me then that I was one of many—just a number. A service number, in fact. But this was the life I had chosen, the life I now couldn't leave, even if I wanted to. My obligatory service wasn't up, and even if it was, I wasn't a writer anymore, so I had nothing waiting for me beyond my professional life in the military. A jaded bitterness coated the back of my throat as I took another bite of fajita and gagged, a chunk of charbroiled beef lodging in my throat until I coughed and coughed, half vomited, but managed to swallow it down. I swished more Coke between my teeth.

"So, Matt gets to be big man on campus while I get painted as the work slut?"

Even Paul slipped into objectifying me the moment he had more than two beers. When he reminisced about our short friendship, he would talk about the night we first met at a unit function. *You were sitting there, smiling, wearing a shirt that, let's be honest, showed what you had to offer!* He would always laugh, and I would too. But each time Paul cracked the joke, I was reminded that my breasts were considered "what I had to offer."

"Ah, Kelly," Paul said, his voice full of sympathy. "You know how this works."

I leaned back in the booth and let the tears slip from my eyes. If I didn't know how it worked before, I certainly knew now.

23

"I'll have you know, you're talking to CFSMI's newest Harassment Officer, at your service," I said to Joe in a British accent. I carried the cordless phone between my shoulder and ear while painting my fingernails for civilian Friday. Instead of Thursdays serving as drunk nights in with Matt, I spent those evenings painting and primping for the one day of the week I was allowed to wear civilian clothing at work.

"You changed jobs?"

"Nope. Another secondary duty." I now had so many extra positions—Gift Fund Coordinator, Event Coordinator, Petty Cash Officer—that these roles took up more of my day than my administration officer job. As Harassment Officer, I was the lead advisor who instructed the CO on harassment issues, and I was sent on a week-long course in Trenton. Most of the men I knew dismissed it as "touchy feely shit," a comment usually followed by elitist sneers about the military that once was, and how we were now pointlessly emotive in a business of war. But armed with information and a week of role-playing and trust games, I felt I'd finally found my niche in the Forces: spreading the gospel of equality and respect in the workplace. "And the unit is going to let me give lectures. I've been so fucking bored at that place

I would have given those 'keep your body clean in the field' lectures for Bruvelle if it let me leave the orderly room."

Joe laughed. "Oh boy, you haven't changed."

I cherished these long-distance moments with Joe, every few months or so. We often made jokes about basic training, that connection a taut cable from his posting in Moose Jaw all the way to me in Kingston. "Oh, I've changed plenty," I said, suddenly feeling sad and sorry for myself. "How's pilot training?" I tried not to be jealous of Joe, who was on his occupational course. When would I be a fully qualified logistics officer?

"It's amazing." I could hear him smile. "I love every minute of it. Being up in the air . . ." He drifted off, and I was uncertain if it was another pocket of lost reception or him being unable to articulate the feeling.

"Well, I'm glad you're living the high life over there while I not-so-secretly hate my professional existence."

"That bad? Still? Captain Murphy not off your back?"

"Captain Murphy is practically my jockey," I snorted. And yet I hid my frustration well, full of smiles and acceptance of whatever task she lay before me.

"Maybe it's time you did something about it. Talked to the CO?"

"Meh." I swept a line of coral polish along my middle finger, keen to leave it there, the only painted nail. The symbolism was a delicious temptation. "Not sure if that would do me any good. Everyone, my CO included, seems to know what she's like, but it's like we've all accepted this is how it is." My commanding officer had actually called me into his office, saying he had noticed Captain Murphy was particularly "difficult." He encouraged me to submit a harassment complaint because, he said quietly, her reserve contract was up for renewal and he didn't particularly have reason not to rehire her in the job.

The opportunity was there for me to snag—make a complaint and get a new boss. But sitting in his sunny office overlooking the CFSMI compound, I found myself wondering why, when he was so aware of her failings as a leader, he didn't employ his own leadership to rectify it. Instead, he wanted the second lieutenant served up on a scapegoat platter.

"Maybe she sees it differently though?" Joe said, his voice gentle. I could hear the rush of traffic zipping by his window. Where was he off to? A hike, maybe. Or kayaking or climbing or something equally outdoorsy. "Maybe she sees it as mentoring you."

"That's what's so fucked up," I said miserably, my polish smeared. I wiped a remover-soaked cotton ball across the tip. "She really does seem to believe she's justified and perfectly rational. What's sadder is when I see her on a personal level, she's really a lovely person. There's a lot of kindness in her. And I really do think she believes that what she does is with the aim of helping me."

"Well, doesn't harassment training teach you to deal with harassment at the source? You can't fix what you haven't said is broken."

I gave up on the polish, my fingernails streaked with a faint haze of colour, wiped off in frustration. "Why are you always so fucking wise? You're like my guru."

"Ah, Thompson. What can I say? I get you."

Once I hung up the phone, I splayed across my bed and stared at the ceiling for hours. I imagined Joe next to me, his voice calm and measured, his presence warm beside me. I fell asleep in my clothes and dreamed of basic training. It was the first time it didn't feel like a nightmare.

—

Part of the role of Harassment Officer was providing an information session to each new serial of students who arrived in Kingston for intelligence training. During the trainees' first week, along with classes on how to complete travel claims and where to redirect their mail, they listened to my lecture about eradicating harassment at the source.

I stood at the front of the room feeling awkward in my khakis and red polka-dot shirt, blonde hair loose around my face and lip gloss attracting dust. Twenty pairs of student eyes blinked back at me—the 6A course for sergeant and warrant intelligence operators, most in their thirties or early forties. My PowerPoint presentation detailed what was considered appropriate behaviour both inside and outside the classroom.

My lecture was going as it usually did—met with rolling eyes, sleepy eyelids, and the repeated checking of watches as they looked forward to getting on to the information that they felt more pertinent to their work. But I would not be silenced on Civilian Friday, my favourite day of the week. A small donation of two dollars to the base-wide United Way campaign offered the chance to wear jeans (no rips or tears), a shirt (collar required), and a little dusting of makeup.

"Harassment can be defined as . . ." I pointed in the air, gesticulating to make up for the lack of interest in the room.

I finished clicking through my slides in record time, less than fifteen minutes into my allotted forty-minute window. I liked to allocate room for a question period, in case I had an unusually participative audience who wanted to engage with my pretend scenarios, although so far I'd never once needed this buffer zone. But with each new batch of students, I maintained a stunted hope for evolution and change.

"So," I said, flicking back my bangs. My voice did little to rouse the crowd from their post-lunch slump. "If a bunch of us were in the mess having a drink and someone said to me that I was just a dumb blonde, and I was upset by this statement, would that be harassment?"

"Of course not," said a student at the front. "People use dumb-blonde jokes all the time. If some chick got offended every time you joked about her hair dye, we'd all be in shit. Hell, my wife would have me permanently in the dog house."

The room tittered with laughter, everyone guilty as much as innocent. I smiled while grinding my teeth into what I hoped displayed generic exhaustion. "Well, that's not exactly the idea," I said slowly. I paused, left space for a student to fill in the blanks with political correctness. Hell, I would have settled for semi-polite. "I can laugh at myself as much as the next person, but you'd be surprised how often I hear this joke, and maybe the first ten times it doesn't offend me, but after the fiftieth and hundredth times, it wears a little thin. Things like this can pick at our insecurities." *Insecurities.* If I hadn't had any before, I was now rife with them. Basic training, Captain Murphy, the men at my unit, and my own expectations of soldierhood had all turned minor concerns into mountains of confidence crises.

What I didn't tell the students was that nearly all of my pretend harassment scenarios weren't pretend at all, but were instead derived from real work experiences. Just a week earlier, I'd munched on a dry baby carrot at the Officers' Mess for an intelligence graduation reception, although as a staff member, I wasn't supposed to eat the food. The ornate wood inside the mess gave way to a wall of windows revealing the waterfront of Kingston, and a recently renovated patio. Captain Murphy eyed me and the carrot from her perch near the bar, nursing a soda water. Her disapproval pulsed in the back of my head like a heartbeat.

"These things are so fucking boring, Ma'am," Master Corporal Dean Rathman said. He was a friend of mine from the unit who was posted in after me. Dean was the only person at CFSMI who was remotely close to my age, and with his 1980s birthday came a different attitude towards women in the Forces. Dean was my friend because not only was he keenly smart and interested in art and culture, but he considered me just as capable as he was. We became regular lunch buddies, but only after I warned him what effect being my friend might have on his reputation at the school. *I'm basically known for having an affair with a former officer at the unit, which means any guy I talk to is presumed to be my next target,* I told him while we sipped fountain pop at lunch one day. *Who fucking cares?* he answered. I knew then that we'd get along just fine. We'd bitch about how our colleagues sneered at us as though being in our early twenties was a mark against intelligence—in the military, wrinkles equalled experience and demanded respect. But at least Dean had the required equipment between his legs. One less hurdle between ambivalence and acceptance.

I nodded. "A parade for the sake of a parade."

Dean poured himself a cup of coffee, slurped at it, and made a face. I could have warned him. "Why don't they just get out of here already so we can clean up and go home too?" A line of newly minted intelligence officers, who would undoubtedly be deployed to Afghanistan within the year, milled around, chatted, offered congratulatory slaps on the back.

"I'm going to walk around," Dean said, jerking a thumb towards the hall and adjusting his glasses. "Send in a search party if I fall asleep in the coat closet."

My uniform tunic was too tight and the humidity was making it worse. It was last tailored to my thin post-basic-training body, forcing me to bend awkwardly towards the veggie tray so

I didn't bust a seam. The gold buttons bulging near my chest threatened to burst across the room and hit Captain Murphy in the eye. The thought gave me a smirk of pleasure.

"Looking good, Ma'am. Lookin' good."

"Pardon?" I whipped around, irritated.

"We don't usually see each other in dress uniform," he said, smacking his lips together. "You make it look awfully good." He was a sergeant. Maybe a warrant. Possibly a fellow officer. They were all nameless, faceless pundits analyzing my makeup, hair, body, as though every part of me was government property and worthy of commentary. Some of the come-ons were water off a duck's back, slipping into the murky pond of borderline harassment. Other remarks left me wanting a shower, feeling shameful. My boobs might as well have been a medal on my chest, presented for valour in the face of countless unwanted sexual advances.

An irritated throat-clearing emanated from the student in front, snapping my mind back to the harassment lecture I'd just finished giving. His eyebrows were arched skeptically, the class clown. "If you hear dumb-blonde jokes all the time, maybe the world is trying to tell you something, Ma'am." He laughed at himself, baring a tiny row of pebble-like teeth.

My stomach lurched as I fiddled with the pen I'd been using as a pointer, and I looked around the room for another female but came up wanting. And even if I'd spotted another woman, she likely would have hung her head as I'd seen so many others do, ashamed, because given the choice it was easier to agree with her fellow troops than it was to admit that the countless harassing experiences did nothing but wear down the fine veneer of self-worth.

"The point is, this scenario would meet the criteria of harassment." I pointed back at my screen for effect, the definition clearly outlined on the overhead in perfect, precise bullet points. I had prepared the presentation expertly, honed it over time, adding a period here, comma there, utilizing my Professional Writing degree whenever the chance arose.

I checked the clock. Time would not pass. It would not pass, I realized, until I stood up to the assholes.

"Seriously?" a man at the back hollered, sporting a tight buzz cut. A number one blade, no doubt, an effort to prove he had nothing to hide. What did that say about the too-long bangs I allowed to dangle in my face? That I was less of a soldier? Less male, and therefore less than? "That's balls and bullshit."

"Is it? Let's go back over the criteria for harassment." Blank eyes. No raised hands. I counted points off on my half-painted fingernails. "One, the person ought reasonably to have known the other member would be offended. Two, the statement was directed at me, a blonde. And three, I was offended. So, harassment." I pushed air between my teeth, frustration prickling at my skin. I shut down the computer in silence, again pushed my bangs from my face. When had they gotten so fucking long? "Well?"

From my audience: Blink. Arm scratch. Sneer. More of the same. I should have been used to it—a bizarre normalcy that should have been comforting in its predictability. Whenever I drove home for visits, Nikki inquired generically about military life. *Do they ever pick on you for being a woman? Hit on you a lot?* she asked me on one occasion. Her blonde eyebrows hovered over her sunglasses, glinting with mischief. *What? Me?* My mouth dry. *Of course not. It's a workplace of respect.* Before that, I had never lied to my best friend. Later, my stomach felt like lead and I called Nikki just to hear the reassuring tone of her voice, the voice of a civilian who could never understand why the women—and anyone else who felt like an "other" in an organization that valued cohesion—stayed silent.

I undid the top button on the collar of my red polka-dot shirt, which now felt stifling. In my degree, I'd learned about the nature of imagery, the use of colour in movies and books to evoke certain feelings. Blue for calm. Green for nature. Black for death and murder. Red for passion and sex and femininity. Red for everything that was wrong with me, with the classroom, and the Forces.

The course warrant popped his head in the classroom. "All done, Ma'am? They ready for the next lecture?"

I took one last look at the men and was met with ambivalence, and my perceived lack of power to change it. *This is what we know. This is the culture.*

"I'm done all right."

The classroom filled with murmurs, which echoed in my mind when back at my desk and even far away from CFSMI, at three in the morning when I lay tucked in my bed. I was haunted by all the servicewomen I knew who had suffered harassment and wore the shame of these experiences as though they were the ones responsible, because they'd chosen to don the uniform in the first place. The outfit designed to make us belong instead reminded us women of how we didn't—our hips filling pocketed spaces, breasts pushing at tunic buttons—encouraging our silence through loyalty to the camouflage. Our uniforms were like full-body tattoos, permanent, even for those of us who wanted the option of removal.

24

My boyfriend, Ben, was coming on course at CFSMI, and with his arrival, I had to provide Captain Murphy with a memo stating I had a pre-existing relationship with an incoming student. I was irritated to yet again have my private life played out like a sporting match through the halls of CFSMI, everyone taking bets. In her office, Murphy took an extraordinary amount of time reading the one-page memo, eyebrows raised in salute, then flipped through his course file with the tip of her finger.

Sergeant Stirling, doesn't he have children?

You're eleven years apart. That doesn't bother you?

He's deployed several times. That can be difficult in a new relationship, you know.

Your career will take priority over his. You're a young officer with a whole career ahead of you.

"He understands that's how it goes," I said. To the other "questions," I had only nodded, unsure of how to provide an answer to judgments on my personal life. "The military comes first." The military always comes first.

"That's what they all say." Under her breath. Sort of. "But it's always harder for men when the moment actually comes, when they're faced with being less important than their wives.

I've seen it." I had no doubt that she'd seen it, men being unhappy with a military spouse whose career surpassed their own, because the wife is meant to follow, right? Stories of the successful female soldier, with her dedicated, stay-at-home husband, were hard to come by in the military. Scrutinizing Captain Murphy's face, I wanted to know how to alter this truth—that my sex life would always be relevant to my career—and yet my short time in the Forces had done nothing to assuage this concern.

"I thought, like me, you didn't want children." Captain Murphy's voice hinted at my potential as an ally. All I needed to do was swear off men and any resultant children; discarded like those with poor recycling habits or the wrong shade of hair. I licked my lips like Pavlov's dog, hungry for her approval but also for my relationship. She only needed to sign the damn memo. I had learned that silence was the easiest route back to my desk, careful not to feed into her pregnant pauses.

She regarded me with irritation when I didn't take the bait. "So, what is it about *this* Int guy?" Her voice extended gratingly across the soft consonants. She could have asked what made Ben special. She could have inquired as to how we met or what qualities about him I cherished. Instead she wanted to know about "this Int guy," as though I'd been lining up a queue of men from the intelligence occupation to fill my bed. *He's sexy as shit. I feel safe with him. He's great in bed.* What did she want to hear? "He's really kind," I said instead.

"Don't you want to feel something other than 'he's kind' for the rest of your life?" I picked at a loose thread on my pants, wrapping it around my fingertip until it cut off my circulation. I wanted to slap her air quotes out of my face.

"Anyway," she said, shaking her head as though she could shake off the conversation, "have you been ensuring you stay in shape? You could be course-loaded any day now."

I looked down at my knee, cloaked in camouflage. It had been nearly three years since the break, and I'd been to the doctor countless times in search of an answer as to why it continued to hurt. Bone scans revealed, puzzlingly, that there was continued mid-range healing activity. *The fact that you're still not healed doesn't make sense,* the doctor said. *You only had a stress fracture.* He ignored my questions that followed: *What about the thirty kilometres I had to march even after it was broken? What about the week of parade practice? What about months of misdiagnosis?* Instead, military doctors suggested I lose weight to relieve the pressure on my still-broken bone. I was smack dab in the middle of the healthy weight range for my height.

"I'm doing my best. Going to all the medical appointments," I said. My knee was now a twist of knots, nerves, and complex scar tissue. I also had a pronounced limp, making my back and neck ache from the altered gait, and with a medical chit declaring me in a state of healing, my career was at a standstill. Murphy occasionally offered to attend my appointments at the pain clinic, even holding my hand while the doctor plunged steroids into my knee. *I'm here as a friend,* she told the doctor, bringing dinner to my door that night when she knew I'd be hurting.

Friend. I had looked at her in shock, unsure of how to embrace the term in relation to my stoic boss. I'd never known anyone so able to compartmentalize work and home.

"You know, if it's not better soon, this will have serious career implications." Her voice was sharp, eyes suddenly angry as though my knee just needed a stern talking-to. "Major injuries usually mean you only squeeze out a few years before you get medically released. Is that what you want?"

I hardly knew what I wanted. The average time an injured or ill member spent in the military post-diagnosis was three years.

Three successive temporary medical restriction categories—each technically six months long, but easily extended by procrastinating the reassessments—would eventually lead to a permanent category, and from then it was approximately a year for the administrators in Ottawa to decide on medical release for members who did not meet the Universality of Service. If a soldier was unable to perform all the physical skills required of Canadian troops, they could no longer be in the military, even with a desk job. "I'm doing everything I can."

"Never mind." She waved her hand at me. "I'll ensure the file references your relationship with Sergeant Stirling." She tersely scribbled in his file and turned to her computer dismissively. The memo was thrust into my hand, giving me a wide paper cut that dripped a drop of cherry blood onto the floor. She handed me a Kleenex, gesturing to the floor. I left with mixed feelings about the fact that I had disappointed her yet again, simply for having what she felt she couldn't or didn't want.

Once Ben came on course at CFSMI, several colleagues visited me under the pretence of needing a claim authorized or a statutory declaration signed, but before long the professional request would segue into discussion of my personal life. *Hear you're dating Sergeant Stirling*, and then they would lean into my workspace, wiggling their eyebrows. I would nod but leave it there, offer them a hard candy from the plastic dish on my desk so I could get back to work.

One of my regular desk visitors was Sergeant Corey Wilden, an instructor at the school. Corey was in the middle of a nasty divorce, a fact he was more than happy to discuss at work, in the coffee room, in the orderly room trailer, and wherever else he found himself. The week before, he had cornered me on my way out of the CFSMI gates, my keys already in hand, moments from escaping back home.

"Ma'am! Hey Ma'am!" He trotted to my side and saluted as he approached. I returned the salute awkwardly.

"Hey, Corey. What's up?" I jingled my keys again, hoping the action conveyed my desire, my need, to get home as soon as possible.

"Well." He looked me right in the eye in a way that was off-putting. "I'm sure you heard about my wife. I'm separated."

He knew that I knew about his wife. Hell, I'd been the one to make the change on his records. I didn't say, *We've all fucking heard about your wife*, but dammit if I didn't want to. "I did. I'm sorry you're going through all that."

"Typical bitch, am I right?" He laughed, but his smile soured when I blinked back at him and shielded my eyes from the sun. "Anyway, I wanted to see if you'd want to go out sometime. Get a drink or dinner." Corey placed his hands on his hips like some authority figure. He'd never actually spoken to me before, not in any sense other than professional discussions in passing, and he sure as hell hadn't expressed any interest or offered too much attention, or Captain Murphy would have been all over that like automatic gunfire. Had my liaison with Matt and my relationship with Ben sealed my fate as the Intelligence Branch equivalent of a groupie? But then I admonished myself for having such thoughts about someone I didn't know well. Too much time with Captain Murphy meant I was absorbing her suspicion of everyone's motives.

"Thanks for asking, Corey, really, but I'm actually already seeing someone." It was easier and kinder than saying I wasn't interested, which was equally true.

"That Ben guy?" Clearly the news had spread beyond Captain Murphy's office. "Well, it's not serious, right? You can still date other people."

"It's serious enough where it's exclusive." I hoped that would be the end of it, smiled, and kept walking to my car, but Corey followed.

"Oh, didn't realize you moved that fast." I let the slight go and kept walking, desperate to get in my car. "Okay, well, have a good night then."

"Yup, you too." I waved and got into my Volkswagen, cursing the entire way home. I didn't tell Ben about the encounter and I wasn't in a position to rock any boats at CFSMI. I still had penance to pay for my previous attempt at love.

"Morning ladies!" Corey burst into the orderly room the next morning beaming, a stack of student folders under his arm. "How goes it today?"

"Fine thanks," chirped the corporal. We were all elbow deep in paperwork, as course reports were filling our inboxes. I eased myself around Corey towards the main building with an apologetic wave of my file folder. *Something to do. Gotta run!* As I crunched across the gravel towards Captain Murphy's office, Corey followed, chuckling to himself.

"Hey, Ma'am," he hollered, and then, more quietly, "So about yesterday, no hard feelings, right?"

"Nope," I said, flinging open the fire door to the building. "None at all."

"Great. Awesome." He sighed, relieved, and I softened. We're all human, and Corey had just asked a person on a date and been turned down. And there I was, making him feel bad about it. Yes, that was it.

He continued to follow me as I walked up the stairs, his own workstation just down the hall from Captain Murphy's. Our boots echoed throughout the stairwell on the short two flights up.

"I'll get over it at some point," he said with a laugh. A laugh can diffuse any bomb of anxiety or miscommunication. "Maybe I should just threaten to fail Ben off his course if you don't go out with me." He laughed real hard from down in his belly, and the noise echoed. I whipped around so fast I nearly fell, my file folder skittering onto the landing.

"Excuse me?" I was calm. I had learned to be calm in these situations, balancing my self-defence with public perception.

"Oh, you know I'm kidding," he said, talking as he would to a child. "I would never do something like that." He disappeared as I stood there, struck dumb. Other colleagues passed and asked if I was okay, handed me my papers. *Fine, totally fine*, I insisted. Then I did what I had come to do: discussed the finer details of the graduation parade with Captain Murphy and executed the graduation ceremony seamlessly.

When a colleague, who had apparently overheard Corey's remark, suggested to him that I might have felt harassed, Corey called me at seven in the morning on a weekend, panicked. *We're good, eh? You're not upset? You didn't feel harassed, right?* The following Monday, upon returning to work, we gathered in the conference room where I assured Corey, our colleague, and myself, that no, no, I didn't feel harassed. *All good here.*

Ben passed his course, and Corey and I slipped into the silent acceptance of so many harassment scenarios, none of them pretend scenarios at all. When Ben and I finally broke up, I couldn't help but feel like I was setting him free from the burden of shame that I felt followed me.

25

Considering most of our unit was within a decade of the compulsory retirement age of sixty, after a couple of years at CFSMI attending retirement functions was routine. The latest was a luncheon for Petty Officer Samuel Victor, an affable, well-liked guy. We sat at Darbar Indian restaurant nibbling on dry pieces of naan as we waited for family-style curry dishes, the officers at one end of the table, the non-commissioned members at the other, and me hovering awkwardly in the middle next to Sam, the guest of honour. I envied him his impending freedom.

"Isn't this place great, Ma'am?" he asked, gesturing around the restaurant, which was empty except for our party of twenty. It was dark inside, not helped by the streaky windows that exposed the upper end of Princess Street and its plethora of pawnshops and thrift stores. "Cheaper than Curry Original but better, if you ask me."

"Yeah, it's great," I said, reaching for an onion bhaji. When I put my fork in it, it gave way to a greasy pool of half-cooked batter. I ate it anyway. "How many years in?" I asked with my mouth full, still chewing. Of course, I knew how many years he had in. As Admin O, I knew the bureaucratic minutiae of their lives, having arranged their common-law separations, set up their children on the dental plan, and seen who was having financial problems after another nasty divorce.

"Twenty-five. Didn't want to give more than that to a job, you know? At the end of the day, the military is just a job." He drained a draught beer and clunked the glass on the table.

"Ah, Sam, if you believed that, you wouldn't have invited all of us to a retirement lunch to celebrate said job."

"You've got me there, Ma'am." He looked away, turned back to his food. He would have a hard time adjusting to retirement; I could tell by the nervous way he fiddled with the collar of his civilian clothing, sprayed with too much starch. I thought of Dad, his own luncheon passed up because he didn't want to face the soldiers who he felt would judge him for his mental health struggles, choosing to slip into the civilian night like a ghost. Dad still used starch on his collared shirts. He still polished his loafers until they gleamed.

"God, can't you call her Kelly now?" Petty Officer First Class Byron Stoddart, Sam's friend at the unit, leaned in, both of them well matched in their prankster ways. "You're just an average guy now. Gotta learn to stop seeing rank."

"Hey, I guess so, eh, Ma'am?" Sam looked to me for approval.

"Of course! I hate this 'Ma'am' shit anyways. I'm twenty-three, for Christ's sake. Kelly is good. Call me Kelly."

"Would feel awkward though, around here."

"Who isn't awkward at CFSMI?" said Byron with a side smirk. "We're all a little fucked up. It's in the water." Byron was always cracking jokes that bordered on inappropriate, depending on the receiver.

"I'll drink to that." The men clashed their glasses into one another and slopped froth across their chests.

"Not imbibing today?" Byron gestured at my glass of water, his own eyes already glassy and red.

"Naw, I have to drive home."

"Ah, always on the up and up," he said. I turned to an offered dish of korma and piled it on my plate. "When are we going out as a crew to have some drinks?"

I almost cried. Just the suggestion of social engagements outside of work, no matter the age or rank of my attendees, made me giddy. My friendship prospects were slim, Paul still present but somehow at a distance, Ray having essentially written me off. I was tainted goods and could feel our friendships had fractured like a bone, permanently damaged. And Dean had a girlfriend, so there was only so much of his time I could occupy.

"Whenever you finally invite me."

"Ah, Sam, you hear that? We've been ignoring the nice second lieutenant here."

"We could all go to my place after this. Have a few drinks? Everyone's invited." I said this a little too fast and with far too much excitement, my voice rising several octaves until I realized I sounded just like my grandmother. I might as well have suggested I make spinach dip and run home to iron my cloth napkins. I'd recently moved into a townhouse in a semi-decent neighbourhood, and had spent the first few months of home ownership battling the condo board to evict the family of squirrels living in my walls. It wasn't much, but it was mine.

"Hey! Awesome idea! Sam, what d'you think? It's your party, after all."

"Can I cry if I want to?" Sam asked, colour rising to his cheeks. The officers' end of the table was stoic, and I hoped Captain Murphy hadn't heard my invite. She'd likely think I was setting myself up for a CFSMI orgy.

"Hell, buddy, you can do whatever the hell you want. It's your big day!" Byron proceeded to whisper invites down the table. I noticed the officers were left out of the after-party.

After the meal came a long speech from the CO. *We all value Petty Officer Victor's service. He will be remembered. He was an exemplary staff member. Blah blah blah.* As soon as the event finished, I zipped into my driveway and rushed to set out glasses and whatever alcohol I had lying around, which wasn't much—a half-empty bottle of piss-warm vodka, three lone beers in the fridge that belonged to Paul, and dark rum in the freezer left over from my time with Matt. The cupboards offered little other than a bag of plain ruffled chips and some Ritz crackers. I threw the chips into a bowl and, within minutes, ten men from the unit poured in like a gang of uniformed misfits. It didn't occur to me to be nervous, that by inviting ten drunken men I might end up like the ill-fated Meerin. I was like an abused wife, always expecting a different outcome.

A casual house party with my colleagues gave me immeasurable joy. At the unit, I felt perpetually on the outside of my own clique, somehow relegated to the children's table at Thanksgiving, except Thanksgiving was every fucking day. So now I sat on an uncomfortable wooden bench on the far side of my living room, smiling like an idiot at every joke, every shared insight into the crazy workplace that was CFSMI. Soon, everyone was glossy with booze, while I was dead sober, wanting to take it all in. Finally, I was one of them.

The sun had set hours before, disappearing behind the hefty maples. Co-workers began to trickle out my front door, calling cabs to deliver them home. Their shadows moved across the street to vehicles that rumbled in wait. *Look at us,* I thought, *being all responsible. We don't drink and drive.* We. Everything was now a collective "we."

"We should get out of your hair," said Sam. Just he and Byron remained.

"Ah, it's been my pleasure. Really, it was nice having everyone."

"But especially this guy?" Sam jerked a thumb towards Byron, who was barely vertical on my couch.

"Ha, yeah, definitely him. Life of the party and all that."

"All right there, Byron, get your damn boots on. Time to go." Sam hooked his arm underneath Byron's armpit to ease him off the couch. "Heave ho, buddy. Come on."

"Kelleee!" Byron wobbled over to me of his own accord and threw his arms around my neck, pulling me in for a tight hug. I laughed and raised an eyebrow at Sam, who shrugged and rolled his eyes. Same old Byron. "Thank you having . . . having us . . . us guys, here." He gestured with his fingers around the now empty room. "Here in your house. Nice house. You're so nice. And smart. Pretty."

"All right there, Byron. Time for you to head home I think," Sam said, leaning in. Next to the couch was half of Byron's twelve-pack of beer, the other half polished off and the bottles stewing outdoors in the recycling bin.

"You're nice. So nice." Byron held me by my shoulders, the air thick with his beer breath. But then his balance began to give way, or he made some intentional, determined choice. Byron leaned forward with his mouth agape, hands up and splayed wide in front of his chest like he was going to give someone a push. And then, as though it were the most natural and acceptable thing in the world, he clasped his fingers around my breasts and squeezed, tweaked, massaged, and I stood there like a fucking idiot and let it happen. "Wow. Nice. Real nice." His hands swirled around, right then left. Back and forth, groping through my cotton button-up that I'd changed into.

As a civilian packed into crowded bars, I was known for fighting off lecherous drinkers, able to handle myself. But as Second Lieutenant Thompson, I said nothing, maybe even offered a nervous titter of laughter with a relative stranger's hands groping my chest. Civilian Kelly would never forgive her silence.

"Whoa, okay there, buddy." When Sam realized what was happening, he stepped between us and pushed Byron back towards the door. "I think it's time we wrapped this party up. Ma'am, thanks for having us." He glanced around like I had hidden cameras somewhere; surreptitious and nervous. *Ma'am.* Any softening of the barriers between us now reverted back to stuffy formality. I had put up with it for nothing at all.

I shut the door behind them and cracked open Byron's beers, depressingly calm after the assault because I saw the action as drunken male bullshit, to which I was nearly immune. Besides, I was lucky, no? I was safe, hadn't been sexually assaulted like so many other women I'd come to know, both inside and outside the Forces. The harassment I'd experienced was on a different level of suffering, so much lower than some of my female colleagues, and suffering in the military was all relative. Yes, my experiences were the lesser of so many evils.

As I poured the hoppy liquid down the sink, I repeated one of the tenets I'd learned on my harassment advisor course. *The person ought to have known that the other person would be offended.* Byron should have known, right? I'd been so caught up in the warm feeling of acceptance that it had only then crossed my mind that being welcomed into the fold was only permitted when my youth, gender, and body were part of the deal. With Matt I'd made a name for myself, a name that meant every part of me was up for grabs. The message had been received loud and clear now. No encryption required.

26

I'd been at CFSMI for almost three years, most days a repetitive routine. According to regular career progression, I was supposed to be promoted to lieutenant one year after university graduation, and captain two years after that. So I should have been Captain Thompson by May, and yet with my injured leg and lack of logistics training, I was stuck, still a second lieutenant in February, after almost thirty-three months at my first unit. I arrived at work each morning with a Starbucks coffee I couldn't afford, ate sugary breakfasts to energize my misery, then trudged upstairs for my daily meeting with Captain Murphy. It was the customer service aspect of my work that helped me wake up in the morning. *Today, I will help someone*, I told myself as I turned off the alarm and donned my uniform.

In my role as administration officer, I received all posting messages, often the first to know who was being moved to and from CFSMI. Military postings rolled around each spring, with the moves occurring in the summer months. Depending on the location, I often hand-delivered these messages to soften bad news, as opposed to sending off an email to the soldier.

Uh, Gagetown. Army bullshit, eh? But I hear they have this great pizza place in town.

*Sorry buddy, Gander. Fucking cold, I know. Maybe the snow-
mobiling is good up there?*

Captain Crumbie's posting message to CFSMI came early in
the season. When the message pinged in my inbox, I recognized
the name but a face would not materialize.

SUBJECT: Posting
Hi Kelly,
Looks like I'm coming your way this posting season! Looking forward to
getting back in touch again. When I was a student at CFSMI, you were
always so great at your job. Kingston will be a nice change. See you soon,
and I'll pop into the office when I'm next in town.
Later

Donovan

SUBJECT: Re: Posting
Hi Captain Crumbie,
Great news! Look forward to meeting you again as colleagues. Let me
know if you need anything related to your move or have any questions
about the unit and I'll do my best to help or point you in the right direction.

Kelly

You were always so great at your job. Those words were like water
after years in a desert. He sent another email almost immediately, wanting to confirm I was the person he thought I was.
Young? Worked in the orderly room trailer? *Do you have a photo?
Just want to make sure I'm talking to who I think I am!* He acted
like we'd had some kind of previous interaction I should have
remembered, and I found myself wracking my brain to make
the connection.

I paused, reading the line of text repeatedly, gut and common sense telling me no, but engrained soldier-to-soldier trust won over. Crumbie wasn't asking for nudity. He just wanted to confirm my identity, right? So I sent a tame shot of me sitting on the back deck of my home, the sun bursting in a halo effect from behind my head. I was wearing a military-issue T-shirt, unadorned by makeup. *This is me!* I typed. Stupid. So stupid and naive.

SUBJECT: It's you.
Ah yes, it is you! Your hair looks great. You cut it shorter, yes? Looking forward to more time together when I arrive at the unit.
Speaking of which, I'm looking to set up an arrangement. I'm in a long-term relationship, with kids, but not married. Not looking to get out of that relationship, but aiming to have something fun and no-strings with a like-minded person, so I thought I'd reach out before I arrive. Interested?

Donovan

I have no idea how long I sat and stared at the words in the email. Harassment must meet the following criteria: *Improper conduct by an individual*—maybe this was the way adults operate, with random requests for casual sex? *The individual knew or ought reasonably to have known that the conduct would cause offence or harm*— I asked for it. I made him think I was into this by sending the damn photo. *Directed at another individual*—he probably asked lots of people to have affairs without so much as a real conversation. He was just testing the waters. *Offensive to that individual*—yes, I must have flirted. Just like Captain Murphy said. *Was a series of incidents, or one severe incident, which had a lasting impact on that individual*—I could just delete this email. *Occurred in the workplace.*

But there was zero room for interpretation. Worst of all was that the compliment about my work now meant nothing at all.

I stood up and sat down twice, and even considered telling Captain Murphy, trying to weigh the pros and cons of bringing this issue to her attention. But no, somehow she would remind me that I had brought it on myself, and the culture of silence and victim-blaming would continue to perpetuate.

My email to Captain Crumbie was clear. I wasn't interested, but thank you for the offer. I actually said thanks. His response was glib. No problem. He'd look elsewhere. *Whew. No problem.* I read my own words several times over. No, I'd not upset him. I'd not been offensive in my dismissal of his advances to a junior officer before he even set foot in the door. Disillusionment flooded every military memory I cherished, as my hand lingered on the mouse before I snatched it back as though I'd been burnt.

I pressed my fingers to my temples and pushed into the flesh, wincing as I blinked back tears. And then I clicked on his series of emails, rapid-fire over our ten-minute message exchange. Delete. Delete. Delete.

27

The orderly room hummed with activity as we prepared for the graduation ceremony for the latest batch of students. Sergeant Zaph walked towards the photocopier while pushing her glasses up on her nose. She leaned in close to the buttons on the machine and punched over and over.

"Not working again?" I stood at my desk to assess the photocopier from a distance.

"Oh, heck, I'm not sure." *Oh heck* was about as close as Sergeant Zaph came to expletives, except when she drank, cheeks rosy like the Syrah she sipped, when she was full of *fuck* and *shit* and other cacophonic words. "Just a jam, I think. Remind me not to order this paper next time. It seems to stick more often."

"Let me know if you need me to call the Ricoh guy."

"Maybe I just need to . . ." She leaned into the machine, flipping open the mechanism to peer into its inner workings. She revealed a chunk of paper gnarled in on itself, streaks of toner lining both sides. "This would be the problem. Out you come." She tugged on the jam and it released like a white flag, whipping in her triumphant hand. "Hope this isn't important to someone." Sergeant Zaph held the document close to her face, waiting for her bifocals to adjust to reading. Her eyebrows furled in, blonde wisps nearly meeting in the middle as her wrinkles gave way to irritation. "What the hell?"

At the hint of stern language, the entire orderly room perked up, eyes darting to Zaph, who was examining the paper more closely, holding it up to the fluorescent lighting. Her fingers whitened where they gripped the edges of the document, teeth gnashing.

"What? What's wrong?"

She wandered over and thrust the paper into my hand. "What the hell is this? Who was printing this here?"

Hurt Feelings Report. Principal Purpose: To assist whiners in documenting hurt feelings. It was presented like a legitimate military document. The form included spaces for apparent relevant info: age, sex, type of whine used. From there, the complainant could document the "time of hurtfulness," if "anyone was sympathetic to the whiner" (with a note to include "paid witnesses"), if the hurt resulted in a "traumatic brain injury," and the "name of the person who hurt your pansy-ass feelings." Next was a list with boxes to check—to indicate the reason for filling out the report:

I am thin skinned.

I have woman/man-like hormones.

The Department needs to fix my feelings.

I am a wimp.

The weather is too cold.

I am a crybaby.

I want my mommy.

I didn't sign up for this.

My feelings are easily hurt.

I was not offered a tissue.

All of the above.

And so it went. On, and on, and on . . . 2009, and still this bullshit was routine. I scanned the list, deflated; all these traits my male counterparts deemed weak, I saw as forms of great strength. Why did crying and having "woman-like hormones" have to be some strike against competence? Holding the sheet, acknowledgement of the futility of my work hung weighty around my neck. For a woman in the military—if not subjected to outright assault—life felt like death by a thousand paper cuts, slicing away at any feelings of self-worth.

"You have to be shitting me."

"What's worse," said Zaph, "is that there are a few other copies waiting here to print. I mean, who was distributing this?"

"Like we don't already have enough problems with people feeling safe reporting harassment." I slammed the paper on my desk and then shoved it into a brown file folder. "Now we have to paint them as complainers. Babies." By military definition, I had been a complainer, a baby, a woman, a pansy-ass, and yet there were so many moments deserving of my anger where I chose to stay silent, not wanting to perpetuate the weak image that seemed to follow me. By not voicing my feelings in those moments, I'd almost convinced myself they didn't matter. How many others had done the same? "I'm going upstairs to talk to the boss and find out who this was."

Captain Murphy didn't look surprised to see me. In fact, she rarely did, as though she had a CCTV camera trained on my desk. "Ma'am, we found this in the photocopier in the orderly room." I thrust the file into her hand and sat without being asked. I could feel my face getting hotter, blood creeping up my ears and tingling in my fingers. "It's unacceptable to be distributing anything like this in the workplace, much less throughout a training environment. I mean, what if the students actually saw this?"

"Kelly, your voice doesn't need to reach fever pitch." Captain Murphy always had a way of reprimanding like an elderly aunt, as though my passion were unwarranted, even when the opposite was true. But as she read the form, her eyes went wide and then angry. I'd seen the darkening mood on more than one occasion, grateful that this time I was not on the receiving end.

"I think this has to be taken to the CO, Ma'am. Immediately, before it's distributed—or, if necessary, to mitigate the impact on students," I said.

"You know, Kelly, I completely agree."

If I hadn't been so angry, I might have fallen off my chair in shock over her acceptance of my suggestion. We knocked on the commanding officer's office, and entered when permitted. Captain Murphy did all the talking while I stood back, light pouring in from the preciously rare CFSMI windows in his office space.

"Kelly?

"Yes, Sir." I snapped to, my legs tightening into an unnecessary attention stance.

"I asked if this meets the criteria for harassment by definition." The CO stood with his hands on his hips as he scanned the paper that was now crinkled and sad-looking.

"Absolutely, Sir. We're trying to encourage dealing with harassment at the lowest level possible. Stuff like this makes everyone less likely to report when they are being harassed because they feel they won't be taken seriously, or that their complaints have career implications. Having a staff member hand this out . . . well, that would keep me quiet if I were a student."

"Well then, we'll launch an investigation, but in the meantime, it might be pretty easy to figure out who was disseminating this. Kelly, once you're back at your desk, let me know what the next steps are in the process, okay?"

"Yes, Sir." I returned to my desk, triumphant.

"Well?" Sergeant Zaph stood up from her chair when I came in.

"We took it to the CO. He's going to find out who put it out there."

"Who put what out where?" Warrant Officer Tabbot stepped into the orderly room, and with him came a waft of stale cigarette smoke. Tabbot was about my dad's age, known for smelling like an ashtray and for spending far too much of his workday on the business end of a Canadian Classic. But his nicotine-stained skin blended in with his tan, which he liked to say was from countless deployments, usually explained to us "girls" like he was talking to children. Typical "old army," unable to make room for change.

"We found a very inappropriate form in our photocopier," Zaph said.

"Oh, you found my Hurt Feelings Report!" he said, roaring with laughter that he seemed to believe would catch like wildfire. "Had to make a few extra copies for my students in there." He plucked one of the extra copies from Zaph's desk and held it close like he'd been reunited with a good friend. "Had enough of their whiney bullshit lately."

As a kid, listening to Dad reminisce about the old army days was like hearing a bedtime story, the tales taking on more colour as I aged. I heard about an officer's wife—who had a hefty bottom—pranked with a tractor seat welded onto her bicycle; and later, the female officer who had her head Photoshopped onto images of pornography actresses and showcased on the overhead screen during the daily Orders Group. In the company of Dad's colleagues, I had laughed along with them, not knowing what I was laughing at. My dad was a good man, respected women on the whole, and yet it was evidently easy to fall into these patriarchal traps. Watching Tabbot before me, I wondered if in another life, I'd be laughing too.

"I'm sorry? Pardon?" I stood and tried to calm my voice. The orderly room staff's mouths hung slack. Tabbot took on a bravado-filled stance—chest out, yellowed teeth dug into his bottom lip like he could hardly contain himself. "You distributed this to your students?" He barely looked at me when I talked.

"Hell yeah I did. Trust me, if you had to teach these morons, you'd have done the same thing."

"You can address me as 'Ma'am.'" Never once had I enforced someone paying me the respect my rank demanded, even when their tone indicated complete dismissal, which Tabbot's often did. And yet I'd also never been put in the position of having to, especially by a thirty-year veteran who ought to know better.

"What's that?" He whirled around on his heel to face me, for the first time meeting my eyes.

"I was just reminding you of my commission, because you seem to have forgotten. And I can assure you, Warrant Officer Tabbot, that I wouldn't have done the same thing, because what you did was harassment."

"Harassment?" He laughed loud and wide, leaning forward with his hands on his knees. But I could tell the laughter was used to hide his anger, which was spreading across his skin like a rash. "That, Ma'am," he said, scrunching his nose like he smelled something rotten, "is the whole point of the Hurt Feelings Report. Everyone acting all wounded over some good old-fashioned army discipline." He looked at me, smug, eyes burning like one of his countless cigarettes.

"I'd argue there's a very large line drawn between discipline and derogatory bullshit like this," I said, taking the paper from him. "A line I'm going to ensure is enforced. You're teaching this garbage to students, to the next generation of the military.

What the hell?" I couldn't tell anymore if I was mad at him or mad at my own silence and being part of the problem.

"This is what's wrong with the military today," he said, leaning close. "This is why it's impossible to get anything done." He didn't say, *It's because of you women demanding respect, because you want to be equal*, and yet he might as well have. If prodded, I'm sure he could be inspired into such rhetoric, but even Tabbot seemed to recognize that I was not a bear to be poked. This was the ever-present issue—faced with the choice to respectfully appreciate the unique contributions women made to the Forces, or to continue promoting the tough-as-nails soldier image, many kept choosing the latter.

"No," I said, aware of Zaph and my staff watching me, silent. "This form is what's wrong with the military. Perpetuating this attitude is what's wrong with the military."

Dad often lamented about Forces life in the 1970s, noting that if you dared to complain about something—whether that was an injury, stress, or some actual issue that needed tending to—you'd be punished. *The sergeant would call us behind the tank and beat the shit out of us.* Dad's voice betrayed ironic pride for having withstood this abuse. And I would nod, because yes, I knew that was how it was, but I also felt this behaviour was an example of why so many people left the Forces and proceeded to fall apart; because they'd never been properly heard and didn't feel safe at work while being expected to protect others. Their mental health came at the price of their silence.

"This is bullshit," Tabbot grumbled as he left, combat boots clomping in anger, letting the door slam behind him. I wonder if he knew it was wrong but just didn't care, or if thirty years in the military had simply made him believe that his actions were totally justified.

—

Tabbot was the first and only staff member in my nearly three years at CFSMI to be posted from the unit in the middle of the year, outside posting season and without warning. Firing a soldier from the Forces is akin to removing a tenured professor from their post and requires a significant administrative process—so, instead, offending troops are siphoned off to other locations to start anew. Tabbot was sent to a hard army unit that provided pre-deployment training, ironically located directly across the street from CFSMI. I imagined his belief system would have him slotting into place at his new unit like a key.

Tabbot waved to me once while I walked through the CFSMI gates, standing at the top of the stairs to the entrance of his new workplace. The wave, the hefty flinging of fingers, appeared genuine, as though I'd earned his respect. I waved back like we were the best of friends.

28

When my bone scan continued to show healing activity, and my continued pain kept stalling my logistics training, doctors ordered surgery on my knee, which was done while I lay awake shivering on the operating table. *Sure is junky in here,* the surgeon said, sucking at the debris-filled joint with a tiny vacuum. I watched the whole thing play out on the television overhead, marvelling as he sliced pieces of skin and chunks of cartilage. *That should help with the pain,* he said, *but sometimes broken bones just don't heal right.* I returned to work within two weeks, but the pain was still there. The pain was always fucking there.

There was no monumental moment in which I was suddenly deemed physically healthy by the military medical authorities, but six months after my surgery, "healthy enough" seemed an agreement the Forces and I were able to reach. I was still on my second temporary medical restriction, the six-month physical fitness reprieve in hopes of healing injuries, which I was forced to carry in my uniform pocket at all times. The paper felt like it would burn through the fabric and leave an indelible mark on my chest. But despite the medical restrictions, nearly three years after my arrival at CFSMI, Captain Murphy called me to her office

and said, "You've been course-loaded for your logistics training."
No eye contact.

"Really? When?"

"In two weeks."

Two weeks wasn't a lot of time to wrap up my current work projects. I was busy trying to find a way to hire a new staff member for the HUMINT trailers, had undertaken a course in tasking software, and was finally proficient in managing the finance system. "That's pretty fast."

"Yes, we've not been provided with much notice." She scanned the course-loading message again. She did not offer congratulations. "You'll likely be posted once you complete training. After all that effort to provide proper on-the-job training by us." She shook her head, somehow irritated about the routine process of on-the-job training, and the career progression that had been in effect for the history of the Forces.

"I'm ready for the change," I said.

"Oh, are you now?" She shook her head again, this time at my apparent ungratefulness. "You know, this is going to be expensive for the unit, paying for your TD fees." While on course, I would receive temporary duty allowance, an extra seventeen dollars a day to make up for being away from home. I gathered I was meant to feel guilty about the impact this would have on the budget that Sergeant Zaph and I had carefully prepared.

"We're very proud of you, Second Lieutenant Thompson." Major Fairchild, the instructor on my human resources course, placed my course report in front of me with a flourish, curly blonde hair pulled into a tight bun.

After more than six months of training, I had arrived at the end of phase four of my logistics training in Borden, Ontario—

the same base where I'd spent most of my childhood. Basic training had taught us to be soldiers, while the general logistics training showed me how to work within my occupation. After that I had learned about logistics as it applied specifically to the air force; and then, finally, this latest report from Major Fairchild proved I'd been trained in my human resources subspecialty. I was now a fully-fledged Log O, the rank of captain a guarantee once I passed my fitness test.

My HR course report was full of glowing statements. *2Lt Thompson displayed a strong academic performance achieving a score of 100%.* "You're the second-top student on the course," Major Fairchild said with a smile. My reports from the other three phases of my training had been equally glowing. *2Lt Thompson was selected as the top student on her serial. 2Lt Thompson's academic marks were consistently above the course average.* How different these notes were from IAP and BOTC.

"Thank you, Ma'am."

"You worked really hard, and I know you're going to excel in your career. You'll be Captain Thompson in no time, considering you've met the seniority requirements. All that was standing in your way was getting trained, am I right?"

"Yes, Ma'am." Also, my knee. I didn't mention the injury to Major Fairchild, grateful that logistics training had no physical component to stall my progress and end my career. And I was so close to success. *This* close.

"I also see you're being posted to JSG."

In the final weeks of my course, I'd received a posting message to the Canadian Forces Joint Support Group. I would return to my home in Kingston but was moving to a unit known as a mecca for logistics officers; it was notorious for exciting deployments for support trades. I felt both excited and nervous at the prospect of leaving CFSMI, my military home of three years.

"Yes, Ma'am," I responded. "Executive assistant to the Commander." EAS travelled often, joining their commanders while they hobnobbed with high-level policymakers, but the role also offered the endless tedium of meetings in which I would have no input, sitting silent while the decisions were made by the important folk. Blending into the background would be part of the job description. A glorified coat-holder.

"Not a human resources job then. Well that's disappointing. But JSG deploys quite a lot. Does that interest you?" She was quizzical, concerned even. I sensed it was okay to tell her the truth, but no.

"I just want to do my job, Ma'am, wherever that is."

At news of my posting, my course roommate had rubbed her hands like I had struck professional gold. *You'll really see some action*, she said. Hell, she'd nearly salivated. I gave the canned and appropriate peer soldier response: *Awesome*. Was I the only one kept up at night by the idea of deploying, nervous about Canadian-flag-wrapped caskets and black vehicles pulling up to the door to tell my family I was dead? Was I the only one who was scared?

Perhaps it was naive of me, but I had hoped to avoid any brushes with death while I served in the Forces, but Afghanistan robbed me of this hope. Once, some colleagues and I were shown one of the refrigerated caskets used to transport dead soldiers on the sweltering twenty-hour flight home from Afghanistan. We'd stared emotionless at the stainless-steel shell, scared to get too close in case we smelled something—or maybe scared that all of that sadness, ensconced inside, would rub off on us. So we pretended the caskets were just another piece of kit while shivers crept up my spine, the image settling into the depths of my memory, where all those dark things hide.

Or there was my first funeral at the National Military Cemetery, for the wife of a co-worker. She'd died of cancer—not war—but even so, barely anyone had mentioned her first name, her home life, her passions outside the Forces. Her spouse had shifted uncomfortably in his chair and I found myself desperate to help him shed the weight of the uniform and all that came with it. If he was just another family member, he could crumple on the floor in tears. He could wear the sweater she liked best on him and get his haircut any way he liked. If she was a civilian, instead of her formal officer photo he could have displayed one of her at the beach or having a barbecue with friends. Anything but the picture with the Canadian flag waving bravely in the background, which millions of soldiers have taken before their deployment. The one no one sees unless you're dead.

Standing at the edge of her grave, I recognized there were other ways to kill a soldier than with a bullet. There was cancer, suicide, heartbreak, mental illness, conformity, loneliness. So many ways to die. I was a prime example: I'd thrown myself into work in which I was not creative. Not an individual. Not a writer. In joining the Forces, I'd given up a part of myself, sacrificed it like an offering. And yet I stayed, despite the fact that in less than six months, my obligatory service was over and I could leave without financial penalty. But now—top student, a potential success—I felt the future might be different. I was torn between loyalty to myself and to an organization I admired, despite its reality proving less-worthy of the pedestal I placed it on.

"Do you have a specific career track in mind?" Major Fairchild asked.

"I'm hoping to work with the injured and ill soldiers in casualty management," I said. Afghanistan meant that wounded troops were more numerous than ever, and I wanted to help them navigate the complicated and anxiety-riddled rollercoaster of the military medical system. I was one of them, in a way. And I felt my empathetic nature would be a boon to the role.

"That's emotional work. Take it from me." Major Fairchild had burst into tears during one of our lectures on return-to-work programs, having recently lost a co-worker to cancer after developing a work-from-home adjustment for her. Fairchild had been embarrassed about the show of emotion, and had tried to cover herself with waves of her uniformed arms. *God, I'm sorry*, she'd said, swiping at her face. Her fellow instructor, also a woman, had stepped in and told her that it was natural to cry over such a loss, then calmly took over the presentation. *Someone you cared about died*, this other officer had said, as though this was a justified reason for a soldier to cry. I idolized them both.

"It's where I feel I'll actually make a difference." We left it unsaid that I feared I wasn't making a difference anywhere else. I signed my course report with a smile, full of hope.

"Guess who?" I popped into the CFSMI orderly room, wiggling comical jazz hands and beaming widely. I couldn't explain it, but I'd missed the unit, the people, the competency I eventually came to feel as Admin O. And now I would leave for a new workplace, new ideals, new acronyms, new bosses.

"Welcome back!" Sergeant Zaph stood alongside the rest of the orderly room and clapped for me, to which I bowed like a Shakespearean player.

"You're looking at a newly minted Log O," I said, spinning around in uniform like I was Vanna White.

"And top of your class in almost every course!" Sergeant Zaph beamed and I felt warm all over, like I'd made her proud. "But now you're leaving us! We just got the message."

"I know," I said. "You're probably annoyed to get me all trained only to have me leave."

"That's how it always works," she said, moseying back to her desk. "But you know Captain Murphy won't think that way."

"Yeah, she'll take it as a personal attack, like I have a fucking choice in the matter."

"She's been down here complaining about it," Zaph said, smirking. "Wondering what we'll do without you."

"God," I replied, hand to my heart. "Little ol' me? I think it was three years of her telling me all the things I'm doing wrong, only to then be pissed when it's time to go."

"I think she'll miss you," Zaph said, already back at her desk working. "She leans on you more than you think."

I settled at my own desk, feeling uncertain about this new power balance now that I could be missed or needed. I looked at the walls of the orderly room trailer, the blinking fluorescent light I'd been asking to be repaired since long before I left on course, the faded slice of linoleum rubbed raw by my office chair, and for the first time in more than three years, I didn't want to leave CFSMI. Even the hint of being needed was an antidote to the venom in my veins.

"I want to say thank you to everyone at the unit," I said, holding my CFSMI certificate that the CO had just presented me with. We'd set up in one of the lecture halls to say goodbye to all the troops posted out for the year, and I was to depart with as much fanfare as I'd got when I arrived. None. "I've been lucky to work with great people, especially all of my staff in the orderly room who worked tirelessly and taught me so much. But I'm looking forward to my future at JSG and hope to see many of you at base functions." All very professional. All very future-colonel-esque. Twenty-four years old, and on to new things. My brief speech felt general enough not to have to address Captain

Murphy directly. There was a part of me that was so angry that I could not give her any credit for the things she had taught me, even where it was due.

A round of applause burst from my colleagues and I turned quickly on my heel to start my first day at JSG.

"Kelly?" Captain Murphy stood with her hands clasped in front of her like a ballet dancer, combat-booted feet splayed outwards in a stance of strength.

"Ma'am?" I checked my watch for effect. I had places to be. My new boss was waiting.

"Is that all you have to say?"

I had no idea what I had to say, other than a jumble of love and hatred and frustration and admiration. She'd made me miserable, sure, but Captain Murphy had become, perhaps, what the military had demanded of her—it was a measure of self-protection. "It's been nice working with you, Ma'am." I shook her hand firmly, eye contact and all, then walked up the street to my new workplace.

29

I walked a few blocks to the Joint Support Group and was greeted by the Commander's civilian administrative assistant, Marie. I followed her quick pace down the hallway to an office at the east end of the building. The walls were dark blue, with dark blue carpeting and mahogany desks, making it appear that the room tumbled in on itself.

"I can show you around afterwards," Marie said. "First, you should go meet the Commander."

At the back of our workspace was the Commander's office, a sunny change from the dark location I'd be sharing with Marie. I knocked and came to attention, noting the large picture windows where CFB Kingston spread out on a swath of green, 1930s buildings all boasting the same peeling ivory paint. The Commander, Colonel Arthur Norman, was in his fifties, quiet but forceful, with a tidy sweep of greying hair.

"Second Lieutenant Thompson, nice to meet you, and happy to have you on board." Colonel Norman did not rise to shake my hand. Instead, I bent awkwardly over his desk to take his, then returned to a semi-at-ease stance.

"Thank you, Sir. I'm looking forward to it."

"Where are you coming in from again?"

"Straight from my training, technically. But I spent three years at CFSMI awaiting training after an injury."

"All better now?" He barely looked up from the papers on his desk as he spoke.

My knee, as if responding for itself, throbbed and pinched with pain. For weeks I'd been practising the step test, the push-ups, the sit-ups, determined to pass the PT test after almost four years on the military career bench. Six years into military service, my injury felt like a life sentence.

"Should be, Sir. Last surgery was a year ago and I think they've determined there's nothing else we can really do." He pursed his lips and laced his fingers into a tent under his chin. I tried to assess if my purposefully ambiguous answer would cut it.

"Well, glad to hear you're soldiering on. Once you get that PT test out of the way, we can promote you to lieutenant. We should have you meet the rest of the team. Marie?" She appeared in the doorway as though she'd been waiting just outside, eavesdropping. "Have the Chief and Driver come in, would you?"

Soon after, a jovial French master corporal arrived, in his fifties with a round belly and hair swept into a comb-over. "Sylvain Tousseau, Ma'am, nice to meet you." He pumped my hand up and down, filling the room with the tart scent of cologne. He turned to the colonel, hands jaunty on his hips. "So, this is the new one, eh, Sir? Young, isn't she!"

They laughed together like I wasn't standing there, just as Chief Warrant Officer Lavoie arrived, entering like a giant, combat boots thumping an earthquake as he also came to attention. Unit Chiefs are notoriously tough individuals, and this behemoth of a man was true to form. While the Commander would be considered king, maker of laws, the Chief served as a type of enforcer and was the most senior non-commissioned member, responsible for discipline and deportment.

"Ma'am," he boomed in English, although he was Quebecois, and offered the fiercest handshake I had ever experienced. I forced myself to maintain eye contact without wincing at the pressure. "We are happy to have you with us, right, Sir?" More nods around the room, but I couldn't help but feel no one was really happy to have me there, as though I'd crashed some private party.

"We travel a lot, as you may have heard," the colonel said. "So you better get used to spending time with these three ugly mugs."

"Looking forward to it, Sir." No big deal, I assured myself. I could get along with anybody. Emboldened by training, I felt up to whatever task was placed in front of me.

"Oh, and did anyone mention you'd be deploying with us for the Olympics? I'm heading up the support unit." The Commander had settled back behind his desk and was jotting wet blue ink across a legal pad. "We leave for Vancouver right after Christmas, but there are a few exercises in between now and then. So make sure you give all your details and passport info to Marie so she can book your flights. That'll be all."

Dismissed, I came to attention and left while the Chief and Driver stayed behind to chat. Marie filled me in on the details. Three week-long exercises would run in Vancouver to practise response to issues that might arise during the 2010 Olympic Games, where the Canadian Forces was assisting the RCMP in providing security. Rooms had been arranged for us in the centre of the action, at Camp Jericho, Vancouver. Prime location. Blocks from the ocean. I could look at it as a vacation, Marie insisted, obviously irritated that she wasn't coming along.

"But I've already been away from home for more than six months this year," I said. The Canadian Forces limited how long troops could be on courses, deployed, or otherwise away from home, to keep divorce statistics from straying too far from the national average.

"Don't worry about that," Marie said, sweeping a hand in annoyance but not bothering to look up from her stack of paperwork. "I have a waiver for you to sign saying you don't mind."

"How long will I be gone?"

"Four months or so in Vancouver, plus the exercises over the next few months."

I missed my bed, my own laundry detergent, my home-cooked meals, but I signed the waiver on the dotted line, just as I was told.

I sat at my new desk uncertainly, adjusting the seat to my height. Marie's eyes were trained on her computer screen. Unwilling to ask the obvious questions—*What is my job, exactly? What do I do?*—I started up my new computer and set to making my desk home. Upon entering my login information, a flood of emails filled my inbox, which I hadn't checked since my week of leave after my course. One name, and my stomach leaped into my throat.

SUBJECT: Olympics

Is this the email of one soon-to-be-Captain Kelly Thompson? How're the new digs at JSG, Miss Fancy Pants EA? Just found out I'm deploying for the Olympics, so really looking forward to that. Other than that, Comox is beautiful and you'd love it! Come visit soon

Joe.

My eyes darted around the room, like I expected Joe to jump out from behind a filing cabinet. If he was going to be working at the Olympics too, then everything would be okay. Better than okay. Our friendship had recently rekindled now that Joe was settled in Comox on Vancouver Island, working as an air traffic controller after switching out of the pilot trade.

SUBJECT: Re: Olympics

Hi! JSG is okay, although it's my first day. To say I'm the odd woman out would be an understatement. But hey, just found out I'm going to be at the Olympics too! Thirteen Platoon reunites! Can't wait to meet up.

Kelly

I stared at the email until the words meant nothing, as I tried to stop smiling like a fucking idiot. The Olympics felt like my own personal competition, a chance to dip my toe into military life.

I was trained as a Log O. I had proved I was one of the best. And now, on the other side of the country, was the man who made change feel not only possible, but necessary.

30

The following months of working at JSG involved so many flights around the country that I was dizzy with the pace, punctuated by days where I was so bored I nearly fell asleep at my desk. When we travelled as the Command Team—Norman, Tousseau, Lavoie, and me—I easily adapted to the feeling of not belonging; oddly comfortable with this persistent element in my career. When we met for meals while on duty, it didn't strike me as odd that I was not asked for my choice in restaurant, and was not invited to join them when they went to movies or met for a Pepsi every afternoon. Being ignored was the most normal part of my day.

Despite my knee injury, I passed the fitness test with flying colours, securing my promotion to lieutenant with captain soon to follow, and afterwards I loaded my military gear into three waiting kit bags, all nearly too heavy for me to lift. We then hopped on the military flight to the 2010 Vancouver Olympics, the plane sweeping over the Rockies, ground springing up in various shades of green, even in January.

There were several temporary military and police bases scattered throughout the Lower Mainland as part of the national security force for the Olympics. Colonel Norman and many of the support services team were assigned to Jericho Beach on the outer edge of the city, nestled in the community of Kitsilano and just minutes from downtown. The only permanent military structure on the base was the headquarters for the reserve unit, 39 Brigade, while temporary trailers were contracted to serve as the gym, mess, post office, laundry room, and barracks. Officers got their own rooms, while NCMs were stacked in bunk beds without enough space to store all their gear, a game of kit Tetris ensuing. I dropped my bags off in my room, which was the size of a prison cell, feeling pleased and excited. In my role as EA, I felt like a glorified coat-holder, sure, but I was in Vancouver, near Joe, for the Olympics.

My pocket chirped—a text message. *You all set up?* Joe. *Three cheers for the Olympics! Can you believe we're a part of this? Gotta say though, living out here in Aldergrove is shit—I'm missing all the action!* Joe had been relegated to a camp an hour and a half away.

I'm here! It's beautiful. Love the mountains. Not what I wanted to say. Not "Come see me. Let's hang out every day. Let's see if we could be something." *Gotta run. Duty calls. Touch base later this week and we'll see what our schedules look like to meet up.*

Sounds good!

Once I unloaded my belongings, I reported to the top floor of 39 Brigade headquarters, where my office adjoined the Colonel's—the Chief on the other side of me. We cobbled together workstations from postwar-era office supplies and, after our first day, fell into a general pattern of meeting daily for breakfast at the mess and heading to the office by 0730 hours. I hadn't been told exactly what my job was as an EA, other than to deal with all of Colonel Norman's requests—and, eventually, to anticipate them like a fortune teller. I spent my days arranging his schedule, coordinating visits to the countless camps he

oversaw, and holding his coat as he chatted with important offi-
cials and my brain turned to under-stimulated mush. At the end
of each day, I would hover on the 39 Brigade steps and stare out
at the North Shore Mountains, or the rise of mist from the
ocean when the temperature dipped below zero; stunned into
silence by the beauty.

When I wasn't visiting with Joe in my precious spare time,
my loneliness was an animate thing, stuck between two worlds:
the officers, who wanted nothing to do with a lowly lieutenant,
and the NCMs, who welcomed me to their dinner table with
laughs and kindness but were deemed to be people I shouldn't
be "cavorting with" in my spare time. *Spend time with people like
you*, the Chief said once, gesturing to the silent table of officers
with their heads bent over the meals. So far, only one captain
had bothered to befriend me, but the sole purpose was to point
out the tainted optics when I brought my friend, Dean Rathman,
a coffee during a night shift in the ops room. The next day,
gossip abounded that I was sleeping with Dean, the apparent
proof in the steaming cup of Sumatra blend at 10 p.m. The
captain who pointed this out bared a charming grin, edged his
tongue into the hole where he was missing a tooth, and mentioned that it might help if we had a drink together at the mess
sometime. You know, officer to officer. He'd failed to mention
his wife, concealing the vacant crescent of white skin where his
ring should have been.

"When will my job not suck?" I said to Nikki over the
phone, my voice whiny. She'd been dodging my phone calls, or
at least it felt that way. I called almost every day, wanted to talk
too long, needed too much advice. She had a husband, a business to run, happiness to exude.

"Lots of people hate their jobs." I could hear her sipping
something from a glass. "Seen Joe lately?"

My smile was impossible to hide, even over the phone. Each evening, as soon as Colonel Norman set me free from work, I texted Joe, asked what his schedule looked like for the rest of the day. *Feel like dinner?*

"You know when you talk about him your voice changes," Nikki said. I ignored her. Picked through some emails on my work BlackBerry, my personal cell phone tucked between my chin and neck. "You just have to be careful," she said, her voice garbled by another slurp of her drink. "You're setting yourself up for a bad situation here. He lives on the other side of the country for God's sake."

"I love him, Nikki."

"I know you do. Hell, we've all always known."

"Who has?"

"Everyone," Nikki said. "Everyone who loves you back."

When we weren't busy at work, I walked around and explored the city, keen to escape the cloak of camouflage. I went to museums, took yoga classes, and feasted on the palpable Olympic energy. I felt most at home when touring Granville Island, where I felt at one with the artistic crowd—no military to speak of. There were peddlers of arts and crafts, tour guide operators, and artisans hocking everything from custom gold jewellery to handmade corn brooms on twisted Manzanita handles.

While stuffing a still-warm donut into my mouth, I passed the Granville Island Psychic Studio, a sandwich board directing me up a steep flight of stairs to learn about my future from a woman who was also named Kelly. I pushed through a beaded curtain, and with forty dollars to burn, held my palm open wide and watched as the psychic cleansed the room with a burnt sage offering, washing smoke over her body as though taking another form.

"You're meant to be with someone you've known for a long time," Psychic Kelly said, jotting the notes down on a piece of paper that looked like a Ouija board. She was matter of fact, unapologetic. "Someone who saved you from something."

Joe.

"I also see you struggle between a very professional job, one you might call militaristic, and a very creative one. You will work one day in Vancouver, doing that creative job. You are a master of words. Is any of this making any sense?" I checked myself for evidence of my prim military life, a camouflage wallet or carbon-laced fingertips. But I was well groomed, with my punky hair spiked, and civilian clothing that said more bohemian hipster than soldier.

I tacked Psychic Kelly's numerology report up in my room on base, waking up each morning to my future mapped out in pen.

The Olympics came and went with little fanfare in our military offices. Since much of our job was to plan and prepare for the worst-case scenario, the actual duration of the Olympics and Paralympics were sleepy in comparison to the months of work beforehand.

After three months in Vancouver, it was time to return to Ontario. To mark the end of the operation, Joe and I went for a hike in Lighthouse Park, driving through the expansive West Vancouver rebuilds, glimpses of ocean bursting between property lines. At the park, we loped down a trail towards the waterfront, wrapping ourselves in layers to protect against the March chill. Spray sprung from the ocean and clung to our Gore-Tex as Joe folded a scarf in two and spread it out across the rocks. We nestled together against the wind as he pulled out our Nalgene bottle filled with Sauvignon Blanc.

"Cheers to the athletes!" We clonked our knuckles together in absence of cups, then each took sips of the wine.

"If you were to get in a boat and wind over that way," he said, pointing to the stream of water, "you'd find my house in Comox. It's weird being so close to home but between ferries and shit, it takes me four hours to get here. It's only about fifty kilometres as the crow flies." He cupped his hands over his mouth, blew warm air and returned them to the warmth of his pockets. His ears were red at their tips, as he'd given me his hat when I'd forgotten my own, despite his bald head. "It's been amazing, hasn't it? Being here during all this?" He gestured at the Vancouver skyline, a Snakes and Ladders game of glass buildings and pockets of greenery. I breathed in and swallowed the lump in my throat, a ball of emotion that the wine couldn't wash away.

"I don't really feel like going home." *Because I could be a writer in this city. Because you, Joe, are just fifty kilometres as the crow flies.* "I want to move out here."

"Oh?" He arched an eyebrow and turned towards me. It was too forward, too much, too everything, and yet he didn't run away. Didn't pack me up into my car with a kiss on the forehead and then watch me drive away in tears. "Military might want to have a say in where you live, now that your career is underway. Top student Lieutenant Thompson. You'll be on the move."

A career underway. It seemed an impossible concept, and yet military life was now being offered to me on a platter. Yet I wanted female friends. I wanted to be taken seriously. I wanted to be unique. I wanted to be more than the sum of my breasts. I wanted to write. I wanted Joe.

"Still," I said, eyes on the horizon, letting the sentence fill itself out. The sun was starting to set. I could make out Jericho Beach directly across the water, lights blinking around the overrun camp. I imagined Lavoie, Norman, and Tousseau camped out in the office, indulging in their afternoon Pepsi and making plans for their arrival back at the unit. Back to routine. They had talked endlessly of their desire to return home, although none of them had family waiting. It was just another thing that set us apart.

"You should give the whole military thing a chance," Joe said, rubbing his palms on my arms to generate heat. "Your opinion of the Forces could change now that you're not always feeling stuck at the bottom."

I hardly heard him over the sound of the waves lapping at our feet, or the noise in my own head. We went quiet, staring out at the water, legs splayed out in front of us. He was letting me hold on to the dream, and I loved him even more because of it.

31

"You're back!" Marie all but threw herself into my arms as the Commander, Lavoie, Tousseau, and I returned from Vancouver. "I've been so bored!" We laid out the gifts we'd bought for her: Olympic logo sweaters and scarves, mugs and key chains, all of which appeased her upset. Upon my return, Marie and I became fast friends.

The Commander and Chief both disappeared to their offices, and Marie pulled me aside near the photocopier. "Wait until you meet the new Chief of Staff," she said, followed by an exaggerated eye roll and a jerk of a thumb towards his office, which connected to our own.

"That bad?" I asked, pouring water into the kettle.

"Worse."

Lieutenant Colonel Forsythe, our new Chief of Staff, had been brought in from another unit, where he'd left a trail of hate behind him. He was known for his "sense of humour," a device he wielded to make snide comments behind a facade of joviality. I met him in passing on his way to the Commander's office, where he introduced himself but didn't wait for my name, as though it didn't matter. Marie and I barely tolerated him from the start of his tenure, both of us irked by his attitude, his snobbery, and his frequent requests for tea or coffee despite the fact we weren't 1950s secretaries. *I'm an administration assistant,* Marie emailed to me with a wink from across the room. *Not a fucking barista.* We laughed about his chauvinistic ways in the manner one would smile at a misbehaving puppy. Annoying, sure, but nothing to get too worked up over—not in the military, where patriarchy was the cornerstone of business. Besides, I rationalized, JSG was going to be different, a sanctuary after years of oppression. I was no longer in a training environment like CFSMI, and I had finally been promoted to captain. Maybe Joe had been right. Maybe the whole military thing was worth a chance. Captain Thompson finally sounded like me, not my father.

Part of my work involved managing all files that came across my desk destined for the Commander, checking for errors and polishing up the staff's work.

"Sorry, Sir," I said to one of the unit lieutenant colonels standing at my desk. "This needs some revision before I can pass it along to the Commander."

He set his jaw and leaned on my desk with his palms. "All it needs, Captain Thompson, is his signature." His rank badge dangled in my face, which I gathered was the intention.

I sighed, tired with this routine. An EA's role was to reduce the workload of the Commander, to be the funnel through which countless documents, files, and emails filtered through for clarity before arriving on the Commander's desk. This meant I had to diplomatically tell high-level officers what to do and how, and even though they understood the nature of the request, they didn't like it.

If I didn't send back shoddy work riddled with typos, then I wasn't doing my job. Yet here we were, day after day, with me having to justify my job to another fifty-year-old man while correcting his shit grammar with a delicious sweep of red pen.

The lieutenant colonel snatched the file from my hand and stormed out of the office, mumbling. Definitely not singing my administrative praises.

"What do they want from you?" Marie said, shaking her head. "They know how it works. They should be learning to use spellcheck if they don't want the EA correcting their work."

"I'd be lying if I said I didn't relish it a little bit." I returned to prepping files, thumping the two-hole punch with a clomp of my palm until the sound bounced around the walls and into the hallway.

"It's a few problems rolled into one," Marie said, clicking away at an email. Her ability to multitask was something to marvel at. "You're young, you're a captain, and you're a woman."

"Kelly," the Chief of Staff hollered from his office, which was within earshot of our own. "Have you ever thought that maybe you're just a total bitch, and that's why they don't listen to you?"

"Excuse me, Sir?" The respectful term turned to slime on my tongue and I tried to rinse out my mouth in a swirl of tea. I stood from my desk as Marie's eyes went wide with shock, or maybe fright, or perhaps anticipation.

"I said it sounds like you're just a bitch." Lieutenant Colonel Forsythe ambled out to lean against his office doorjamb, calm eyes blinking. The office lights flickered behind him and his skin was ghostly pale, as though a layer of flour had fallen from the sky. A smirk appeared on his lips, curling them up at the edges.

I swallowed my shock but my face must have given my feelings away. The military thrived on cursing, on *fuck you*s and *shit*s and *dickwad*s. But it always felt different when the words were used about something, not someone, or when those terms didn't assault the insecurities and worries that I'd clung to since basic training: that being an assertive woman trying to do her job made me a bitch, which is why I had always skated too close to the other extreme of overt friendliness, which others labelled as flirty. I stood there, staring at the Chief of Staff, knowing I couldn't win.

"I'm not sure that term is appropriate for the workplace," Marie said, my words stolen from my mouth. I could do nothing but blink, rapid-fire, and lick my dry lips.

"Oh, ladies, you know I'm just kidding," the Chief of Staff said with a dramatic flop of his hand. He walked back into his office, point made. As usual, he wasn't kidding at all.

Emails flew between Marie and me, even with our desks only five steps apart.

What the fuck was that? That's harassment, Kelly.

I literally had no idea what to say. I actually hate him.

You need to talk to the Commander. Immediately. And then, perhaps sensing I wouldn't report harassment for my own comfort: *You have to say something for both of us. He makes me so uncomfortable that I don't want to be here when you aren't.*

Faced with protecting my co-worker, I prepared the perfect statement for the Commander, lodging my complaint professionally and devoid of emotion. The Chief of Staff's comment was abusive but also a pattern of behaviour that made Marie and I hate our workplace. I used the term *harassment*, because that seemed to make a difference to how seriously a complaint was taken. And the prevention policies indicated I was doing the right thing: bringing the issue to my direct chain of command.

The Commander shook his head, clearly disappointed in someone's behaviour. "I'll speak to him immediately." The assurance in his voice comforted me.

The next day, Lieutenant Colonel Forsythe called me into his office, placing me squarely in his playing field. He looked smug behind his desk, a cheap model made of clunky plywood boards overlaid with veneer. I felt grown, officer-like. Prepared for the apology that was coming my way so that we could move on, professionally, without sexist slurs tossed about like confetti.

"So, Kelly, I hear you don't like the way I talk."

"Pardon me, Sir?" My face felt hot, like a reprimand was coming, one I'd come to believe I deserved. Emotions mixed in my stomach like sludge.

"I've been told that I make you uncomfortable. The Commander was telling me that you and Marie think I'm difficult and rude."

What could I say? I stared at his degree framed on the wall behind him, wondered if he got it out of a Cracker Jack box for a toonie. He wore a simple gold wedding band and I tried to formulate a vision of his perfect family, but it would not come to mind.

"Here's the thing. What you two need to appreciate is that I'm a bit different. I don't do things the way everyone thinks I should, you know what I mean? So sometimes I say things as a joke, but it's sarcasm. You have a writing degree, right? You know what *sarcasm* means?" I tasted bile in the back of my throat. "So, we'll have to learn to get along, is my point. For the boss's sake. You, my dear, have to learn how to take a joke." He gestured to the door, dismissing me, and said nothing when I didn't salute as I returned to my desk.

He did not apologize. He did not acknowledge any wrongdoing.

Countless times I'd witnessed that policies dictating that harassment complaints are best managed on the lowest level did nothing for women in the Forces, when complaining only highlighted a woman's ability to "not be able to take a joke." I couldn't count the number of times I'd walked that line, not wanting to disturb the tender balance between equality and feminism, between belonging and segregation. I returned to my computer knowing I couldn't keep this up much longer, that I was running out of passion for the career that was constantly squashing it.

I'd been told in countless ways that the military was not the life for me. But sitting in the Chief of Staff's office that day, I finally listened.

I got a break from the JSG offices when I was told I required a second knee surgery, which led to an infection that had me off work for several months. *Not sure what all this swelling and fluid are about*, said the surgeon, without offering much of a prognosis. I would have pain forever, he assumed, seeming not at all broken up about the news. I emerged from the operating room without a solution but sporting new pink lines over the previous scars.

After a few months, my military doctor called with the aim of meeting for a medical update. I sat in Dr. Burndock's MIR office sucking on a Jolly Rancher, the smell of blue raspberry filling the room, bouncing my bad leg in a nervous twitch. I stood when she arrived like she was a judge passing a sentence. I felt claustrophobic, unable to escape.

"Please, please, have a seat." She gestured to the plastic chair I'd clung to more than once, waiting for results that would determine my future. My GP was a civilian contractor, and her short grey bob floated around her cheekbones as she flopped onto a wheeled stool and pulled up my chart on the computer.

"Kelly, after this latest assessment from your surgeon, I think we need to have a serious talk about your career."

"What do you mean?" I knew what she meant. She held a permanent medical category form in her hand. The form that ended careers with a few marks of a pen. I couldn't tell if I was happy or heartbroken, and I looked around the room frantically for something certain to hold on to.

"Well, you're officially in breach of the Universality of Service, without any avenues for continued medical improvement. We've sort of taken you as far as the healing will allow, and you can't do all the things required of a soldier physically. You might be able to squeeze out another few years, but you have to consider at what cost to your future health. I'll have to submit this paperwork to the medical folks in Ottawa, which will then be handed over to the career people. Essentially, once the paperwork winds its way through the administrative track, you'll be medically released in about a year's time."

I nodded as she marked up the form in silence. In one year, I'd be a twenty-seven-year-old veteran with more than eight years of military service. Dr. Burndock patted my knee and I had to bite my lip to keep from crying, surprised by the surge of emotion for a job I felt such conflict over, which pitted me against my female colleagues and partially alienated me from my male ones. For a job that gave me friends I'd have for a lifetime and which had made me into the woman I was now. But simmering in the background was the knowledge that it wasn't just a job; it was the life I knew, the life I'd grown up in. My devastation lay in all the accomplishments I'd never achieve, the people I wouldn't help, the uniform I'd no longer wear.

"You'll get through all of this," she said.

My mind flooded with concern, and everything from the job I would do to the place I would live presented themselves as terrifying, exciting choices. I could move to the other side of Canada. Hell, to Comox even—3,651 kilometres as the crow flies.

The paperwork was thrust into my hand and I shuffled away, not bothering to return to work. I dialled Dad's cell without looking, my eyes never leaving the comfort of the road, the definiteness of streets and cement, pedestrians and four-way stops.

"I'm out, Dad." I gasped for air, foreshadowing the kind of sobbing that would rake over every part, every cell. "Med"—sniff—"ical . . ."—sniff, sniff—"re-re-lease." I was a failure. I was the fuckup course staff had always assumed. I was a whiner. A MIR Commando. I couldn't soldier on. I'd failed Dad in making this phone call, and for meeting the same fate as his own career. I was, in that moment, the representation of so many things I'd grown to hate.

Dad let me cry the whole way home, until I had to pull over on Bath Road, car idling in a bakery parking lot.

"So, what's your plan?" Dad always wanted a plan. A plan meant things wouldn't go haywire, that they would follow a simple trajectory as outlined by attention to detail. I had planned a career in the Forces, planned to succeed, planned to get a pension, but none of that was materializing. I watched through the window as bakery staff wielded piles of dough like mottled white flesh, palpating it back and forth on wooden slabs. I focused on the minutiae of their task until I caught my breath.

"God, who knows," I said after a long pause. "After JSG and CFSMI, I think I left my soul somewhere back in university."

"Understood." His voice sounded clinical, cold in a way that was designed to hide what he was really feeling.

"I've been thinking about these new Integrated Personnel Support Centres. They look after all the injured and ill troops." My voice turned up like a question, hoping Dad would answer it for me. And then, to fill the empty space: "If they would post me there until I retired, I could finally do casualty administration and actually help people. The job I always wanted." IPSCs had been created in response to the war in Afghanistan, for the new veterans who were coming home physically and mentally damaged. They were intended to guide soldiers towards a smooth transition into civilian life, or help ease them back into a military routine. As an injured person myself, facing my own medical release, I felt this would make me the perfect IPSC staff member, like the guy from the spray-on hair commercial. *I'm not only the Hair Club president, but I'm also a client!*

"Leave the operational world of JSG? You want to do that?"

"I just want to do my job and do it well. I can do that at an IPSC."

"It's just that"—Dad's voice was quiet and pinched—"I don't want this to happen to you. Not like it did to me. Not like this, without a choice."

Through the bakery's expansive window, I watched as an elderly woman entered the shop and ordered a loaf of bread. The staff member wiped his hands on his apron before pushing the bread through the slicer. Jagged steel teeth sawed back and forth rhythmically while I drummed nervous fingers on my dash, transfixed. "You can't really compare a thirty-five-year career with an eight-year one, Dad. It won't be nearly as hard for me as it was for you."

But then why this lump in my throat?

"It's different. It's different when you don't make the choice to leave, when they tell you it's time to go because of things beyond your control, especially when it's been your whole life." He sniffed twice, moved the receiver away from his mouth to cough. "And having your career robbed like that . . . well. Plus, military life is comforting, in a way. The familiarity. The rules you know don't change."

"Dad, we've had really different military experiences. You loved your job, your work. You had peers. You fit in. I haven't loved it like you did." But I did. But I didn't. Even I couldn't make sense of my feelings.

"You fit in, Moo." Dad didn't sound convinced, and yet hearing the words from his mouth cemented that not fitting in wasn't necessarily a bad thing. And then, finally, I could breathe.

"Maybe this is my body's way of telling me that the military was never really for me." Saying it out loud felt like running a marathon, my whole body desperate to collapse with the weight of speaking this single truth.

"You made a choice to join, and I wanted you to have the choice to leave. That's all."

"It's all beyond our control, Dad. What happened with my leg, what happened with you, it couldn't be helped. I just have to wait for the administrative side to catch up to be given my official release date. Then all I can do is move forward."

I said I had to go, got him off the phone with some excuse about needing to get home. Housework that needed doing or dinner that needed fixing. Move forward. That was all I could do.

Days later, I put in a transfer request for the IPSC. My wish was granted the following week and I left Marie like she was a stray cat. At least she was a civilian. That fact alone would shield her— knowledge that, in my mind, justified my exit. I wasn't leaving a man behind; I was actively making a choice to save myself.

32

A week later, I arrived at the IPSC to find my new colleagues sitting in the entry area, chatting over cups of coffee. The reception lounge was bright and warm, neutral art on the creamy walls and cozy leather seating arranged in sections that encouraged conversation.

"Hi, I'm Captain Thompson, reporting for my first day." I waved, suddenly feeling stupid in uniform, back to that kid-playing-dress-up feeling.

"Kelly! We've been looking forward to having you." My new boss, Major Drummond, stood to greet me, short blonde hair circling her slim face. I felt as though I'd stepped into an alternate military universe of acceptance.

"I'm excited to be here. Thanks for accepting my transfer so quickly."

"Well, who better to understand the medical release process than someone who is living it." By the time I went around the room and learned the names and jobs of my co-workers, I had received several hugs as hellos, each one more welcoming than the next. "This'll be your office," Major Drummond said, directing me to a room off a wide corridor. I had my own office for the first time in my career, cupboards naked and new, begging to be filled with mementos and other small parts of my identity. "Feel free to make it your own, however you please. We thought we'd put you in charge of all of the Depart with Dignity ceremonies. Ordering all the certificates, arranging the events, that kind of thing. Ensuring military members are sent to civilian life with the honour they deserve. And considering our workplace, we have a lot of releasing members. How does that sound?" I could only nod. I would have scrubbed the IPSC coffee pot, mopped the floors, and shaken out the mats.

"Well, I'll let you get set up and then later this morning we can go over the details of your role. Any questions?"

My job was later explained to me, in clear and finite detail, complete with charts and contact information for subject-matter experts. Understanding my role before launching into it felt like a glorious luxury I'd not been previously afforded.

"I think I'm good, Ma'am." I looked at my computer, the empty space around it begging for photos and colour. "Do we have coffee together like that every morning?" I asked, swirling on my heel.

"Not every morning, but often. You'll find the work here really emotionally challenging, so we like to recharge our batteries as a team. Honestly, some of our clients are suffering emotional injuries, and PTSD. Sometimes they just want to come here, be around other non-judgmental military people, and talk about what they're going through. Half of your job will just be lending a kind ear. We can all relate to that, right?"

We could. PTSD was a term I felt had been imprinted on my skin like a family birthmark. "I hope we can make it better. I hope we can make a difference." It sounded naive, and yet for the first time I wasn't embarrassed to show my sensitivity.

She smiled and squeezed my arm. "You're going to fit in just fine here."

—

Over the following months at the IPSC, I organized Depart with Dignity events like I was a wedding planner, meticulously choosing seating arrangements and picking up framed retirement certificates; finding complete happiness in the role and in being amongst my co-workers. I loved every day of work—a place where I was allowed to be bubbly because it put nervous soldiers at ease. *You're not like the other officers I've met in my career,* said a corporal as he chatted to me about his latest, horrific deployment. I took the statement as the highest of compliments.

Release numbers increased as the war continued, and the messages collected in my inbox. When my own release message was solemnly delivered to my desk by Major Drummond, I was shocked to discover it was just one page long, shorter than the message that had welcomed me to service in the first place, although there now seemed to be loose ends that needed weaving into the tapestry of my career.

Release date of September 12, 2011, six months left as a soldier, releasing just after the anniversary of 9/11, a catalyst for my enrolment. Eight years of service to my country. As part of my vocational rehab, I could leave the military immediately and take six months to train for civilian life, while still receiving a salary from the Forces.

I could leave. I was free. I was soon to be jobless. I was scared shitless.

"Plans for the future?" Major Drummond asked.

"I'm going to move to Vancouver and be a writer." The words tumbled from my mouth, verbal vomit on the office linoleum. I'd lined up an internship at a publishing house in Vancouver—to start when my release message came in—with the hope of a life as a book editor, a dream that until that point had felt permanently out of reach. A career in books. Joe. A new life with so many possibilities. A flush rose up my neck and I swallowed, waiting for her to throw her arms up at my preposterous aspirations. I felt teary, excited, raw.

"It's okay to be sad, Kelly," my boss said. "There's a real sense of grief that comes with leaving a military lifestyle. A lot will change, but that doesn't mean it's for the worst." I grinned weakly and rolled the edge of the paper message between my thumb and middle finger until it felt as soft as Egyptian cotton. I used the edge to dab at my inexplicably moist cheeks. "Don't worry," Major Drummond said. "We all cry here. Fuck the uniform."

"Yeah, can I have a minute?" I asked. I thought I might be sick, a dribble of perspiration meandering down my inner thigh. "Just need a second alone."

"Absolutely. You come talk if you need anything. We, of all people, understand." Major Drummond put her hand on my shoulder and squeezed gently until I looked up at her. No competition. No pity. Just compassion. It was an act from a fellow female soldier that felt so foreign and yet impossibly welcome.

Major Drummond shut the door to my office and I cried until my eyes swelled and I could barely see. I had finally found my place in the military just as I prepared to leave it.

I pulled pieces of kit out from underneath the basement stairs, trying to sort out anything that appeared army green in the hazy light—tactical vests, ballistic glasses, helmets—shades of green relish that blurred in the diffused basement light.

Dad had come to Kingston to help me sort out my kit and uniforms for returning to the clothing depot, and wouldn't relent when I said help wasn't needed. My name and service number would be crossed off all my gear with another black

Sharpie, replaced with new alphanumeric identifiers for the next soldier. I ran my finger impatiently over my name, emotion blooming on my skin like an allergic reaction.

"Finding everything back there?" Dad leaned into the crawlspace and took the items I handed to him to sort into a pile.

"Uh, not sure. Where in the hell is my webbing?"

"Language, Moo."

"Seriously, Dad. Not in the mood." I hit my head on a beam and bit my lip to contain the profanity, then wrenched my webbing from a pair of crutches left over from my last knee surgery, the canvas straps wrapped around the aluminum frames like a python on a vine.

"Just trying to help," Dad said, offering a hand as I climbed over the pile of gear. I sat cross-legged on the floor and separated items into a kit bag while Dad stood over me with his hands on his hips and doing nothing of value, from what I could gather. His presence was inexplicably grating, but then in recent weeks everything in the house had felt somehow invasive and out of place as I prepared for my move to Vancouver. My Kevlar helmet skittered across the floor towards Dad's feet, the sound a dull thud—just like when my head connected with the ground during my ruck march fainting spells at Saint-Jean. Each time I woke, Joe was there, waiting with concern. I smiled dumbly at the memory, webbing clenched in my fist.

Dad dangled my tactical vest over his head. "Didn't have anything like this when I was in."

"A lot's changed since then." I didn't try to soften the snide tone. Didn't Dad see he was doing to me what his own father did before he died? Pretending they were still military-relevant when we all knew being out of the profession for a month had veterans lagging behind on the trail of constant change? *Soon, I won't understand either.* I motioned to Dad for the vest and pushed it into the depths of the kit bag, releasing a plume of army smell that made me dizzy.

"Before you go to Vancouver, we should do that trip to the Canadian War Museum." Dad inspected the house's sagging support beam and traced the drywall cracks with his fingers. "I wouldn't want to go with anyone but you. Two crippled vets cruising the halls. We'll have to call and have them roll out the red carpet." Dad chuckled at his lame joke, the laughter dying in his throat.

I'd been dodging this same request for years, knowing neither of us was ready to stumble through the experience of our military family history. I'd already been to the museum with my IPSC co-workers, where we trolled through the exhibits solemnly, scattering to private spaces of worship like churchgoers. I'd pushed through the set-up surrounding Hitler's limousine and the corner that allowed kids to dress up like First World War soldiers in bowl helmets, then found what I'd been looking for in the Peacekeeping section. A piece of the Buffalo plane was encased behind Plexiglas, shot down over Syria in 1974, killing all nine Canadian peacekeepers on board. The metal glinted underneath its beam of light, but I'd felt its presence all my life; a veritable monument in the Thompson household. The placard tacked onto the wall detailed the history of the soldiers who'd tried to collect the bodies of their comrades, coming under heavy gunfire. I tried to reconcile what I was reading with the father I knew, who nearly forty years earlier had been picking up his friends' body parts, scattered across the desert when their plane burst into flames. He was meant to be on the plane, but overcrowding and his generalized fear of flying meant he'd driven to their destination, only to return under gunfire to attempt to collect the serial number off the plane for proof. For decades, Syria denied launching that missile, and for just as many decades, my father suffered.

Meanwhile, back in the seventies, Mom was waiting at home, planning their wedding. She sent Dad letters about how the flowers were going to match the napkins, how the church ladies would make the meal to be served at the reception in the church basement, how they would take photos in Simcoe's Wellington Park. She was crossing the days off the calendar, sending those letters in loopy cursive where she tried to express bridal excitement combined with the unsaid words: *Life continues on without you here.*

Cool. Your dad is a piece of Canadian history, my civilian co-worker had said, snapping a picture of me standing next to the Buffalo remnant.

He was. I was. We all were.

"We'll have to see if I have time for the museum, Dad. I'll be moving soon."

"Yes. Moving." He snapped my webbing belt together and then separated the plastic pieces, over and over, the sound akin to fingers on a chalkboard. "Feeling nervous?"

I fiddled with a strap, stuffed more gear into the kit bag. "A little."

"Your mother and I are worried about you. You don't know anyone out west."

I didn't mention Joe. I didn't say that we'd been waiting for each other for years, that this was finally my chance to write, to love my job, to be in love. I didn't talk about Joe to my family because it felt silly and shameful and childish—a pipe dream. But then, so had joining the Forces in the first place. So had a degree in writing. So had seeing the Olympics live in my home country. So had a career in the military that it pained me to let go.

"I'll meet people, Dad." I led us upstairs while I made tea Dad wouldn't drink.

"Paperwork ready to go then? Everything all set for the move?"

"I'm a logistics officer. Of course the paperwork is done." I had a stack of said paperwork in a lime-green folder, stashed somewhere in the household chaos. I looked around me, the house in shambles and my life upturned. It was the end of so many things, and the start of so many others. "What about you, Dad? You applied for your disability pension with Veterans Affairs yet?"

"It's not the same," he said, almost a whisper. "Your injury is physical. Mine—well, it isn't."

"And?" My eyebrow arched in a question and I flicked the lid on the kettle so I wouldn't have to hear its plaintive whistle.

"I know I have depression. But I don't know about this PTSD thing." His voice was staccato, nothing like the Dad I knew, but his denial of having PTSD—something he associated with shame—was a common military refrain. When I missed his previously confident and reassured tone, I called Grandma's house to access her voicemail, which Dad had recorded years earlier. *You have reached the Thompsons. We are unable to come to the phone right now. Leave a message and we will return your call as soon as possible.*

"Dad, I don't know how to break the not-so-gentle news, but you're a textbook case. Stigmatizing it only stops people from coming forward when they're struggling." My fingers curled into angry air quotes. "'Soldier on' and all that garbage, telling people to keep it all in. Where did soldiering on get me? A broken leg that won't heal and a career that's over. And it got you in a mode of still dealing with shit more than thirty years after it happened."

His face went red and he leaned in closely. "In my day, when someone couldn't handle things, the sergeant took you out back and beat the shit out of you until you snapped out of it." His small fists were tight, body rigid. How many times had

Dad relayed this story, holding it up as proof that not being able to handle things meant a need to be put out to pasture?

"Afghanistan changed things, Dad, at least a little. There's more compassion for people going through what you deal with."

"It will never change enough."

"That's true." I hugged him, smelled his cologne and the familiar smells from home. "So I guess that's up to us."

"What is?"

I leaned in close and gave him a hug. "Changing the culture, Dad. Change is up to us old vets." I kissed him on the cheek and, tea in hand, returned to the basement to finish packing.

Weeks later, I got into my car and looked back at my family, who stood with their arms around one another.

As I drove, my feet itched with the restless need for postings that would never come again. But I would arrive in the new province and make a living. I would write. I would press my lips to Joe's and be home. I would be free, and that freedom would be terrifying and somehow unwanted. I knew even then, sobbing as I waved goodbye to my family, that I would miss the military in a way that would drag me into dark mental places, but that would be okay. I would learn. And I would write.

Epilogue

Kelly S. Thompson-Shorrocks
May–Sep 2014

Joe took the remote from me and clicked off the television, then took my hand and brought it to his lips.

"Did you look at that website? For the kayak?"

I'd recently learned of Soldier On, a program that helped injured and ill soldiers and veterans maintain active lifestyles through equipment grants, no matter if the injury was mental or physical. Years earlier, kayaking had made me feel powerful, but that was before my medical release, the diagnosis of Graves' disease, and the depression that I still battled although I'd resigned my weapon three years earlier. The thyroid illness affected all my body's hormones, and nothing had tamed the gland's wild nature; not radiation, not medication, not rest. So it was easier to blame the illness for the depression. It was easier than saying I missed the military with a chronic ache, especially as I watched Joe don his uniform each morning.

"That would be crazy expensive," I said to Joe, who was shedding the tunic from his own uniform. "Who asks for a kayak? They'll think I'm greedy."

I nervously fiddled with the fringe of a throw blanket. Out the window, Vancouver's mountain ranges loomed—mountains I had once appreciated from the steps of 39 Brigade, just down the road from where we now lived. Back when I was military. Back when I belonged to something. Release files sat in my desk drawer, tucked underneath a stack of pens and more boxes of staples than I would ever use in a lifetime. Once a week I would pull out the file and breathe in the smell of military order and precision. Everything was as it should be, and yet it wasn't.

"Just try. We could save and buy me one too. Go on trips together. You love kayaking, and it's something you could manage—you know, physically. What happened to your sense of adventure?"

He left the room, shedding his CADPAT tunic across the back of the dining room chair, the Canadian flag a splash of colour on the shoulder and his nametag Velcroed over the chest pocket. I willed the camouflage shirt to disappear, become a figment of my imagination, or, better yet, something I wasn't at all familiar with. I didn't want to know about the secret Velcro pocket over the heart where I'd imagined I would stow love letters during tours in Afghanistan that never materialized. I wanted that uniform to be shrouded in mystery, as it had been the first time I donned it and it took me half an hour to get dressed between all the buttons, strings, pockets, and elastics.

I felt unjustified in my depression, especially when I thought of all the soldiers I'd helped at the IPSC, not to mention my father and grandfathers. Their depression was a product of war, which somehow meant it was okay. Mine was rooted in something else entirely: health issues and devastation, aimless career dreams jumbled in my mind. I felt especially guilty when my sadness forced Joe to bear the weight of putting joy into our marriage. I deserved nothing. Not the veteran's licence plate on my car.

Not the lovely home that overlooked Vancouver's mountains. Not the kind husband to whom I would always be dead weight.

After a decade of loving him, Joe and I had finally married on Quadra Island. Thirty friends and family came to celebrate with us during a lazy September afternoon, the sun slipping behind the mountains an hour after the ceremony. Joe swept tears from my face, spun me around the dance floor to a crooning Sarah Slean, and tipped back celebratory champagne as we sliced a Swiss dot lemon cake. I had been so happy, and yet depression was there, beyond the cheery face.

Once I heard Joe in the shower, I sent a nervous email to the Soldier On program director. Two weeks later, I received the cheque and permission to purchase my Epic 18X Sport kayak and all the accessories. I stared at the sum blankly, as though the hefty gift had arrived in pennies.

The speedboat clunked against the resistant wake resulting from the storm, which had been following us all day from Vancouver, up to North Van, onto the Sunshine Coast ferry, up to Earls Cove, onto the ferry along the choppy Powell River, and into the small village of Lund. We loaded a week's worth of food and survival gear and hired a tour company to haul us to our final destination of Desolation Sound, our kayaks strapped to rigging overhead. The boat was manned by a weathered couple in their late thirties, tanned and confident in their sea legs, the wife in charge of the operation. Her husband sat to the side and obeyed her orders, which she needed only to mime before he was tightening ropes and adjusting weight loads in response.

"How you two doing down there?" she hollered to Joe and me. We weren't certain the trip would go ahead, considering the relentless winds, but she pushed the throttle harder and we tugged our merino wool toques over our ears, leaning in to one another while jostling between our bag of dried fruit and nuts. We gave simultaneous thumbs ups.

We'd saved all year to buy Joe a matching kayak, bright white and yellow like mine. We called them Roxanne and Stella and giddily ordered name decals for their golden sterns, which I had plastered on the day before our big trip while Joe organized kit into dry bags. He'd sat in the basement for two days, packing and unpacking, stuffing then loosening, going over his kit list like Santa. All the while, his face gave away his childish elation, a return to passion for the outdoors that hadn't been trampled by midnight bug outs and thirteen-kilometre rucksack marches.

An hour later we arrived at a rocky outcrop on one of the Curme Islands, with rudimentary tent pads constructed from wooden slabs. Our research had indicated it was a perfect jump-off location for touring the area, with short two-hour paddles and promises of rest and relaxation in between.

"This is the spot," our guide said, wiping sea spray from her face. She eased the boat into an inlet that provided us with meagre protection from gusts of wind. "Best location I can get you to considering the weather and fact that the tide is out."

I resisted the urge to consult my tide chart or one of the maps we'd brought along. Instead, I wordlessly helped gather our gear and tossed it onto the rocks while the couple unloaded our kayaks and tied them off to a nearby Arbutus. With a wave, our guides zipped away, and with them went my hopes for an easy way back to the mainland.

"This is going to be so relaxing," Joe said as he prepared his camp stove for a pot of tea. "An adventure."

"It feels like basic training," I said, sweaty from the fifteen trips I'd made in a stumble to recover another dry bag from the inlet. We set up our tent, ate a dehydrated meal, and made love during the sunset overlooking the Sound before Joe drifted off. I fell asleep listening to the rhythmic hum of the ocean mixed with Joe's sleeping bag rustling against his mat. It really was like basic training, but this time, I could breathe.

The storm abated overnight, leaving behind a milky trace of cloud that snaked through the sky in a thin line. At nine in the morning, it wasn't too hot, and the water was silky and calm, slopping lazily against the rocks of the surrounding islands' shores.

"Ready?" Joe asked as he drained his instant coffee.

"Ready."

I snapped on my lifejacket, the air temporarily squeezed from my chest and my arms puffing awkwardly from my sides. Joe looked the part of ocean-farer in his kayaking uniform, fluorescent emergency whistle slung around his neck and a sticky layer of sunblock smeared on his dotted skin, while I felt like a kid playing dress-up, spray skirt dangling from my waist. We edged the boats down the path of rocks and I stepped tentatively into the water, knee deep, the cold shock of the Pacific clamouring its way into my bones.

"Good to go?" Joe asked, fists on hips, steadying the boat between his legs.

"I think so. Be nice to me, Roxanne," I said, caressing her yellow stern.

Joe laughed and pulled me in for a kiss before I approached Roxanne with caution, a potential enemy with the element of surprise in her favour. Heat dried ocean spray into a salty crust on my cheeks as I maneuvered into the cockpit, snapped on the skirt, and hovered while Joe did the same. Wordlessly we pushed away from the island with an eye towards Tenedos Bay. We'd heard there was a lake there, perfect for filtering drinking water and a swim. From the Curme Islands, it appeared to be a short jaunt.

Fifteen minutes into the paddle, I wanted to stop. Correction: I felt like I had to stop. My muscles shook with weakness and I cursed the fact that I hadn't trained for longer distances, lamely certain of my kayaking abilities. My heart raced at breakneck speed and my hands rubbed raw on my carbon paddle, blisters forming in the webbed area between my thumb and pointer finger.

Ahead of me, Joe skimmed in an effortless straight line towards the bay while I muddled forward in the general direction. Desolation Sound was almost entirely silent except for the grunt of seals that sunned themselves on boulders birthed from the ocean floor. Occasional glimpses of the rocky bottom revealed multicoloured starfish, their suction-cupped arms raised and flattened as though they were caught mid-wave, and sea kelp swarmed and grabbed at the boat as I moved.

"Isn't this awesome?" Joe called out.

It was awesome, but I could only nod. All of my energy needed to be diverted to maintaining momentum. Basic training had taught us that if pushed, anyone could find the extra strength to complete the mission, no matter the personal cost. But I'd done that before and all it had done was bring me to this moment, broken as fuck, paddling across the smooth Pacific with my husband out of reach.

"It's over here!" Joe shouted across the water. I pushed harder to catch his boat as it disappeared around a peninsula. As I approached, he was taking a long gulp from the Nalgene bottle he had strapped onto his hull, assessing the waterproof map. "Whoops."

"What do you mean, *whoops*?" I was breathing heavily, my arms aching and my neck singed by the sun.

"I misjudged a bit," Joe said. "We have to go back that way about two nautical miles." He pointed towards a northwest inlet with a pale arm that throbbed with well-defined veins. He did not look tired. He did not look stressed. I could not hate him for it.

"Are you fucking kidding me?"

I was overwhelmed with the urge to cry. If I had asked Joe to tether our boats and tug me along, he would have. But the words would not form on my lips. I could not ask to be rescued.

"Come on, it's not that far. You can do it."

I wanted to both slap him and hug him for his faith in me, this misguided sense that I was capable. Hadn't he figured out that he'd married a broken-down piece of equipment? But there was no other option but to go back, retrace our steps, and right the course. Joe grabbed his paddle with expert grip and I followed slowly behind, the sun at our backs. I watched him as I would study a character for one of my books, tattooed arms peeking out from his life vest, the rusty colour of his shirt underneath, the gentle sway of the rudder behind him. I memorized every detail as I'd done more than a decade before, lined up in our ranks at basic training, Shorrocks and Thompson. Throughout basic, I'd spent hours staring at Joe's broad back and where it narrowed in at his hips, the dot of endearing moles that led a trail up his neck and peeked out from his thin blonde hair. I loved him without ever needing to see his face.

Back on the ocean, I looked ahead to where Joe bobbed on the surface like a buoy. Then we heard it at the same time. The unmistakable sputter of a whale blowhole somewhere south of us. Our heads swivelled, assessed, calculated the approximate distance.

"Over there!" I shouted, and pointed at the pod of five orcas, their black dorsal fins breaking the water. Joe swept his paddle deep to quickly spin around until the tips of our boats met. We watched, stunned and silent, as the mammoth animals slipped under the water then back up to the surface, moving in our direction.

"Well, come on!" Joe shouted as he paddled towards them. They were a few kilometres away but we would meet in mere minutes. They could have been under us that very moment, rising from below to swallow us up, black blubber glistening like ink blobs. Joe was already moving full throttle in their direction, excitement palpable in his neck and arms.

I watched and planned how I would write about my first whale encounter. In the days since completing my Masters in Creative Writing from the University of British Columbia, everything in my mind was narrated and scripted. I would capture it all with my keyboard, trap this moment as a reclaiming of myself, scrubbed new by each crested wave that broke against the hull of my kayak.

I paddled forward, nerves rising up but exertion pushing them down. The military taught us that too: a way to cope, a matter of necessity in a life full of new and unnerving experiences. Also, the knowledge that I could make it under my own steam—could meet the orcas like a gentle challenge, the reward being in getting there, accomplishing the task. As I skimmed across the sea, I felt eerily calm, as though anything could happen and Joe and I would simply ride the wave in a steady, equal tandem, mapping out a life of adventures.

There was a story in this experience, this trip, my new cultivated relationship with Roxanne. I would write it, craft it, nurture that story into existence. No one else would tell me otherwise or control the narrative, give me orders around structure and dialogue. No, this story would be mine. And it was going to be beautiful.

ACKNOWLEDGEMENTS

Early on, I learned the necessity of teamwork. Writing a book, it turns out, isn't much different from military life in that regard, so I have many people to thank.

A good agent is the unsung heroine of the publishing world, and I am indebted to my mine, Stephanie Sinclair, and the Transatlantic Agency folk, for bringing this book to fruition. Stephanie, you saw a memoir in my fictional pitch years ago, making me realize it was my story to tell and not that of a fictional character. Thank you for nurturing this book into existence.

To Jared Bland and the other kind-hearted people at M&S and Penguin Random House Canada, thanks for believing in me and the importance of this book. My editor, Jenny Bradshaw, edited with such grace and gentleness, ushering in new ideas and concepts that honed the manuscript. Kim Hesas was also vital, as well as Sam Church. You've all been such a pleasure to work with and I know I've found my publishing home.

Thank you to the Ontario Arts Council for your financial support, and to the Banff Centre for the physical space in which to churn out the first draft.

Short sections of the book have previously appeared in Canadian anthologies including: *Embedded on the Home Front:*

Where Military and Civilian Lives Converge (edited by Joan Dixon and Barb Howard, Heritage House Press, 2012); *Boobs: Women Explore What it Means to Have Breasts* (edited by Ruth Daniell, Caitlin Press, 2016); *Everyday Heroes: Inspirational Stories from Men and Women in the Canadian Armed Forces* (edited by Jody Mitic, Simon & Schuster Canada, 2017). Thank you to these publishers, editors, and other professionals.

Biggest of thanks to my family. You are the people of all people, my mini fan club. I'm lucky to have parents who never stop telling me how proud they are, even when I perceive failure. Dad, I am a soldier because of you, and Mom, I am an artist because of you. Thank you both for those gifts.

And to my sister, Meghan, thank you for being my biggest cheerleader, for championing my words. Thanks for being my first reader, for giving me so much more to write about, for never trying to censor me. I know you'll be watching. I know you'll be proud.

And of course, my Joe. I'm grateful for the practical support you've provided along the way, including helping me to check my memory on our shared basic training experience, walking the dog so I could work, and providing endless cups of tea. But also for assuring me that this book was important, that you stood by me no matter the content, and that I really was a soldier in your eyes. Your faith in me set a new standard by which I've learned to measure myself. I didn't want or need to be rescued, but I always wanted you.